# Sites of Statelessness

SUNY series in Global Modernity

---

Arif Dirlik, Ravi Arvind Palat, and Roxann Praziniak, editors

# Sites of Statelessness

## Laws, Cities, Seas

Edited by

Ayşe Çağlar
Sabyasachi Basu Ray Chaudhury
Ranabir Samaddar

SUNY
PRESS

Published by State University of New York Press, Albany



Printed in the United States of America



For information, contact State University of New York Press, Albany, NY
www.sunypress.edu

**Library of Congress Cataloging-in-Publication Data**

Names: Çağlar, Ayşe, editor. | Basu Ray Chaudhury, Sabyasachi, editor. | Samaddar, Ranabir, editor.
Title: Sites of statelessness : laws, cities, seas / edited by Ayşe Çağlar, Sabyasachi Basu Ray Chaudhury, and Ranabir Samaddar.
Description: Albany : State University of New York Press, [2024]. | Series: SUNY series in global modernity | Includes bibliographical references and index.
Identifiers: LCCN 2024009209 | ISBN 9781438499895 (hardcover : alk. paper) | ISBN 9781438499901 (ebook) | ISBN 9781438499888 (pbk. : alk. paper)
Subjects: LCSH: Statelessness. | Stateless persons.
Classification: LCC K7128.S7 S58 2024 | DDC 342.08/3—dc23/eng/20240402
LC record available at https://lccn.loc.gov/2024009209

# Contents

# Acknowledgments

The idea for this book emerged from a number of academic exchanges organized by the Europe-Asia Research Platform on Forced Migration, jointly launched by the Calcutta Research Group (CRG), India, and Institut für die Wissenschaften vom Menschen (Institute for Human Sciences, IWM), Vienna, Austria. The research platform hosted several collaborations, including a hybrid workshop on "Sites of Statelessness: Laws, Cities, Seas," held at IWM in Vienna in 2021. The coming together of scholars focusing on a diverse set of areas, topics, and approaches has been an impetus for this publication.

Our thanks go especially to our contributors for sharing their research with us, and for their patience throughout the process of organizing this volume. Our colleagues, both at IWM and CRG, have constantly supported us, especially Ana Ćuković and Samaresh Guchhait. We also convey our thanks to Debasree Sarkar for helping us polish the manuscript to make it presentable.

Above all, this has been the teamwork of the CRG and IWM. We are grateful to everyone on this team.

We profusely thank the editors and staff at SUNY Press for their constant support, encouragement, and dedication. We are especially grateful to Dr. Michael A. Rinella and Diane Ganeles. We also thank the unknown referees of this manuscript for their encouraging words and insightful comments that improved this work as a whole and opened avenues for future work.

Sabyasachi Basu Ray Chaudhury
Ayşe Çağlar
Ranabir Samaddar
May 2024

# Introduction

## Abandoned to be Stateless

Sabyasachi Basu Ray Chaudhury, Ayse Çağlar,
and Ranabir Samaddar

The postcolonial experiences of statelessness, now witnessed in the countries of Europe and the Northern American hemisphere, tell us what is happening to the institution of citizenship in the wake of massive displacements and migratory flows. This volume examines the entanglements of citizenship policies and practices with the spread of statelessness today, which defy any kind of a citizen/stateless binary. Citizenship policies almost everywhere reflect the desire to achieve a perfect fit between the "right" kind of population and the "right size" of territory for a nation-state. These policies become significant in the background of a shift in emphasis from *jus soli* to *jus sanguinis*, the existence of borderland populations and the no-where people, population flows across (post)colonial border formations and boundary delimitations, and the growth of regional, formal, and informal labor markets, characterized by migrant labor economies. The questions looming large over this edited volume is: In what way is the production of statelessness (its actors, instruments, and discourses) in this postcolonial global time of ours different from the classical idea of statelessness originating from the succession of states? What are the sites of statelessness and how are they produced and reproduced? What are the implications of the drive to firm up the national registers of citizenries in various countries in terms of international human rights laws and for key instruments on statelessness—the 1954 UN Convention Relating to the Status of Stateless Persons and the 1961 Convention on the Reduction of Statelessness? Will the international legal understanding of statelessness be adequate to theories the growing phenomenon of statelessness in the postcolonial world? What are the fault lines of confining statelessness to a legal status/condition? How do legal infrastructures themselves contribute to the production of statelessness?

Conventional discussions on statelessness as a form of refugee existence move around definitions and legal histories. This volume proposes to move away from these definitional accounts and aims to focus on *sites of statelessness*, bringing out in the process the inadequacy of our present understanding of statelessness. Three such sites are examined: law, city, and the sea. In each site, the making and re-making of statelessness take different forms and involve different actors, mechanisms, practices, and institutions whose dynamics we can capture once we approach statelessness beyond a legal condition.

Therefore, one of the strengths and the edge of this volume is that it addresses the distinctive dynamics of the different *sites* in the production of statelessness; that is, it considers the impact of the sites as critical and does not simply treat them as a backdrop. Different sites evoke different histories and repertoires and bring different possibilities of alignment with the problematics the volume aims to address.

The first two decades of the twenty-first century have witnessed more and more refugees, more asylum seekers, and even more stateless persons with more dispossession, unfreedom, and precarity, in search of the "right to have rights." The remnants of coloniality and raciality rather have continued to criminalize the movements of human beings. In an age dominated by big data and artificial intelligence, new synergy of the neoliberal economy and illiberal populist politics have intensified the legislated exclusion of the "undesirable" minorities through different means of geo-juridical approaches and new algorithms of control and oppression. When state sovereignty has been challenged in view of the neoliberal economy, its sovereignty has been transformed by the state to control the borders with growing securitization of refugees and migrants. As nationalism has quite often been blended with the politics of fear, negotiating the empire of new borders has been a challenge for different minorities within a state, both in the Global North and Global South. The neoliberal neglect embedded in the politics of unfeeling (Yao 2021) has changed the border optics with respect to the movement of human beings. Over and above, the newly emerging biometric border regime has been creating fresh mindless gaps between citizenship and its others in the Global South in the name of nation-building (Samaddar 2020, 2003; Chaudhury 2022).

On their part, the states in the Global North have opted for legislated injustice, constructing new "illegalities" of migration through the techno-politics of border control (Godin and Donà 2021). New algorithms for excluding refugees, migrants, and asylum-seekers, through constant demonization, new documentations of "nativeness" leading to exclusion, and through rewriting histories of convenience have facilitated the omission of the existing communities and groups of people from the territory of a state. On another plane, the soft legality of international law has been a major impediment in the path of supranational laws, which meanwhile have turned more people stateless, thereby constantly creating and shifting sites of statelessness. Moreover, neither the 1951 Refugee Convention nor other international legal instruments have recognized conditions of extreme poverty and material deprivation as grounds for legitimate asylum of human beings. Therefore, economic migrants remain considered worldwide as individuals who simply demand "illegitimate" claims to protection and refuge, using the language of rights discourse (Benhabib 2004, 114).

The existing international legal regime on refugees and stateless persons primarily emerged in the context of the evolving situation in Europe in the immediate postwar era. The 1951 UN Convention on Refugees or the 1954 Convention on Statelessness or, for that matter, the Universal Declaration of Human Rights (UDHR)—all were instant outcomes of the crises faced by Europe during and immediately after the Second World War.

Article 1.1 of the 1954 UN Convention relating to the Status of Stateless Persons defines a stateless person as "a person who is not considered as a national by any State under the operation of its law" (UNHCR 1954). The 1954 Convention establishes minimum guarantees in areas such as education, health care, employment, identity, as well as travel documents. While it does not oblige states to provide nationality for stateless persons in their territories, it asks them to facilitate naturalization. The 1961 Convention sets out important safeguards that can be incorporated into nationality laws to prevent statelessness (UNHCR 1961). For example, in relation to acquisition of a nationality at birth, or loss of nationality on marriage, or as a result of prolonged residence abroad. In addition, international human rights law plays a significant and complementary role. Its guarantees apply to all persons, with very few provisions restricted to nationals alone. Key human rights standards include the obligation to ensure birth registration, the prohibition on arbitrary deprivation of nationality, guarantees of equal treatment for women in relation to nationality laws, and protection against arbitrary detention. Yet, despite these and other global initiatives, new risks of statelessness have emerged. The level of ratification of the UN statelessness conventions is also low. In this way, statelessness points to a major weakness in the power and effectiveness of international law on refugees. While efforts have been mounted by the UNHCR (United Nations High Commissioner for Refugees) and the global humanitarian community to help and assist the victims of forced eviction through relief, rehabilitation, and integration in the host country and third-country resettlement, the problems stateless people face do not go away. The problems, in fact, increase. A major part of the displaced population across borders is stateless (a few years back, of the nearly 43 million refugees, about 12 million were stateless). As a large number of refugees and migrants have no chance of going back, after a protracted period of displacement, they became *de facto* stateless.

But, perhaps equally significantly, people do not have to cross the borders in order to become refugees and/or stateless. Losing their citizenship status, or never enjoying it, many become refugees even when they have not crossed international borders. They become "refugees" in their homes, stripped of their citizenship, and rendered *de facto* stateless. In fact, statelessness has emerged as a serious issue within several countries. The citizenship laws of several postcolonial countries, moving from *jus soli* to *jus sanguinis*, are highly influenced by the self-perception of the "majority" who claim to constitute the "nation." Ethnic bias, cultural, linguistic, religious prejudices, gender discrimination, and political concerns of the emerging ruling elites shape policies for granting as well as denying citizenship.

On the other hand, the international community's engagement with the problem of statelessness is rather recent. One of the major weaknesses of international protection mechanisms for the stateless persons is the non-applicability of international law within the sovereign jurisdiction of states where the majority of stateless persons live. The states control their borders, frame the immigration policies, and decide who should be allowed to enter and whose entry should be rejected. The present immigration laws, policies, and practices of most states do not make a distinction between stateless persons and other migrants. Involved in such situations like this, is the issue of responsibility: responsibility of the state that forces displacement, responsibility of the state that has to give shelter, responsibility of the region (think of various regional initiatives and solutions), responsibility of institutions in charge of global governance, and finally, responsibility of the international legal arrangements. These failures combine to produce massive *de facto* statelessness, where the lives and experiences of the *de facto* stateless people and those in legal limbo converge.

In other words, one of the major sites of statelessness is the very field of law. Relatively few scholars of refugee studies have so far attached importance to critical jurisprudence. "Precarity," the pervasive marker of statelessness, is a non-legal condition. The law fails to incorporate the "condition of precariousness" in its understanding of statelessness. In the same critical vein, we can note the phenomenon of innumerable stateless people undertaking risky sea journeys, in the Bay of Bengal, in the Mediterranean or the Aegean, in leaky, dilapidated boats, sometimes arranged by smugglers, fleeing hostile and violent regimes to reach other countries on the other sides of the maritime space. While such maritime movements have been a common feature of the Bay of Bengal or the Mediterranean, and on the Aegean over the last five years, again few studies have been conducted to explore the position of migrants at sea and how seas become the sites of the production of (*de jure* as well as *de facto)* statelessness. The lack of permission to disembark on the shores of the intended destination puts migrants on hold in unimaginable precarity and legal limbo, and has done so even more in the times of the COVID-19 pandemic.

Precarity is not a fixed status. Most migrants experience oscillations in their levels of precarious existence over time and through space. The scalar and temporal aspects of precarity are experienced by a wide range of temporary urban migrants, from low to high-skilled, refugees, asylum seekers, and stateless persons. Cities tend to receive the majority of the world's migrants, either through internal or international migration. Urban settings, especially the informal settlements of the displaced, are reproductive spaces that influence levels of precarity. The realities of such city spaces mirror the structural vulnerabilities and similarities shared by those framed as stateless, refugee, migrant, or as citizen. Cities are also the settings where multiple forms and levels of precarity intersect and overlap. Spaces within the cities are possible sites of contact and contestation, but also of alignment and sociability among migrants, refugees, the stateless, and people categorized as "local." Such spaces and localities determine who belongs to the city.

Precarious forms of labor often associated with the city thus become another major site of statelessness. The right to work is guaranteed in the 1948 Universal Declaration of Human Rights, and by other global legal mechanisms, the migrant labor has the right to protection against labor exploitation. Yet the gaps in protection mechanisms are telling. These deficits lead the migrant labor to extreme precarity, particularly in the neoliberal times. The feminization of migration puts women and children in a more vulnerable position through dispossession and bondage. Marked by the lack of citizenship rights, these conditions tell us of a situation of *de facto* statelessness. Statelessness leads to a precarious existence—this is not surprising. But what the law leaves out is the problematic of structural precariousness leading to statelessness. In this way, we are back to where from we started, namely, the game of citizenship that makes a part of the population within a national territory stateless.

One of the most infamous sites of statelessness in cities is sex work, and sex work is one of the most crucial forms of urban subaltern labor. Statelessness robs people of their rights over their bodies and dignity of life, while depriving them of the ability to protest rampant exploitations. Stateless people become insecure because they can be displaced at any time that the state or the majority community so desires. Space, in its physical and mental form, is organized by race, class, and gender among other factors. When women are displaced, they are destabilized from their moorings, and such destabilization is often made an occasion for their sexual exploitation. Trafficked people, regardless of their gender affiliation, are marked as aliens in all the countries of South Asia, but it is the women and the transgender people whose alien-ness translates into sexual vulnerability. By markings, women, transgender, and underage people are viewed as sexually available, and their sexual exploitation is facilitated. Victims of trafficking, sex workers, a majority of whom are migrants, are almost natural subjects of statelessness. Legislations fail to ameliorate the conundrum. The gender dimension of the issue of statelessness brings in the question of the subaltern forms of urban labor. Sex work is one of the glaring instances of the close relationship between statelessness and subaltern forms of labor.

Finally, we have the phenomenon of erstwhile citizens "lost in the seas." Does the sea provide a safe haven to stateless populations or refugees inhabiting camplike spaces that are bereft of basic civilian rights to undertake voyages? What are the avenues of protection for migrants lost in the high seas, be it the Aegean Sea, the Mediterranean, the Andaman Sea, or the Bay of Bengal? Search and rescue operations have paradoxically increased fatalities. Often, migrants jump into the sea in desperation, failing to comprehend the reasons for interception. Recently, some scholars (Choi 2017) have written how maritime governmentality is shaped by complex legal infrastructure for which the responsibility of states to protect is often difficult to detect or prove, resulting into variegated forms of rightlessness and loss of lives. In contexts of protracted "migration crisis," akin to, for example, the Rohingya situation, when all states, including Myanmar where the Rohingya belong to, deny them citizenship rights, individuals can actually be compared with empty vessels sailing in the sea without any state flag or state protection. Experts in international law have thus been aiming at reducing migrant casualties in the sea while simultaneously trying to establish and institutionalize new legal encasements of seas and to uphold the legal right to asylum. These journeys on the sea are penal journeys, much like resettling the refugees and unwanted subjects on penal islands. They recall a much earlier history of a voyage, such as that of the *Komagata Maru*, or the history of the Vietnamese boat crisis.

Today, with the changing times, and in view of the large-scale omission of the Global South, the existing international legal framework seems archaic and powerless in spite of its earlier limited achievements and contributions. The usual sites of statelessness tend to emerge more from the concept of modern citizenship in the first two decades of the twenty-first century, and from the erasure of basic entitlements of ordinary people from the frame of human rights, from the state's racialized policing and digital surveillance based on artificial intelligence. Therefore, the refugees, migrants, stateless, and asylum-seekers, the "suspected" subjects of the Global South, quite often jostle with one another to cross the Mediterranean to reach the shores of the Global North.

Against this backdrop, the present volume containing twelve chapters, is not a collection of dry legal documents with technical legal arguments and debates, but a mixture of legal and social dossiers, which are testimonies of dispossession, unfreedom, and precarity of people without citizenship, and people who are *de facto* stateless (Chaudhury 2021). These dossiers contain legal and social narratives of dispossessed people, brushing with sovereign power, which refuses to recognize human beings, or to be answerable to anyone other than itself. While the global discourse on human rights intends to make sovereigns accountable to the universal principles of justice, it fails to exceed the order of the state, challenging its real and conceptual borders. This volume, in a way, challenges this paradox of sovereignty and questions the quest for recognition of the rights of people and human dignity in the face of the state-instigated proliferation of statelessness. In other words, this volume highlights, drawing from the multiple experiences not only from Europe, but also from Asia, that the position of stateless people across the globe, hinges on the margins of political community and its other. It tells the stories of these people living on the edge and the challenges they pose to the new legal and political frames.

The growing securitization of refugees, migrants and asylum-seekers, and in some cases, even a state's own citizens and/or subjects, have been pushed beyond the frontiers of basic rights on the ground of being the "usual suspects." In this context, this book attempts to bridge a critical gap between the sites and experiences of statelessness in the Global North and Global South through the everyday experiences of the *de facto* stateless, refugees, migrants, and asylum-seekers in Europe and Asia. The volume, therefore, indicates that, the situations of statelessness, or being at risk of statelessness, render these human beings more vulnerable to harm and detention, and prevent them from seeking refuge because of a lack of documentation, or the concerned states' unwillingness to allow refugees and/or stateless persons to enter their territory.

## Overview of Chapters

### Part I: Law as a Site of Statelessness

In his chapter, Sabyasachi Basu Ray Chaudhury has written about legalizing illegality through borders, boundaries, and legal and constitutional methods in the Global South In this connection, he discusses the postcolonial territorialization and exteriorization through which territoriality and sovereignty turn into a great disconnect with the inhabitants of South Asia. He has argued that, although Europe was the major site of statelessness in the immediate postwar era, in recent times, more and more people, living historically at a certain geographical space for generations in the plural societies of Asia and Africa, are becoming stateless in the context of nation-building exercises, the consequent enactment of new citizenship laws, or the modification or amendment of the existing ones, simultaneous growing populist and xenophobic politics, and the increasing securitization of migrants and outsiders. According to him, the postcolonial "state-nations" in South Asia are still unfolding, thus regenerating the traditional cleavages in the societies, with the objective of homogenizing of the heterogeneities. He also indicates that the juridicalization of citizenship by postcolonial constitutional and legal processes has made the concept more and more contested and complex, ignoring the histories of continuous mobility of people across the region. He thus concludes that the hegemonic (re)production of Western epistemologies across the globe, largely ignoring the specificities of different geographies, and the continuous silencing and erasure of the other histories of displacement, and other knowledges and traditions of hospitality, perpetuates a sense of inferiority of understanding displacement in the Global South. To him, the liminality of the postcolonial space of the Global South, as evident from South Asia, divided among different state territories, has become the site of surveillance and discipline through (il)legal means. Therefore, there is a need to take into account the discourses of diversities, making inclusion underscored in the international laws governing refugees, migrants, and the stateless, and not to be lost in the overwhelming geopolitics of knowledge originating in the Global North.

In the chapter entitled "The Production of Statelessness in Europe," Elspeth Guild and Sandra Mantu argue that, from an international legal perspective, citizenship is part of national constitutional arrangements. Through a legal framework, deprivation of nationality is prohibited, and states have an obligation to reduce or avoid statelessness. European legal traditions constitute citizenship as an expression of loyalty between the individual and the state. However, European states, in particular, are creating situations of statelessness for their citizens on the grounds of increasing securitization of migrants and refugees. When the state constitutional rulers fail the individuals, a claim is often made to supranational human rights law as a source of obligation on the states not to abandon its citizens. But the existing international legal instruments treat nationality as a bastion of state sovereignty, and in the European context, nationality is not expressly included among the rights protected by the European Convention on Human Rights (ECHR). This leads us to a hierarchical state of humanity, as the state's obligations to its citizens tend to differ depending on the socially constructed racial and gender identity, thus enabling the demotion of a citizen to homo sacer in view of the exceptional security politics of the contemporary times.

Nergis Canefe in "The Banality of Statelessness and the Impossibility of Counting the Dispossessed" considers the exclusionary forms of the state and political membership as they emerge in contemporary reformulations of temporary labor regimes and capital accumulation, questioning the very idea of approaching statelessness from international refugee regimes. As such, "statelessness is neither time-bound nor geographically distinct in origin." Building on the conceptualizations of denizenship, Canefe argues that statelessness should be considered beyond the state-citizen duo, and instead in terms of the dynamics between the relationships of state, society, and the individual. A perspective centered on processes of dispossession through precarity and violence, moves beyond the dichotomies tied to the state and [erasure] of subjecthood.

## Part II: City as a Site of Statelessness

According to Paula Banerjee and Sangbida Lahiri, citizenship is central to the statist imagination, and hyperstatism can lead to statelessness. In "The

Conundrum of Trafficking and Statelessness in West Bengal," the authors argue that the alienness of women and children leads to their sexual vulnerability. Taking the case of West Bengal, endemic deprivation and lack of rights place populations in vulnerable positions, making them targets of the traffickers. While human trafficking is illegal in India, its illegality does not prevent trafficking. For instance, the increasing vulnerabilities of women and children, particularly in the Sundarbans in West Bengal, where multiple cyclonic storms and natural calamities, like the sea water flooding the agricultural land in the recent times, have damaged the cultivable land with salinity, thereby making the land uncultivable in the foreseeable future, leading to more vulnerabilities of the inhabitants, specifically the women and children. Similar is the case of the women and children in Bangladesh. The authors argue that, poverty, deprivation, hunger, and environmental disasters all lead to erosion of rights, in general, generating situations conducive to human trafficking. On the other hand, cities are never formed without the presence of a trafficked population. These vulnerable souls deliver all the essential services for the city. Therefore, according to Banerjee and Lahiri, statelessness and trafficking often work as a dyad.

In "Can Undesirables Inhabit the World? From Camps to *Instant Cities*," Michel Agier focuses on the figure of the undesirables, their location in space, and their spatiality through the framework of "wasted lives." Embodied through legal and social conceptualizations of the internally displaced persons, irregular migrants, and refugees, the figure of the undesirable is inscribed on space as camps and *instant cities*. Taking Patrick Chamoiseau's novel *Texaco* and Liberian refugees in camps in Sierra Leone, as examples, Agier shows the construction of lives, "cities," and futures taking place on the margins, borders, and fringes. The conceptualizations of cities challenge the dominant attitudes and knowledge in Europe vis-à-vis the "other" territories and populations that are shaped over the course of centuries of conquest, colonization, exploitation, and exclusion. These *instant cities* experiments reduce or eliminate the gap between time and space, and the temporal parameter becomes one of the factors used for classifying space. These urban communities and their inhabitants together make the city which enables us to rethink the model of instant cities.

Efadul Huq and Faranak Miraftab, in "Stateless in Informal Settlements," consider *de facto* statelessness as spatially produced and experienced through rightlessness in the urban informal settlements of Dhaka, Bangladesh. Statelessness leads to a lack of all the rights that the nation-states usually promise. The authors show the structurally precarious position of informal dwellers as akin to forms of statelessness. With the example of Korail slum in Dhaka, Bangladesh, Miraftab and Huq indicate the banality of making distinction between *de jure* and *de facto* statelessness. They also argue that exploring statelessness beyond the legal histories contributes to the Southern turn in theorizing city-making and urban citizenship. To them, statelessness can result from various geopolitical alignments among states, and on account of racialized and ethnicized persecutions.

In "Statelessness and Camp Settlements: The Curious Case of South Asia," Nasreen Chowdhory and Shamna Thacham Poyil highlight the stateless, as the other of the citizens, while discussing the everyday experiences of statelessness. Statelessness, to them, is an extreme form of rightlessness—precarious legal, political, and human standing of individuals, who are denied the protection, rights, and privileges of citizenship. The authors, however, argue that rightlessness emanating from the lack of citizenship does not necessarily signify total exclusion from the polity. Rather, taking on South Asia as its site, the refugee camps entail expectations of citizenship in spite of spatial and temporal indeterminacy, and the camps exemplify "unfinished citizens."

## Part III: Sea as a Site of Statelessness

In his chapter "The Tragic Journey of *Komagata Maru*: Empire, Immigrants, and Anxiety," Subhas Ranjan Chakraborty takes us to the journey of Kamagata Maru, which prefigures the experiences of refugees, migrants, and the stateless population of our times. Its journey began like most journeys but ended with a tragedy in 1914. Chakraborty shows that migration was predicated on coercion from the very beginning, used to recruit labor for various projects in the colonies. A majority of these emigrants were from rural areas, marked by crop failures. Chakraborty shows the strong correlation between emigration and harvest conditions, with frequent famines making the situation worse. Under such circumstances, most migrants left their villages for the first time in their life. Quoting Hugh Tinker, Chakraborty concludes that, the entire international labor system and the Indian diaspora were the consequences of British exploitation.

In chapter 9, "Subjects at Sea: Jahaji Relationships and Their Discontents," Samata Biswas discusses indentured labor through the Ibis trilogy of Amitav Ghosh, an anthropologist and novelist. Biswas's chapter highlights the vulnerabilities of the subjects of the British Indian empire, who were taken to different Indian Ocean and Caribbean Islands, and forced to produce sugar, coffee, tea, rubber, and opium. She reminds us that, while indentured workers were primarily men, many wives accompanied their husbands on their dangerous sea voyages, as did many single or unattached women who migrated to avoid unwanted marriages and other hardships. Biswas further discusses how the slave-carrying ships gradually turned into ships carrying indentured labor. These modern forms of enslavement are an outcome of the racialized forms of the trans-Atlantic world, becoming a global phenomenon through the very crossing of trans-Atlantic boundaries. These crossings within and beyond states, subject women to multiple forms of state, colonial, and patriarchal authorities, rendering their location within the frames of statelessness visible.

Sibel Karadağ, in "Governing Migrant Mobilities in the Aegean Sea: From Moral Rhetoric to Blatant Use of Violence," brings to the fore new technologies to monitor, expel, and manage migrants at sea, as well as tactics implemented by border enforcement. She points out that the spatial and juridical configurations of the sea lead to certain power projections and political technologies in the Aegean Sea. The distinctive semi-closed geophysicality of the Aegean Sea maps out its spatial and juridical configuration, leading to specific border practices, whereas the changing infrastructures and political technologies seek to deter, discipline, and police the migrant mobilities in Turkey and Greece. The everyday practice of pushback, along with a novel infrastructure and technology of expulsion, has been transforming the political space both at the sea, and on the land, in the region. The life rafts used by migrants to cross the Mediterranean have practically turned into floating carceral spaces, put into necropolitical intervention in the Aegean Sea, turning the sea into a "death-world." Sibel argues that the scope of its surface, insular geography, and close proximity with the territorial waters have a decisive impact on the art of governance and juridical mapping of space and are closely related to the impossibilities of disembarkation.

In "Sea, Refugees, and Stateless Migrants on the Bay: The Rohingya," Sucharita Sengupta highlights the trajectory of the Rohingya refugees from Myanmar to Bangladesh. The author questions when and how can the status of statelessness be considered in relation to being stranded in the sea for prolonged periods of time and the implication of international legal instruments in addressing the statelessness of refugees at sea. By taking on the example of the crossing of the Rohingya refugees in the Bay of Bengal, Sengupta's work ponders on the "legal and humane implications of statelessness vis-à-vis the state," and how statelessness becomes produced at sea.

In the book's final chapter, "Logistics of Maritime Capitalism: Flags of Convenience and the Statelessness at Sea," Joyce C. H. Liu, Yu-Fan Chiu, and Jonathan S. Parhusip show the location of FOCs in global capitalism. By taking the case of Taiwan as a major receiving country of foreign fishery, statelessness of foreign workers is reflected through policy and legislative processes as connected to global capitalism. By placing these events relationally and investigating Indonesia as a labor-sending country, Lou, Chiu, and Parhusip engage the complex logistical network of the global supply chain and their position in producing statelessness within the industry of Flags of Convenience.

Taken together, chapters in this volume indicate that although no human being can be "illegal,'" the stamp of "illegality" is very often given to a number of unwanted, undesirable, or disposable people within or arriving in a state's territory. The "illegality" is produced through law and the ambiguity in the status of predominantly minoritized people living within marginalized spaces, whereby their basic rights, through suspension of law and its ambiguity, enable the state to easily detain those individuals. It abandons them, with no "right to have rights." Through this legal suspension of law, the extra-legal sovereign power, constituting the political in the modern state, becomes supreme. The prerogative of sovereign power is quite dispersed, and sometimes invisible. But this process of criminalizing the innocent, and/or disenfranchising them simply dispossesses them of their rights in the context of increasing racism, xenophobia, and populism.

This volume also shows how the states deny basic rights to non-citizens and the *de facto* stateless, within their borders, while the international legal architecture imposes very limited responsibilities on the states with respect to those fleeing persecution. Citizenship studies have been quite common in the Global North for a long time. However, that has not been the case in the Global South, including South Asia. Therefore, the everyday practices and experiences of citizens need to be more closely studied apart from the citizenship acts and/or their amendments. There are yawning gaps between the legalized and institutionalized forms of citizenship, on the one hand, and the everyday experiences and practices of citizenship (Sadiq 2016). A few enforceable protective mechanisms are sometimes more significant than a bunch of unenforceable lofty ideals to provide to the stateless people.

In September 2016, the United Nations took a major initiative to prioritize the issue of migrants and refugees globally. The subsequent New York Declaration generated a fresh framework for further deliberations. Accordingly, in 2018, many states agreed to a Global Compact for Safe, Orderly and Regular Migration (GCM), and another separate Global Compact on Refugees (GCR) (United Nations 2018; International Organization for Migration 2020). However, the two Global Compacts have mainly been drafted to address the refugee and migrant crisis in the Global North, highlighted through the Mediterranean crisis of 2015, and therefore, the concerns in the Global South have again mostly been neglected. First of all, the formulation of two separate Global Compacts denied the reality of mixed and massive flows of refugees, migrants, and asylum-seekers across the globe. Second, this initiative to formulate Global Compacts again failed to take any special note of the refugees and migrants in the Global South, thereby ignoring the other legal geographies. This raises the question of how "global" are these Global Compacts (United Nations 2018; International Organization for Migration 2020; Chaudhury 2022).

In other words, even the recent initiatives of the UN failed to move beyond the citizenship's Westphalian basics. Both the national and international regulations and initiatives still help to sustain the dominant mode of political community in the contemporary world, and the system of sovereign states remains the most important actor within the international legal order. Therefore, the Kolkata Declaration 2018, adopted after a conference organized by the Calcutta Research Group (CRG) on "The State of the Global Protection System for Refugees and Migrants" in November 2018, pointed out that any global compact aiming at sustainable resolutions must be "based on wide-ranging dialogues involving refugees, migrants, stateless persons and groups defending them" (Calcutta Research Group 2018: 6). Although the contemporary global politics and the international legal framework governing statelessness are definitely gathering momentum, several inadequacies, ambiguities, and unconcern for the stateless in the Global South still remain, which are unmaking citizens, and making hundreds and thousands of people stateless across the globe. In this connection, one may be reminded of Étienne Balibar's observation twenty years ago: "Whereas traditionally, and in conformity with both their juridical definition and 'cartographical' representation as incorporated in national memory, they should be at the edge of the territory, marking the point where it ends, it seems that borders and the institutional practices corresponding to them have been transported into the middle of political space" (Balibar 2004, 109).

The present volume contains chapters that clearly indicate that even the status of citizen is very often that of a "subject," as political participation gives way to the rule of police, and their inclusion in the society, and in the "nation" is purely discretionary. Statelessness of another kind, *de facto* statelessness, is therefore quite common, which does not usually find space in the definitional discourse of statelessness. This condition of continuous dispossession, unfreedom, and precarity calls for pushing the frontiers of the debates on statelessness, which can only change and emancipate their conditions.

## References


Balibar, Étienne. *We, the People of Europe? Reflections on Transnational Citizenship.* Translated by James Swenson. Translation/Transnation. Princeton, NJ: Princeton University Press, 2004.

Basu Ray Chaudhury, Sabyasachi. "Dispossession, Un-Freedom, Precarity: Negotiating Citizenship Laws in Postcolonial South Asia." *South Atlantic Quarterly* 120, no. 1 (2021): 209–19.

Benhabib, Seyla. *The Rights of Others: Aliens, Residents, and Citizens.* Cambridge: Cambridge University Press, 2004. https://doi.org/10.1017/CBO9780511790799

Calcutta Research Group. "Kolkata Declaration 2018."

Chaudhury, Sabyasachi Basu Ray. "Governance of Migration in South Asia: The Need for a Decolonial Approach." In *Displacement, Belonging, and Migrant Agency in the Face of Power*, edited by Tamar Mayer and Trinh Tran. London: Routledge, 2022.

Choi, Young Rae. "The Blue Economy as Governmentality and the Making of New Spatial Rationalities." *Dialogues in Human Geography* 7, no. 1 (2017): 37–41.

Godin, Marie, and Giorgia Donà. "Rethinking Transit Zones: Migrant Trajectories and Transnational Networks in *Techno-Borderscapes*." *Journal of Ethnic and Migration Studies* 47, no. 14 (2021): 3276–92. https://doi.org/10.1080/1369183X.2020.1804193

International Organization for Migration. "ILO and IOM Sign Agreement to Strengthen Collaboration on Migration Governance," 2020. ww.iom.int/news/ilo-and-iom-sign-agreement-strengthen-collaboration-migration-governance

Sadiq, Kamal. "Limits of Legal Citizenship: Narratives from South and Southeast Asia." In *Citizenship in Question*, edited by Benjamin N. Lawrance and Jacqueline Stevens, 165–76. Durham, NC: Duke University Press, 2016. https://doi.org/10.1215/9780822373483-010

Samaddar, Ranabir, ed. *Refugees and the State: Practices of Asylum and Care in India, 1947–2000.* New Delhi ; Thousand Oaks, California; and London: Sage Publications, 2003.

———. *The Postcolonial Age of Migration.* London & New York: Routledge, Taylor & Francis Group, 2020.

UNHCR. "Convention Relating to the Status of Stateless Persons." United Nations, 1954. www.unhcr.org/ibelong/wp-content/uploads/1954-Convention-relating-to-the-Status-of-Stateless-Persons_ENG.pdf

"UNHCR Fact Sheet: The 1961 Convention on the Reduction of Statelessness." UNHCR. *Refworld*, 1961. www.refworld.org/docid/612608084.html

United Nations. "Global Compact for Safe, Orderly and Regular Migration," 2018. www.un.org/en/ga/search/view_doc.asp?symbol=A/RES/73/195

Yao, Xine. *Disaffected: The Cultural Politics of Unfeeling in Nineteenth-Century America.* Durham, NC: Duke University Press, 2021.

# Part I

# Law as a Site of Statelessness

Chapter 1

# Revisiting (Il)legal Sites of Statelessness in South Asia

Sabyasachi Basu Ray Chaudhury

## Introduction

The postcolonial experiences of statelessness in South Asia mainly originated from the process of decolonization and the enactment of the new citizenship laws, or the amendment of the existing ones. With the transition from colonial to postcolonial times, the rhetoric and techniques of discipline and governance were reimagined and reinscribed in the postcolonial space. The postcolonial states have mostly expanded the basic institutional arrangements of colonial law and administration after their decolonization. This chapter illustrates how, in these changing circumstances, the "unwanted" minorities were excluded from the space of the new "state-nations" and from the discourses of postcolonial "nationhood." The continuous process of "othering" of the religious and ethnic minorities, and their systematic dispossessions, pushed these "unwelcome" populations to the frontiers of law and nation, rendering them stateless. The minorities or "unauthorized migrants" of the colonial period were "illegalized" through the techniques of postcolonial governments in South Asia. Thus, illegality turned into a status resulting from the political decisions made by the postcolonial states leading to the criminalization and liminality of the minorities. The structural violence inherent in the condition of their "illegality" crossed swords with their nostalgia of belonging and their desire to live with dignity. This chapter thus argues that the existing responses, inherent in the dominant legal ecosystem, crafted primarily in the postwar era, fall short of addressing the contemporary situations of statelessness, and calls for decolonizing the epistemologies of statelessness.

The national laws in countries around the world and the international and regional legal instruments are supposed to be framed in order to foreclose the policies that may render more human beings stateless. The judicial decisions are also supposed to be usually proclaimed for the same purpose. In spite of these initiatives, the number of stateless people has been on the rise. The people did not become stateless overnight only in the context of the Second World War, when it came to the forefront to encourage the formulation of international legal instruments on this issue. In spite of this, human beings are still becoming stateless in the recent neoliberal times. Europe was the major site of statelessness in the immediate postwar era, which provoked Hannah Arendt to foreground the causes of the people without the right to have rights. In the recent period, more and more people, living historically at a certain geographical space for generations in the plural societies of Asia and Africa, have turned into *sans papiers* in the background of nation-building exercises, the resultant enactment of new citizenship laws, or modification or amendment of the existing ones, and growing populist, often xenophobic politics, and increasing securitization of migrants and "outsiders."

When the "inside" of a state is freshly distinguished from its "outside," even the human beings inhabiting a space within, begin to be considered as "aliens," "outsiders," and therefore the usual suspects for the "national security" of the state. In this scenario, we shall revisit the legal sites of statelessness, mainly in South Asia. In doing so, we shall also look back at the binaries of legality/illegality and examine how the boundary-making exercises, both territorial and sociocultural, can rob groups of people of their "citizenship." Drawing examples from South Asia, we would indicate how subsequent policies of postcolonial states in South Asia, through their new legal ecosystem of citizenship, impacted the "bare life" of various groups of people in the region by rendering more and more human beings stateless. The disrobing of hundreds and thousands of people of their citizenship deprives them of their sense of belonging, branding them "illegal," and thus "outlawed." And, making them disenfranchised, in fact, pushes them to precarity generated through the operations of powers that be, constituted by the majority or dominant community in a designated postcolonial space. Our examples would elucidate the major trends addressing how groups of inhabitants in South Asia have gradually and systematically been dispossessed of their basic rights as human beings—and have thus been expelled to a world of unfreedom and precarity—in the name of the discourse of modern nation-states and citizenship framework derived from the Global North.

## New States of South Asia

As postcolonial societies of the Global South largely inherited colonially demarcated and sometimes arbitrarily partitioned territories, as in South Asia, they legitimized and reproduced the colonial boundaries and laws of governance. Spatially bounded parameters of belonging, based on the ideas of nation-state, borrowed from the Global North, have only excluded more people from the "nation" and its citizens in South Asia. Therefore, the history of statelessness has turned into the other side of the history of citizenship in the region.

The anticolonial movements in the Indian subcontinent, mainly during the early twentieth century, had huge potential to be emancipatory for the autonomy of the people (Werbner and Yuval-Davis 1999). But the decolonization of South Asia simultaneously generated irreconcilable strains between communal solidarities and primordial sentiments, on the one hand, and the ideas of democratic citizenship, rule of law, and individuality, on the other. In order to have homogeneous nation-states in South Asia, following the footsteps of their European counterparts, the postcolonial states gradually started relying upon majoritarianism, even when democratic ideals and models of governance were experimented with. Democratic experiments quite often turned into the means of establishing a rule only by the majority or by the dominant ethnic community, side-tracking the ideals of inclusiveness, a core value of modern liberal democracy. These new "state-nations" of the region were more passionate about building nations, mainly on the basis of forging a majority based on identarian politics, thereby privileging some citizens over others, thus very often creating an unbridgeable gap, and generating mutual suspicion and mistrust between the majorities and minorities.

Through this process of segregation, the minorities of this region have further been pushed to the margins of the system of governance, sometimes leading to the exclusion of the long-term inhabitants of a territory from the idea of the new "nation." Therefore, citizenship has been the site of extreme contestations in the postcolonial South Asia, where the minorities can perhaps mainly survive, either being co-opted through a process of "mainstreaming" or being entirely subservient to the politically dominant majority community. There thus has been a systematic exteriorization of the interior through the laws of citizenship and the process of nation building in South Asia. The foreignness of the "other" has been produced by and reflected in the institutions of immigration and citizenship laws, discursive representations, political commentaries, and academic discourses. In fact, the people who inhabit the *exteriority* (i.e., the outside invented in the process of defining the inside) have hardly any control over the knowledge ecosystem (Mignolo 2011). Citizenship, therefore, has taken on multiple meanings, as it is "not only a legal definition conferring a relationship to the state; it is also a practice, a concept of belonging and a context within which other activities are made possible" (Ng'weno 2013, 156–75).

## Borders and Boundaries

The tensions became more intense in the borderlands of South Asia, where boundaries were drawn or redrawn by the rulers, who were hastily leaving their mines of prosperity, in the immediate aftermath of the Second World War, thus not only partitioning the land but also the communities traditionally residing in those borderlands. This rush of the British colonizers "only exacerbated the chaos" (Dalrymple 2015). Drawing new borders posed cartographical challenges and anxieties in South Asia, as freshly demarcated lines on maps only nebulously followed ethnographic contours. It also raised issues concerning relations between new states and their citizens as subjects of colonies, who were legally turned into citizens of the new postcolonial nations. Thus citizenship has remained a contentious issue since the decolonization of the region, which has given rise to new instances of statelessness in South Asia. This is evident from the issues relating to a section of Tamils in Sri Lanka, Chakmas in Arunachal Pradesh of India, Lhotsampas of Nepali origin in Bhutan, Rohingyas in Myanmar, and the very recent example of 19 million inhabitants of the Indian state of Assam becoming people without a state through newly enacted citizenship laws or through existing acts that were amended. All such initiatives by the postcolonial states were parts of a nation-building process that involved the inclusion of certain communities within the fold of the new state and the instantaneous exclusion of the remaining ethnic or religious communities from the same political space (Basu Ray Chaudhury 2021). In fact, the nation-building in South Asia has been intended to homogenize a plural society comprising different religious and ethnic communities, which were historically sharing the same territorial space.

## Legalizing Illegality

Sir Cyril Radcliffe, a British judge assigned to draw the borders of the two new states of India and Pakistan, was given barely forty days to remake the map of South Asia. The Bangla-speaking people living in the undivided Bengal and the adjoining areas got divided when the partition of the Indian subcontinent was thrust upon them in 1947. They were henceforth compelled to live in the new nation of Bangladesh (earlier East Pakistan), on the one hand, and in West Bengal, Tripura, Assam, and Meghalaya of India, on the other. Similar has been the case of Naga and Chakma communities in the east of South Asia and Punjabis and Pashtuns in the west. The redrawing of boundaries has left the Nagas in Nagaland, Manipur, Assam, and Arunachal Pradesh states in India, on the one hand, and in Myanmar, on the other. Against this background, we shall take the examples of the Chakmas in Arunachal Pradesh and the Rohingyas in Myanmar to show how the developments in history along with the constitutional and legal mechanisms have, in fact, triggered their dispossession and erasure of citizenship.

## Deprivation of Chakmas

The Chakmas are spread over the Chittagong Hill Tracts (CHT) of Bangladesh, on the one side, and Tripura and Mizoram states in India, on the other, due to alteration of the boundaries and the postcolonial policies adopted after the partition. The Chakmas of CHT, in anticipation of the merger of their territory (being a Buddhist-majority region at that point) with India, hoisted the Indian tricolor national flag at least for a week in August 1947 at Rangamati, the district headquarters of CHT until the Pakistan army pulled it down on August 21, 1947. Moreover, Chakma leaders such as Sneha Kumar Chakma and Kamini Mohan Dewan took initiatives to merge the CHT with India and went to Delhi to meet the Indian national leaders to convince them about this merger. However, the CHT ultimately became part of East Pakistan according to the decision taken by the Boundary Commission chaired by Sir Cyril Radcliffe. But their suffering did not end there.

Subsequently, when the Government of Pakistan decided to construct the Kaptai dam over the Karnaphuli River in the CHT in the 1950s with assistance from the United States Agency for International Development (USAID), about 54,000 acres of arable farmland belonging to the Chakmas was flooded, and more than 100,000 people were displaced. At least 40,000 of them crossed over to India in 1964, and the Government of India settled them mainly in Tirap, Lohit, and Subansiri districts of the North-East Frontier Agency (NEFA), now the state of Arunachal Pradesh (Hindu Net Desk 2017). This was primarily due to their perceived loyalty to India that could be utilized by the Government of India in the context of the immediate aftermath of the Sino-Indian border conflict, when almost the entire NEFA came under the control of China's People's Liberation Army (PLA), at least for a few days.

Until the early 1980s, the Chakmas in Arunachal Pradesh could have a job, a ration card, and access to a few other rights enjoyed by the Indian citizens in a sparsely populated, remote, and bordering province of India. They were also allotted some land in consultation with the local Indigenous communities. The Government of India also sanctioned one-time financial assistance to the displaced families. In this context, by the mid-1990s, the number of Chakmas in Arunachal Pradesh had increased to around 65,000. Meanwhile, in 1994, the All Arunachal Pradesh Students' Union (AAPSU), a local students' organization, had issued "quit notices" to all alleged foreigners, including the Chakmas, asking them to leave the State by September 30, 1995. The AAPSU also threatened to use force if its demand was not acquiesced. In fact, the Chakmas were being perceived as "illegal immigrants" in spite of being there for three decades. When this issue, in the context of the *National Human Rights Commission (NHRC) vs. State of Arunachal Pradesh and Anr*, was referred to a bench of the Supreme Court of India, the apex judiciary in the country, led by Chief Justice A. H. Ahmadi and Justice S. C. Sen, the bench observed that the Chakmas had been residing in Arunachal Pradesh for more than three decades, having developed close social, religious, and economic ties. Therefore, to uproot them at this stage would be both impracticable and inhumane.

## Expulsion of Rohingyas

The Rohingyas were once residents of Arakan State, which is now called Rakhine State in Myanmar. Their exclusion from the new nation of Burma was formalized in 1982 when the country's military junta enacted a new repressive citizenship law that practically robbed the Rohingyas of their rights in Burma and rendered them stateless. As a consequence, and on account of the structural violence against these Muslim minorities in a Buddhist majority state, about 250,000 Rohingyas fled the country in the early 1990s. However, the mass exodus of the Rohingyas from Myanmar, to the tune of at least 730,000 since August 2017—once their houses were burned down, properties destroyed, resources plundered, women tortured and raped, and even children not spared from heartless torture—has perhaps changed their lives forever.

The escalation of violence and a simultaneous humanitarian disaster forced the Rohingyas to take shelter in the makeshift and already over-populated refugee camps in the neighboring Cox's Bazaar in Bangladesh. Myanmar's (name changed from Burma subsequently) refusal to recognize the Rohingyas as its legitimate citizens made the Rohingyas stateless. With the reticent, as well as nonchalant, attitude of the Government of Myanmar, the return of Rohingyas back home and their regaining citizenship are as remote as the Moon. The status of Rohingya refugees in Bangladesh, Malaysia, and many other countries is that of refugees, whereas in India, they are considered "illegal immigrants." Be that as it may, all these Rohingyas are *de facto* stateless people in a world of nations.

## Postcolonial Territorialization and Exteriority

It is hardly difficult to ignore the words of Ayesha Jalal on the partition of the Indian subcontinent. According to her, partition has been a "defining moment that is neither beginning nor end, partition continues to influence how the peoples and states of postcolonial South Asia envisage their past, present and future" (Jalal 2013, 4). Jalal also rightly said, "There can be no real understanding of India, Pakistan, and Bangladesh without a full grasp of the lasting impact of partition on their self-imaginings, political contestations, and national projections" (4). 'Partition-refugees' became integral elements of nation-building in South Asia (Samaddar 2003, 27). Similarly, Yasmin Khan has argued that Partition "stands testament to the follies of empire, which ruptures community evolution, distorts historical trajectories and forces violent state formation from societies that would otherwise have taken different—and unknowable—paths" (Khan 2017, 210). In other words, the partition left a lasting imprint, not only on the frontier areas of the former colonies alone but also on those countries, which could not entirely escape a close brush with coloniality, like Nepal and Bhutan, in spite of not being ever directly colonized by the European powers.

In fact, territorialization of states has perhaps been less about drawing geographical or spatial boundaries than it has been about drawing social distinctions between peoples. Territory has primarily been a way of dividing up and governing people, not space, in South Asia. The postcolonial states in this region are, to a great extent, the leftovers of the Age of Empire, which, in a way, is yet to end. Imperial histories have given birth to the complicated nature of the relation between colonial sovereignty and border making in South Asia (Baud and Van Schendel 1997; Leake and Haines 2017). The postcolonial state-nations in this region are still unfolding, offering pathways of emancipatory ideals of entitlements for individuals, and yet regenerating the traditional cleavages in the societies with an objective of homogenization of the heterogeneities. In fact, border epistemology is a framework that emerges at the juncture of oppression and resistance. It is composed of the "plurisversality" of local colonial histories in South Asia entangled with imperial modernity (Mignolo 2007). Living in the borderlands implied higher risks of dispossession, persecution, and violence for many during and after decolonization.

As indicated earlier, in this context, the transition of the majority of traditional inhabitants in South Asia from subjects of a colonial society to citizens of the modern state-nations was brought about through the juridification of citizenship by postcolonial constitutional and legal processes, sometimes making the concept more contested and complex, ignoring histories of continuous mobility of people across the region. Apart from the natural flow of people in search of livelihood opportunities, the British colonial rulers, dominating South Asia in the colonial age, also resettled groups of people for their own commercial interests as indentured labor. Therefore, the Tamils were taken to Sri Lanka, or people from Nepal were encouraged to move to Darjeeling Hills, Dooars, and Assam for plantation activities.

This juridification is a form of constitutionalization that can take many forms and involve many legal and regulatory practices with regard to citizenship. The creation of an "exteriority" outside the territory of the new postcolonial state, under the new circumstances, was also to be negotiated within its own borders. In spite of the actual end of colonial administration, a colonial logic of governing through ethnic and "racial" divides has remained quite common in many postcolonial societies in South Asia. Against this backdrop, tendency is growing in South Asia to endorse the ostensible binary between the "legal" and the "illegal," due to the anxiety of the negative value judgment the term "illegal" carries. This tendency overlooks the process of how "illegalization" operates alongside "legalization," as if conversing with each other, as part of a larger process of making and unmaking of particular relations of power through the operations of law.

In short, the dominant legal discourses often illegalize different groups of people in postcolonial South Asia. This becomes quite evident from the perspective of critical jurisprudence and the premise of legal pluralities. Our brief references to the postcolonial states in the region, their power, ethics, and the relevant laws help us to indicate how the new borders and boundaries, and citizenship have together excluded a large number of people from the state-nation, "illegalizing" and thereby rendering them stateless, although law seems to suppose the generality of a rule, a norm, or a universal imperative. We would also argue that it is not due to certain categorical imperatives that human beings are "legalized" or "illegalized" (and thus, the citizens and the stateless), but they are rendered so within specific contexts of power and politics. In addition, the national laws and international legal discourses are, in many ways, products of late modern coloniality, and have been crucial for dispossession and precarity of the stateless, as neoliberal economic arrangements have been.

## Territoriality and Sovereignty

We thus argue that South Asia is a product of the empire, conceived as expressing all forms of subordination effected by the capitalist world system (Santos 2014). On the other hand, the history of international law has largely been dominated by the states and ideas of Europe. There has also been a centrality of states in the historiography of international law (Hanley 2014). As a consequence, two major international legal instruments—namely, the 1954 Convention Relating to the Status of Stateless Persons and the 1961 Convention on the Reduction of Statelessness—primarily govern the issue of statelessness.

Statelessness, as we know, is closely related to the significant issues of interactions among states, and the relation between people and their governments. The phenomenon of statelessness, or the lack of recognition as a citizen of any state, as we have seen, is inherently tied to broader questions concerning the regulations and substance of citizenship. Citizenship defines the legal relationship between the citizen and a state. However, the question of citizenship has largely remained within the exclusive domain of states. The International Court of Justice (ICJ) indicated in the *Nottebohm* case that nationality "serves above all to determine the person upon whom it is conferred enjoys the rights and is bound by the obligations which the law of the State in question grants to or imposes on its nationals" (International Court of Justice 1955). According to the ICJ, nationality "is a legal bond having as its basis a social fact of attachment, a genuine connection of existence, interest and sentiments, together with the existence of reciprocal rights and duties" (International Court of Justice 1955).

In this connection, however, we must remember the difference between citizens and nationals.[1] It is also important to recall the three principal methods of acquiring citizenship. They are either through the principle of *jus soli*, by birth on the territory of a particular state; *jus sanguinis*, by descent or parentage; or *jus domicili*, via naturalization by virtue of long residence. All these three methods, however, indicate the primacy of territoriality and sovereignty derived from the modern nation-states, emerging in Europe since the Treaty of Westphalia (1648). This perhaps generates a gray area beyond the territorial limits that is also beyond the jurisdiction of any particular state, and also ungovernable by the international legal framework largely bounded by the concept of state sovereignty.

Therefore, the international laws on statelessness have thus far failed to find a dignified position in the international legal regime. In fact, the international legal instruments governing statelessness are at the margins of the international legal regime. At least, the international laws governing refugees, human rights, and migration have established themselves quite solidly in the international legal framework. On the other hand, statelessness has been primarily viewed as the outcome of state succession and armed conflict. But in India and the other postcolonial states of South Asia, there have been instances of the systematic erasure of members of minority ethnic groups from the citizenship registers. This was the case for the inhabitants of Assam through the implementation of the National Register of Citizens (NRC) in the larger context of the stringent anti-immigrant stand of successive governments in Guwahati and New Delhi, or the official deprivation of nationality by constitutional means and legislative enactment.

## The Great Disconnect

We often forget that there is a world with an overwhelming majority of people beyond the Euro-American world. We tend to overlook the fact that the origin and nature of the stateless are diverse in character across different geographies and histories. Therefore, it would be better to look at the issues from a pluriversal perspective, taking seriously into account the different legal geographies and separate anthropologies of uprootedness. Perhaps the recent decolonial thinking, in contradistinction to most modernist ideas, may help us revisit the legal sites of statelessness in South Asia.

These decolonial and pluriversal arguments have two basic premises. First, the dominant Western theory and practice depend on a Euro-modern ontology that has particular ethical and political effects. Second, it also maintains that the Western ontology's claim to universality is false (Hutchings 2019). In this context, our argument would be that, even in the postcolonial societies, the production of knowledge has predominantly been subject to the colonial blueprints and geopolitics that are Eurocentric. Most of these accounts of postcolonial times, like their colonial counterparts, tend to disregard the existence of other knowledges, as do the postcolonial states in connection not only with stateless people but also with regard to different minorities within the boundaries of the state.

On the contrary, the pluriversal approaches claim to recognize and appreciate other cultures, and the existence of other legal approaches originating from other knowledges, histories, and experiences (Mignolo 2011). The legal sites of statelessness in South Asia, and the precarity and helplessness of the stateless population, perhaps may be better understood taking into account the geographies of reason and law (Mignolo 2007). An emancipatory blueprint of governance must appreciate the pluriverse of legal geographies. There is thus an urgent need for an alternative, decolonial, and pluriversal approach to statelessness that takes into cognizance the various histories, experiences, and occurrences across the world.

## Decolonializing Statelessness

The context and process of engendering statelessness in the Global North quite often differ from that in the Global South, including South Asia. The hegemonic production of Western epistemologies—evidenced by the categorization of the uprooted and displaced population across the globe, without considering the specificities—as well as the continuous silencing and erasure of the other histories of displacement, along with other knowledges and traditions of hospitality, perpetuated a sense of inferiority of understanding displacement in the Global South. This, in a way, offers structural frames through which the Global South has been conditioned and trained to consider the replication of Western ideas of displacement and statelessness, although the dominant discourses emanating from the Euro-American contexts may not entirely capture the experiences of statelessness in the Global South, as briefly evidenced in our discussion above.

Decolonization, in general, means decolonization of a territory that was under colonial rule for a certain period of time, mostly by the economically advanced countries of Europe. It does not usually imply decolonization of minds and thoughts. Colonialism, understood as imposition and domination, did not end overnight with the return of political sovereignty to the newly emerging state-nations of the Global South. Rather, colonialism and recolonizing projects very much manifest themselves in the postcolonial societies in a variety of ways, through the many ways in which knowledges are produced and receive validation, the particular experiences of different groups of people that get recognized as (in)valid, and the identities that receive official recognition from the states.

Colonialism, in the contemporary era, manifests itself in different ways, from the dominance of the English language in the knowledge industry to the rise of the mainly state and global capitalism managed by the Global North. The disturbing trends in this context emerge from the homogenizing trend of corporate capitalism. As a consequence, the individuals themselves become complicit in the reproduction of colonial norms. The hegemony of the emerging trend of education, and more so of the knowledge industry that conditions the education system, reduces shared local, particularly Indigenous, knowledge.

This politics of subversion of knowledge and the delegitimization of the knowledges of the colonized calls for a politics of decolonizing the definitions of stateless persons that would take note of their precarity and unfreedom in largely different contexts. This is, however, not to disregard or discard the discourses of the Global North. This is rather to indicate the inadequacies of these discourses to comprehend the complexities of different human histories and experiences of displacement and statelessness. This is why it is necessary to decolonize the epistemologies and the standards developing almost entirely in the context of the Global North.

## Universal or Pluriversal?

The experiences and histories have very often been co-opted within the universal concepts, emanating primarily from the Global North. In fact, an intrinsic connection exists between modernity and globality. "Modernity once deemed itself universal. Now it thinks of itself as global. Behind the change of term hides a watershed in the history of modern self-awareness and self-confidence. Universal was to be the rule of reason—the order of things that would replace the slavery to passions with the autonomy of rational beings, superstition and ignorance" (Bauman 1998, 24). The discourses on universalism should be taken into account in this context.

Discourse, on the other hand, denotes a historically contingent social system that produces knowledge and meaning. Discourse is distinctly material in reality, producing "practices that systematically form the objects of which they speak" (Foucault 1972, 39–140). It is, thus, a way of organizing knowledge that structures the constitution of social, and thereafter global, relations through the collective understanding of the discursive logic and the acceptance of the discourse as social fact. Legal discourse, therefore, is the logic emanating structurally from a broader episteme, or structure of legal knowledge, at a juncture of history. In other words, the effects of power within a social order produce discourses. This power prescribes particular rules and categories that define the criteria for legitimating knowledge and truth within the discursive order. Therefore, in every society, the production of legal discourse is controlled, selected, organized, reproduced, and redistributed. Within every discourse there is always a relation of power (Foucault 1972).

Coloniality reshaped the modes of knowing, of producing knowledge, and producing perspectives (Quijano 2007). The transformation of colonial territories into sovereign states is central to claims that statehood and state formations are universal because all societies, whether European or non-European, participate as equal sovereign states in world systems (Anghie 2005). But, with every specter of difference comes the possibility of hierarchies as well as relations of domination and subordination (Mongia 2007).

Decolonization should have indicated the production of knowledge practices suitable for the task of decolonizing. However, decolonization quite often turned oppression into hierarchies. Oppressions indeed differ in scope and magnitude, but creating hierarchies may themselves be forms of suppression by limiting the range and breadth of experiences. Therefore, even in the postcolonial era, the law itself, including the laws of citizenship, has been used as a weapon and a tool of dispossession. In this sense, the task of decolonization requires the development of alternative concepts and tools that provide a broader foundation for the study of humanity.

## Liminality of the Stateless

The governance of postcolonial societies with the support of colonial documentation and laws was also central to the monitoring of the people and their movements in South Asia. The ontology of statelessness was thus defined by a constant state of liminality between being and nonbeing. The stateless population, who have been dispossessed and then uprooted from their homeland, had to be excluded from the new nations in South Asia they struggled to produce. The birth of the postcolonial states was central to narrating stories of discipline and governance in this region. The liminality of the South Asian space, divided among state territories, thus became the site of surveillance and discipline through (il)legal means.

Although the historic moment of decolonization of these postcolonial states generated infinite optimism, these states required disciplined citizens. In the context of the transition from colonial to postcolonial states, the rhetoric and techniques of discipline and governance were reimagined and reinscribed in the postcolonial space. As a result, a sense of nationalism emerged, through which the majority communities and their privileged classes started effectively silencing the personhood of the "others." This has been one of the major colonial projects in the postcolonial state-nations.

In the process, the ecosystem of surveillance and discipline emanating from this project began calibrating the spatiotemporality and geography of the "new nation." Therefore, in many ways and instances, the postcolonial states have "expanded and not transformed the basic institutional arrangements of colonial law and administration" (Chatterjee 1993, 15). These colonial technologies of spatial control and repression traveled from Europe to the colonized spaces of South Asia during the imperial era. Therefore, with the making and remaking of borders during the decolonization of territories, the citizenship laws and/or their subsequent amendments have been useful to exclude the unwanted minorities from the space of the new states and from the discourses on nationhood. Their systematic dispossessions pushed them to the frontiers of law and nation, rendering them stateless.

When national laws themselves caused dispossession and statelessness, international laws, marked by Eurocentric characteristics, felt abysmally short of addressing the complex developments and issues emerging in the context of the decolonization of a number of states in Asia and Africa. The origin of international law, after all, "lies in the constitution of the modern/colonial world and of Western civilization" (Mignolo 2011, 79). Over and above, cultures similar to the West European system were considered to be closer to modernity, whereas cultures less similar were considered closer to tradition. These dissimilar cultures were thus placed further back in time along an imaginary continuum toward progress and granting them an inferior standing by the nature of this remoteness (160). In other words, coloniality did not cease to exist because of the exit of formal colonial states (Grosfoguel 2017, 219).

As a consequence, the so-called discourses of diversities and inclusion to be underscored in the international laws governing refugees, migrants, and the stateless are more often than not lost in the geopolitics of knowledge originating in the Global North. Therefore, when the Chakmas, Tamils, Lhotsampas, or Rohingyas have been uprooted, criminalized, exterminated, dehumanized, or relegated to the margins of the new "state-nations" of South Asia, the international legal regimes on statelessness have not bothered to take note of these other specificities and experiences to accommodate diverse situations.

In addition, the events of 9/11 triggered a global tectonic shift, which largely modified the existing ideas about nation, space, borders, risk, and the embodiment of terror. This derivative discourse subsequently has not only been part of the geopolitical statecraft but also has percolated into everyday life of South Asia. Islamophobia may have gathered renewed strength in the Global North after 9/11, but it has also manifested itself in the Global South since then. South Asia is no exception to this development. Rather, it has been the basis of one of the newer forms of racialization across the globe.

## In Lieu of Answers

The methodological problem facing us today is sometimes not one of answers but of questions (Scott 2004). The answers we appear to have for the contemporary situations of statelessness in the international legal framework are somewhat deficient, as they were crafted mainly within the narrative framework of Europe at a different time. This pushes us to ask newer questions about the states and their citizenship discourses, ones that reflect the stakes of contemporary times and the diverse experiences of the stateless people both in the Global North and South. We must also perhaps ask what makes certain narratives more powerful to pass as accepted history and law (Trouillot 1995).

The inhuman experiences of the stateless Rohingyas across the Bay of Bengal are as important as the insensitive practices toward the migrants and refugees in the Mediterranean. These pluriversal global approaches to international legal regimes concerning refugees, migrants, and the stateless are now urgently required, and not the traditional universal perspectives, which have become the reigning orthodoxy. Hence, pluriversalism may be based only on epistemic democratization and decolonization of democracy.

## Note

1. For a detailed discussion, please see Alice Edwards and Laura Van Waas (eds.), *Nationality and Stateless under International Law* (Cambridge: Cambridge University Press, 2014).

## References

Anghie, Antony. *Imperialism, Sovereignty and the Making of International Law.* Cambridge: Cambridge University Press, 2005.

Basu Ray Chaudhury, Sabyasachi. "Dispossession, Un-Freedom, Precarity: Negotiating Citizenship Laws in Postcolonial South Asia." *South Atlantic Quarterly* 120, no. 1 (2021): 209–19.

Baud, Michiel, and Willem Van Schendel. "Toward a Comparative History of Borderlands." *Journal of World History* 8, 2 (1997): 211–42.

Bauman, Zygmunt. *Life in Fragments: Essays in Postmodern Morality*. Reprinted. Oxford: Blackwell, 1998.

Chatterjee, Partha. *The Nation and Its Fragments: Colonial and Postcolonial Histories*. Princeton Studies in Culture/Power/History. Princeton, NJ: Princeton University Press, 1993.

Dalrymple, William. "The Mutual Genocide of Indian Partition." *The New Yorker*, June 22, 2015. www.newyorker.com/magazine/2015/06/29/the-great-divide-books-dalrymple

Edwards, Alice, and Laura Van Waas (eds.), *Nationality and Stateless under International Law*. Cambridge: Cambridge University Press, 2014.

Foucault, Michel. *The Archaeology of Knowledge*. Translated by A. M. Sheridan. New York: Pantheon Books, 1972.

Grosfoguel, Ramón. "The Epistemic Decolonial Turn: Beyond Political-Economy Paradigms." *Cultural Studies* 21, no. 2–3 (2017): 211–23. https://doi.org/10.1080/09502380601162514

Hanley, Will. "Statelessness: An Invisible Theme in the History of International Law." *European Journal of International Law* 25, no. 1 (2014): 321–27. https://doi.org/10.1093/ejil/chu015

Hindu Net Desk, 2017. Who are Chakmas? www.thehindu.com/news/national/who-are-chakmas/article19682129.ece. Accessed December 11, 2021.

Hutchings, Kimberly. "Decolonizing Global Ethics: Thinking with the Pluriverse." *Ethics and International Affairs* 33, no. 2 (January 2019): 1–11. https://qmro.qmul.ac.uk/xmlui/handle/123456789/57996

Jalal, Ayesha. *The Pity of Partition*. Princeton, NJ: Princeton University Press, 2013. https://press.princeton.edu/books/hardcover/9780691153629/the-pity-of-partition

Khan, Yasmin. *The Great Partition: The Making of India and Pakistan*. New Haven, CT: Yale University Press, 2017.

Leake, Elisabeth, and Daniel Haines. "Lines of (In)Convenience: Sovereignty and Border-Making in Postcolonial South Asia, 1947–1965." *The Journal of Asian Studies* 76, no. 4 (2017): 963–85. https://doi.org/10.1017/S0021911817000808

Liechtenstein v. Guatemala (*Nottebohm* Case), Second Phase (International Court of Justice Reports 1955).

Mignolo, Walter D. *The Darker Side of Western Modernity: Global Futures, Decolonial Options*. Latin America Otherwise: Languages, Empires, Nations. Durham, NC: Duke University Press, 2011.

Mignolo, Walter D. "DELINKING: The Rhetoric of Modernity, the Logic of Coloniality and the Grammar of de-Coloniality." *Cultural Studies* 21, no. 2–3 (2007): 449–514. https://doi.org/10.1080/09502380601162647

Mongia, Radhika V. "Historicizing State Sovereignty: Inequality and the Form of Equivalence." *Comparative Studies in Society and History* 49, no. 2 (2007): 384–411.

Ng'weno, Bettina. "Beyond Citizenship as We Know It: Race and Ethnicity in Afro-Colombian Struggles for Citizenship Equality." In *Comparative Perspectives on Afro-Latin America*, edited by Kwame Dixon, John Burdick, and Howard Winant [first paperback printing], 156–75. Gainesville: University Press of Florida, 2013.

Quijano, Aníbal. "Coloniality and Modernity/Rationality." *Cultural Studies* 21, no. 2–3 (2007): 168–78. https://doi.org/10.1080/09502380601164353

Samaddar, Ranabir (ed.). *Refugees and the State: Practices of Asylum and Care in India, 1947–2000*. New Delhi & London: Sage, 2003

Santos, Boaventura de Sousa. *Epistemologies of the South: Justice against Epistemicide*. London & New York: Routledge, 2014.

Scott, David. *Conscripts of Modernity: The Tragedy of Colonial Enlightenment*. Durham, NC: Duke University Press, 2004.

Trouillot, Michel-Rolph. *Silencing the Past: Power and the Production of History*. Boston: Beacon Press, 1995.

Werbner, Pnina, and Nira Yuval-Davis. "Women and the New Discourse of Citizenship." In *Women, Citizenship and Difference*, edited by Pnina Werbner and Nira Yuval-Davis. London & New York: Zed, 1999.

"Who Are Chakmas?" National. *The Hindu*, September 14, 2017. www.thehindu.com/news/national/who-are-chakmas/article61473775.ece

Chapter 2

# The Production of Statelessness in Europe

Elspeth Guild and Sandra Mantu

European states have been increasingly concerned to find ways to address terrorism and the radicalization of their citizens. Since the attacks in London in 2005 and Paris in 2015, there has been an increasing focus on the question of citizenship: do citizens suspected of engaging in terrorism "deserve" to retain their citizenship or is this a privilege that should be reserved only for citizens not considered a threat by the state? From the perspective of law, citizenship is a matter of national constitutional arrangements. Deprivation of citizenship, however, does engage international law where there are two UN conventions on the subject of statelessness and one Council of Europe convention on nationality. In line with Article 15 of the Universal Declaration of Human Rights, the common standards of protection distilled from these legal instruments are that arbitrary deprivation of nationality is prohibited and that states have an obligation to reduce or avoid statelessness. Yet, notwithstanding these commitments, some European states have taken action that in practice results in statelessness of their former citizens on the basis of terrorism risks (e.g., former British citizen Shamima Begum), while the European Court of Human Rights seems to be ceding to national sovereignty on the issue of human rights in the deprivation of citizenship (see *Ghoumid and Others v France*).

In the European controversy regarding the entitlement of states to deprive people of their citizenship, one aspect is (so far) consistent. European states have accepted in principle that they cannot use their deprivation powers if the individual becomes stateless. The UK is something of an exception in this regard as it permits the deprivation of citizenship even where the person would, as a result, be stateless if the person had acquired citizenship by naturalization (S 40 British Nationality Act 1981 as amended proposed legislation currently before the UK Parliament would extend the right further). The assumption here is that although the British state has granted the person citizenship, the person is or used to be the responsibility of some other state, so taking away British citizenship is not so problematic. However, people born British are protected from this route to statelessness and can be deprived of their citizenship only if they hold another one. This intersection of citizenship and immigration status arises since the actual use of deprivation powers by European states is almost exclusively reserved for people who have been migrants at some point in their state of citizenship (before acquiring the status) or are the children of people who were once migrants in the state. This relationship with migration constitutes what European states consider to be a legitimate ground for the weakening of the bond between the individual and the state. Most European states differentiate between citizens by birth and citizens who have acquired citizenship later in life when it comes to the grounds upon which nationality can be lost (Meijers Committee 2020). Activities that touch upon national security and are carried out by citizens with a migration background are claimed by the authorities to justify the deprivation of citizenship even where those affected will be rendered stateless, while "real" citizens (by birth) are shielded from this use of state power.

In this chapter, we examine the issue from the perspective of the production of statelessness focusing on three main issues. First, as statelessness is the condition of not being able to claim the citizenship of any state, we will examine the gap between individuals and some European states regarding their entitlement to an effective citizenship. Second, in European legal traditions, citizenship constitutes an expression of loyalty between the individual and the state. The development of European laws and practices of deprivation of citizenship is founded on a rupture of this relationship on the basis of national security. We will look at the assessment of national security and those state bodies charged with making the call. Finally, the deprivation of citizenship in the European context is resulting in the creation of "stranded" migrants without citizenship or even durable links to the places where they are physically present. The consequence is to create situations of profound vulnerability for the individuals caught in the process. In all three cases, where state constitutional rules fail the individual, a claim is made to supranational human rights law as a source of obligation on states not to abandon the citizens they no longer want.

Worldwide, states have become more and more interested in using citizenship deprivation in the fight against terrorism. This has resulted in the judicialization of nationality claims at the national and supranational levels, as individuals affected by citizenship deprivation orders have challenged them in court with varying degrees of success. On the one hand, nationality law is deployed by state authorities as the tool through which citizenship status and rights (e.g., passport denial, entry bans) are taken away from citizens deemed dangerous or lacking loyalty. On the other hand, human rights law is mobilized by applicants and called upon to step in and effectively protect them from their state. While from a national security perspective, home-grown terrorists and foreign "terrorist" fighters (which is to say their own nationals who have gone abroad and engaged in political violence elsewhere) are treated as security threats, depriving them of citizenship nonetheless encroaches upon their human right to nationality. We can thus ask: What are the respective roles of national and supranational law in the governance of citizenship altogether and on what grounds? How has the loyalty characteristic of citizenship been transformed by state bodies seeking to fight terrorism? How do the newly stateless become stranded migrants in vulnerable situations? Finally, do supranational human rights standards that states must observe in the exercise of their powers protect affected individuals, or does the claim of national security as a central dimension of state sovereignty silence human rights?

## Understand a European Human Rights Dimension to Citizenship Deprivation

This section takes a closer look at the European Convention on Human Rights (ECHR) as a source of protection for the right to nationality and at the European Court of Human Rights' (ECtHR) case law on citizenship deprivation from our three vantage points. The ECtHR's engagement with nationality issues from a human rights perspective is an important development when considering that international law treats nationality as a bastion of state sovereignty and that states have been generally reluctant to adhere to enforceable nationality standards that limit their leeway in deciding who should be part of the citizenry (Ersbøll 2007; Kesby 2012; Spiro 2011). In the European context, nationality is not expressly included among the rights protected by the ECHR. The unsuccessful attempts to remedy the absence of nationality from the ECHR by adopting an additional protocol on nationality subjected to the Court's jurisdiction led to the adoption of the European Convention on Nationality (ECN) in 1997 as a separate Council of Europe instrument. The ECN is considered to provide a higher standard of protection against loss of nationality than its UN counterpart, namely the 1961 UN Convention on the Reduction of Statelessness, because it limits the cases in which state parties can take away nationality while producing statelessness to only one accepted situation: fraud during the acquisition of nationality. In respect of all the other situations in which states can legitimately deprive citizens of nationality, statelessness functions as a barrier, and state action is allowed only if it does not create statelessness. The ECN's low number of ratifications—for example, the UK is not a state party, while France has signed but not ratified the convention—suggests that the strong link between sovereignty and nationality continues to inform the position of European states on this matter.

The types of claims addressed by the ECHR touch upon different aspects of the human right to nationality, ranging from the treatment of statelessness in the context of state succession (*Makuc and Others v. Slovenia, Kurić and Others v. Slovenia*) to denial of nationality (*Karassev v. Finland, Genovesse v. Malta*) and loss of an already acquired nationality on grounds of fraud and national security (*Ramadan v. Malta*; *Ghoumid and others v. France*). The Court has developed a body of jurisprudence on the protection of the human right to nationality as part of Article 8 ECHR—the (qualified) right to private life, but without going as far as acknowledging a right to acquire a particular nationality under the ECHR. Nationality is treated as part of a person's social identity, while the notion of private life under Article 8 ECHR is wide enough to embrace aspects of a person's social identity (*Genovesse v. Malta*). An arbitrary refusal of citizenship may in certain circumstances raise an issue under Article 8 ECHR due to the impact of such a denial on the applicant's private life (*Karassev v. Finland, Slivenko and Others v. Latvia, Genovesse v. Malta*). Loss of a citizenship already acquired or born into can have the same or possibly more significant impact on a person's private and family life (*Ramadan v Malta,* para 85), but to find a violation of Article 8 ECHR, such a measure must be arbitrary and its consequences for the applicant's private or family life serious enough to outweigh the margin of appreciation recognized to states under Article 8(2) of the ECHR.[1] Thus, similar to international human rights law, what is relevant in the ECHR system is the arbitrary nature of state actions, the interpretation of which is contested in cases involving terrorism, as illustrated by *Ghoumid and Others v. France*.

## Loyalty and Citizenship

*Ghoumid and Others v. France* concerns five applicants who were dual nationals (four of them French Moroccan and one French Turkish). Two of the applicants had been born in France and acquired nationality by declaration upon reaching the age of majority, a third applicant acquired nationality in his teens because of his father's naturalization, while the remaining two applicants acquired French nationality via marriage (para 15). In 2007, they were convicted of participation in a criminal conspiracy to commit an act of terrorism because between 1995 and 2004 they had provided support to GICM—the "groupe islamiste combatant marocaine," which had links to the organization responsible for the 2003 Casablanca terrorist attacks. Besides financial support, the applicants illegally hosted other GICM members and procured passports to be falsified but had not participated themselves in the Casablanca bombings. They served prison sentences of six to eight years and were released in 2009–2010. In October 2015, as a response to the Charlie Hebdo attacks that had taken place in January 2015, the French government decided to deprive the applicants of nationality as part of its efforts to reinforce measures against persons convicted of terrorist offences. The applicants complained that their terrorism convictions, some ten years earlier and with no direct link to the January 2015 attacks, had a symbolic character. Their attempts to have the citizenship deprivation orders annulled on grounds of misuse of authority were rejected by French courts and the French Council of State, leading to the ECHR challenge.

In Strasbourg, the applicants complained about the violation of their rights to family and private life, considering the arbitrary nature of the citizenship deprivation measures and their disproportionate consequences. The Court unanimously found no violation of private life under Article 8 ECHR and found the complaint inadmissible in respect of the family life limb of Article 8 ECHR. The Court equally rejected the applicants' argument that citizenship deprivation constituted criminal punishment that, combined with the criminal sentences they had already served, violated Article 4 of Protocol 7 of the ECHR. This provision enshrines a fundamental right guaranteeing that no one is to be tried or punished in criminal proceedings for an offense of which they have already been finally convicted or acquitted. The Court accepted without any great scrutiny that despite its severity, citizenship deprivation is an administrative measure under French law, which puts it outside the scope of Protocol 7.

In relation to both sets of claims, the Court's reasoning relies heavily on the seriousness of terrorism itself, which is depicted as an attack on democracy itself, which undermines its foundation, and on the bond of loyalty that unites the citizen and the state that is expressed by the legal status of nationality. French nationality law accepts that the bond of loyalty between state and citizen can be questioned depending on how nationality was acquired and that persons who are not born French but acquire nationality later must be successfully assimilated and show respect for French republican values (Article 24 of the French Civil Code). Only persons who acquire nationality later in life and hold a second nationality can be deprived of French citizenship in cases where the law assumes a lack of loyalty evidenced by conviction for certain crimes, including for acts of terrorism (Article 25 of the French Civil Code). After repeated changes, French law stipulates that citizenship deprivation can occur for acts committed prior to naturalization and, concerning acts of terrorism, deprivation must occur within a fifteen-year limit from the acquisition of nationality and commission of acts (Mantu 2015). The result is that French law treats citizens by birth and citizens who acquire their status via naturalization, marriage, or reintegration into French nationality differently in the fight against terrorism by treating the latter as conditional citizens. Despite the creation of a hierarchy of citizens, the French Constitutional Council does not consider this different treatment to be discriminatory or unconstitutional because of its objective to combat terrorism, the specific seriousness inherent within the acts of terrorism, the fact that citizenship deprivation is limited in time, the existence of a conviction, and the protection against statelessness (Decision 96-377 of 16 July 1996; Decision 2014-439 of 23 January 2015).

It is noteworthy that in its judgment, the ECtHR does not once mention the issue of different treatment depending on how citizenship was acquired when discussing the potentially arbitrary nature of the citizenship deprivation measures. Instead, the Court upheld the arguments of the French government that the commission of terrorist acts coupled with their duration and the fact that the applicants had only recently acquired French nationality showed a weaker link of loyalty between them and the French state (para 50). This position whereby loyalty is questionable in the case of "new" citizens should be discussed in light of the Court's decision in *Biao v. Denmark*, where it ruled that differences in the enjoyment of the right to family reunification between persons born Danish and persons who acquired Danish citizenship later in life amounted to indirect discrimination on the basis of ethnic origin. In the *Biao* case, non-Danish-born applicants fell within the scope of the so-called twenty-eight-year rule before they could claim a right to family reunification. This rule was found to place at a disadvantage or have a disproportionately prejudicial effect for non-ethnic Danes (para 138). What explains the fact that in *Biao* a twenty-eight-year limit to enjoying family reunification amounts to ethnic origin discrimination, but in *Ghoumid and Others*, a fifteen-year limit within which the right to nationality is conditional is not? Is this simply a question of numbers: had French law allowed for deprivation to occur within a twenty-eight-year limit, the measure would have been discriminatory? What about legislations that do not set a time limit but where naturalized citizens are always under threat that they may lose their status? Or is this a question of the interests at stake: in *Biao*, the state's interest in regulating migration and integration, whereas in *Ghoumid and Others* the fight against terrorism, the latter allowing for more extensive state actions?

What is clear is that discrimination and arbitrariness never cross paths in *Ghoumid and Other*. Although in international human rights law, discrimination is considered an important element when assessing arbitrariness (Foster and Baker 2021). Moreover, in its own jurisprudence, the Court has found that the Maltese legislation that prevented children born out of wedlock to acquire such nationality, where the mother was not Maltese, was discriminatory (*Genovese v. Malta*). Instead, arbitrariness is mechanically broken down into four elements: (1) the time frame of the measure, (2) the legality of the citizenship deprivation measure, (3) respect for procedural safeguards, and (4) the proportionality of the consequences of the measure for the applicant's private life. Because the steps provided for in national law had been followed, the Court found no violation concerning legality (para 46) and respect for procedural guarantees (para 47) but without assessing the appropriateness of national legislation. The celerity with which the French government acted in depriving the applicants of citizenship proved a more contested issue, but not the fact that in French law such a limit existed in respect of persons not born French. Although in *Ramdan v. Malta* the Court ruled that a stricter proportionality test may be applicable in respect of the loss of a nationality previously held, this turns out to be a fig leaf because it does not translate into a stricter review of the circumstances in which a state can deprive a person of citizenship on national security grounds. On the contrary, the Court recognizes a right for the state to reexamine the loyalty of citizens convicted for terrorism offences and take measures not originally envisaged (para 45), while the obligation to act swiftly in such cases is set aside by the exceptional circumstances of being the target of terrorist attacks, which allows the state to deprive citizens of citizenship for acts committed some ten years earlier. For all the talk in *Ghoumid and Others* of linking the reexamination of loyalty in the context of the fight against terrorism to a strict control of proportionality, this control is purely mechanical and technical without questioning why the state should be allowed to reexamine the loyalty of some citizens via administrative law.

## Creating Stranded Migrants

One of the few rights recognized by international law exclusively for nationals is that of entering their own country, which includes a prohibition for states to expel their own nationals (Kesby 2012). Being deprived of nationality transforms the citizen into a migrant or a stateless person with a questionable right to be present on state territory. Politically, the possibility to expel or to prevent from returning home that is opened by citizenship deprivation has motivated legislative changes in France and the UK because it is considered that citizens who engage in terrorism are disloyal and should be punished by having their nationality (and the privileges that come with it) removed (Mantu 2018).

While politically the link between expulsion and citizenship deprivation is acknowledged, legally there has been a reluctance to accept that citizenship deprivation is motivated by the desire to expel, which would amount to a violation of the prohibition of expelling own nationals. The applicants in *Ghoumid and Others* complained that the citizenship deprivation orders were arbitrary because of their consequences for their private lives, including their precarious residence status in France, the possibility of facing expulsion to Morocco, and the denial of civil, political, and economic rights (para 33). After losing French nationality, as irregular migrants they applied for permission to remain in France, and expulsion procedures were started against two of them (para 49), highlighting their vulnerable situations.

The Court ruled that in the absence of actual expulsions, citizenship deprivation has consequences only for the applicants' private lives, but these were not judged serious enough to find a violation (para 50). For the Court, the applicants did not attach a great deal of significance to their French nationality because of their criminal convictions for long-term engagement in acts of terrorism and the fact that they committed those acts close to the time of acquiring French nationality (para 50). The interpretation whereby citizenship deprivation leads only to the loss of an element of one's identity but not to other rights (to vote, to work, to social protection, to reside) is a shocking failure to recognize its profound consequences, which transform the citizen into a migrant who needs state permission to continue to reside legally and enjoy rights more generally. Loss of rights is seen as a consequence of a potential expulsion measure, which according to the Court, the applicants are at liberty to appeal. While it is true that the applicants cannot be made stateless under French law and in theory can rely on their other nationality, in the situation where they cannot return to the country of their other nationality, their immediate condition in France is that of stranded migrants—*de facto*, stateless.

## Statelessness and the British State—Examining the Case of Shamima Begum

Who is Shamima Begum? On February 26, 2021, the UK Supreme Court handed down a ruling on the claim of a young woman, Shamima Begum, to be entitled to challenge the British Government's decision to deprive her of British citizenship on grounds of national security and for this purpose to enter the UK. The Court ruled against Begum but in doing so revealed much about our three questions: the gap between alleged and effective citizenship and the entitlement to decide who has citizenship; the entitlement to determine who is a national security threat sufficient to justify withdrawing citizenship; and the vulnerability of stranded migrants created by the loss of citizenship.

Shamima Begum is a woman born as a British citizen in the UK but who, as a child (fifteen years old), ran away to Syria to be the bride of an ISIL fighter. As the civil war in Syria began to come to an end and ISIL (Islamic State of Iraq and the Levant) was increasingly deprived of territory, the UK Government decided to deprive Begum of her British citizenship on the basis that this was conducive to the public good. The ground was based on the fact that she had voluntarily associated herself with ISIL (which the UK Government considers a terrorist organization) by going to ISIL-held territory and marrying a fighter there. Although no evidence indicated that Begum had engaged in terrorist activities as such, nonetheless, her close connection with ISIL fighters was considered sufficient for her to be deprived of the possibility of returning to the UK. As a British-born citizen, the UK

Government had to establish, in accordance with its own laws, that Begum was entitled to a second citizenship. The decision of the Government states that the Home Secretary is "satisfied that such an order [of deprivation] will not make you stateless." The claim was that as Begum's parents had been Bangladeshi citizens, the British Government's reading of Bangladeshi citizenship law permitted the Home Secretary to make the statement that she would not be stateless.

Unlike the *Ghoumid* case, there was little clarity on whether Begum also held a second nationality. The British government argued that as her parents had been born in Bangladesh, according to their interpretation of Bangladeshi nationality law, she was entitled to Bangladeshi citizenship. Begum had never sought a Bangladeshi passport or claimed Bangladeshi citizenship. Indeed, when inquiries were made of the Bangladeshi authorities, they confirmed that their law did not extend citizenship or the right to acquire citizenship to persons in Begum's situation (BBC 2019). Nonetheless, the UK Supreme Court held that she was indeed entitled to Bangladeshi citizenship, so the deprivation of British citizenship would not render her stateless. However, in fact, Begum is now stateless. She lives in a refugee camp in Kurdish-controlled Syria in very poor conditions (McKernan 2021).

The choice of the UK authorities to prevent Begum from returning to the place where she believes herself to be a citizen and to share an identity on the basis of deprivation of citizenship reveals the function creep of citizenship deprivation rules. Although citizenship deprivation was originally designed for clear cases of national security, by the time Begum's case came before the UK courts the legal standard had already been reduced by legislation to "conducive to the public good," a much lower threshold than the previous (national security) and one more flexible for state use. The opportunity that the state gave itself was to choose its citizens at any age and stage of their lives, and to reject them where the public good (not national security), as determined by the state authorities themselves, would be enhanced by such deprivation. The willingness of the Supreme Court to approve this approach to citizenship reveals, as in the case of the ECtHR judgments, a reluctance to protect citizens who on constitutional grounds have been excluded from membership of the community (Macklin 2014).

Academic interest in the Begum has been substantial, without exception (for the moment) critical of the position of both the UK authorities and the courts. Masters and Regilme (2020) criticize the decision and judicial consideration on two main grounds: first, that it establishes and confirms a hierarchical state of humanity, where a state's obligations to its citizens differ depending on socially constructed racial and gender identity. Second, they consider that it reveals the extent to which exceptional security politics enables the demotion of a citizen to what Agamben described as the position of *homo sacer* (Agamben 1998). Labenski (2019) has attacked the treatment of Begum as indicative of gender violence against women in citizenship law. The relation between political rhetoric and hate speech has been examined by Murphy (2021), as revealed in the UK authorities' (and court's) treatment of Begum. It is difficult to find academic consideration of the case that supports either the position of the authorities or the decision of the Supreme Court.

## Loyalty and the Determination of National Security Needs

As a continuing and future national security threat, Begum is a somewhat unlikely choice. As the Supreme Court noted, she was only fifteen years old, and therefore a minor, when she ran away to Syria to be an ISIL bride. In light of her age, she should also be considered a victim of ISIL. She married a "foreign fighter" (a Dutch national) when she lived in Syria and gave birth to three children, two of whom died before the proceedings began and the third while the courts were considering her situation. All three children had been born British citizens because they were born to a British-born woman, although their births were outside the UK. The Supreme Court considered at some length the assessment of Begum by the UK Security Service. Although the Service acknowledged that Begum had been "radicalized" while she was a child and so might be considered a victim, nonetheless it assessed her as a threat to UK national security. According to the Service, she came within a class of persons who constitute such a threat—British citizens who traveled to ISIL-controlled territory to align with ISIL. In the Service's view, anyone who traveled voluntarily to ISIL-controlled territory to join them was aware of ISIL's ideology and aims, as well as the attacks and atrocities that it had carried out. Thus, the threat is a collective one, applying to a class of people and one where extensive knowledge is implied to the group irrespective of their individual circumstances. In the view of the Service, "Anyone who travelled to ISIL-controlled territory even to fill non-combatant roles, was actively supporting a terrorism organization that was engaged in mass murder and grave human rights abuses with an agenda to intimidate and attack governments and citizens globally" (para 17 [2021] UK SC 7). Thus, the human rights–based legal principle that state punishment of an individual must be based on their specific behavior and all relevant factors of their personal circumstances taken into consideration before the punishment (here deprivation of citizenship) is meted out and has not been respected. Begum, according to the Service's assessment of the needs of national security, is to be punished because, irrespective of her personal circumstances, she is characterized as part of a group considered a security risk.

## Stranded Migrant

The third strand of our argument, citizenship deprivation and the creation of stranded migrants in vulnerable situations, is especially evident in Begum's case. It has been alleged that the UK Government has intentionally used its deprivation powers against British citizens while they are outside the UK in order to prevent them from returning home (Yeo 2019). This has certainly been the case in a number of high-profile cases. For Begum, this was clearly the situation. When Raqqa, the final ISIL-held city in Syria, fell, Begum was transferred and held at the Al-Hawl Internal Displaced Persons Camp in Syria under difficult conditions (para 16). It was here that her third child was born and died. She had little chance of leaving the camp because she was being held by the Syrian Democratic Forces (SDF, mainly Syrian Kurdish forces). The British authorities, having issued the deprivation of citizenship order against her while she was in the camp, then refused her a visa (and travel document) to return to the UK to appeal the decision because she had failed to provide a record of her fingerprints and a photograph of her face (para 4). This ground of refusal certainly casts a rather unpleasant light on the UK authorities' good faith regarding this young woman. Had the issue really been one of fingerprints and photographs, any of the British agents who regularly visited the camp would have been able to take the necessary equipment to fulfill this condition for her. Clearly, any argument was good enough to prevent Begum from escaping her internment camp.

As a person deprived of her birth right citizenship—British citizenship, and rejected by the government of her parents' country of birth, Bangladesh—Begum became trapped as a stranded migrant with no country to go to. Since her arrival in Syria, she was a migrant. With the fall of ISIL, she became an unwanted migrant and was placed in a displaced persons camp. When Begum sought to argue before the Supreme Court that her human rights were being infringed because leaving her in the internment camp constituted subjecting her to inhumane and degrading treatment contrary to the ECHR, the Court revised its standard of proof in favor of the Government. It held that the only duty of the Government was to assess whether Begum would be exposed to a real risk of such treatment, and having made the assessment that there was not, the Court held that the Government had done its job. The assessment, not the reality on the ground, was sufficient to justify abandoning Begum to her fate as a stranded migrant (para 129–130). Further, the Court found that it was not for the Supreme Court to interfere with that assessment once it had determined it was made on reasonable grounds, the only applicable test.

From a constitutional perspective, this is a retreat from the obligation of courts to examine not only the legality of state action (whether it appears to comply with formal rules) but also to consider the facts of the case and apply the law to them. The Supreme Court turned its back on the facts when considering administrative decision making. To justify this position, it found that the decision to deprive Begum of her citizenship and leave her stranded in Syria was a matter of policy, not law. The UK authorities were entitled, according to the Court, to depart from policy should they wish to do so with much greater impunity than in respect of the law (para 124). The only check that the Court was willing to place on such a departure from policy was whether or not the authorities had behaved in a manner that was unreasonable (not the unlawful test). This meant that the Court could wash its hands of the consequences of the authorities' decision for the individual because its only duty was to decide whether the authorities had acted within the limits of discretionary power conferred on them by statute (para 126). It did not need to consider whether Begum was at risk of treatment contrary to the ECHR (e.g., being deprived of her life or being subject to torture, inhumane or degrading treatment, or punishment) or indeed a national security risk, as it needed only to decide if the British authorities exercised their powers in accordance with their policy at the date of the decision. Thus, the fate of Begum after the taking of the decision and her plight in Syria was no longer on the judicial table and could safely be ignored by the Court (para 129).

## Conclusion

In this chapter, we have examined the creation of statelessness in Europe from two vantage points. First, the failure of the European Court of Human Rights, a supranational court responsible for determining claims of human rights violations in thirty-seven countries in Europe, to engage seriously with the problem of citizenship deprivation by state authorities. The argument of the states engaging in the practice is that they no longer want citizens who have acted in a manner of which the state disapproves. The division between the criminal law as the constitutionally accepted avenue for the punishment of people who act in breach of the state laws and the abandonment of the individual through deprivation of citizenship has become blurred. At the supranational level, the ECtHR has accepted that the limits of the criminal law are not co-terminal with the entitlement to identity. The fact that a citizen has been convicted and served the sentence accorded by the criminal courts for an offense has not been held to be the end of the individual's punishment. The ECtHR has accepted that state authorities can proceed further and deprive an individual of citizenship. The racial overtones of these acts, in that the individuals affected by such measures are the children of immigrants often born in the country of origin of their parents who mainly originate from North African states, are both denied by this supranational court and state authorities, yet permeate the cases like a nasty scent.

Second, we have looked at a specific case in the UK that has raised many questions, both nationally and internationally, about the creation of statelessness—that of Shamima Begum, who was deprived of her British citizenship notwithstanding birth in the UK as a citizen and always having been one. Her offense was running away from home as a child to become an ISIL bride in Syria. In this case, the determination of loyalty as an inherent component of citizenship and on the basis of which its deprivation can be justified is particularly relevant. The state authority—the Security Service—charged with determining the effectiveness of this loyalty, took the blanket decision that any British national who stayed in ISIL-controlled Syria lacked the necessary loyalty. Thus, it is a collective decision that leads to a complete destruction of belonging—the deprivation of citizenship.

Finally, we have examined the outcome of these decisions as regards the creation of stranded migrants. This is particularly blatant in the case of Begum, who remains in a displaced persons camp in Syria with no place to go—a person who her state of citizenship intentionally transformed into a stranded migrant. In respect of the ECtHR, the young men deprived of their citizenship were deprived of a remedy against that deprivation on the weak premise that should the state where they were living seek to expel them, maybe they would have a remedy in supranational human rights law.

In conclusion, our research reveals the precariousness of citizenship in particular as an identity claim of migrants and their children in Europe. Notwithstanding European and international standards set out in conventions to prevent statelessness, a number of European states are resorting to transformations of membership of their states through citizenship deprivation with only cursory regard to the wording and spirit of their international commitments.

## Note

1. Article 8(2) ECHR allows for state interference with the right to respect for private and family life in as a much as it is in accordance with the law and is necessary in a democratic society in the interests of national security, public safety or the economic well-being of the country, for the prevention of disorder or crime, for the protection of health or morals, or for the protection of the rights and freedoms of others.

## References

Agamben, Giorgio. *Homo Sacer: Sovereign Power and Bare Life*. Stanford, CA: Stanford University Press, 1998.

BBC. "Shamima Begum 'Will Not Be Allowed Here, Bangladesh Says.'" *BBC News*, February 21, 2019, sec. UK. www.bbc.com/news/uk-47312207

Ersbøll, Eva. "The Right to a Nationality and the European Convention on Human Rights." In *Human Rights in Turmoil: Facing Threats, Consolidating Achievements*, edited by Stéphanie Lagoutte, Hans-Otto Sano, and Peter Scharff Smith, 249–70. Leiden: Brill | Nijhoff, 2007. https://doi.org/10.1163/ej.9789004154322.i-299.83

Foster, Michelle, and Timnah Rachel Baker. "Racial Discrimination in Nationality Laws: A Doctrinal Blind Spot of International Law." *Columbia Journal of Race and Law* 11, no. 1 (2021): 83–146. https://doi.org/10.7916/CJRL.V11I1.8018

Kesby, Alison. *The Right to Have Rights: Citizenship, Humanity, and International Law*. Oxford & New York: Oxford University Press, 2012.

Labenski, Sheri. "Women's Violence and the Law: In Consideration of Shamima Begum." *LSE Women, Peace and Security Blog*. November 20, 2019. http://eprints.lse.ac.uk/103903/1/WPS_2019_11_20_women_s_violence_and_the_law.pdf

Macklin, Audrey. "Citizenship Revocation and the Privilege to Have Rights." *Queen's Law Journal* 40, no. 1 (2014): 1–54. https://doi.org/10.2139/ssrn.2507786

Mantu, Sandra. *Contingent Citizenship: The Law and Practice of Citizenship Deprivation in International, European and National Perspectives*. Leiden: Brill | Nijhoff, 2015. https://doi.org/10.1163/9789004293007

———. "'Terrorist' Citizens and the Human Right to Nationality." *Journal of Contemporary European Studies* 26, no. 1 (2018): 28–41. https://doi.org/10.1080/14782804.2017.1397503

Masters, Mercedes, and Salvador Santino F. Regilme. "Human Rights and British Citizenship: The Case of Shamima Begum as Citizen to *Homo Sacer*." *Journal of Human Rights Practice* 12, no. 2 (2020): 341–63. https://doi.org/10.1093/jhuman/huaa029

McKernan, Bethan. "Isis Women Languish in Dire Conditions with Nowhere Else to Go." *The Guardian*, February 26, 2021. www.theguardian.com/world/2021/feb/26/isis-women-languish-in-dire-conditions-al-hawl-shamima-begum

Meijers Committee. "Policy Brief on 'Differential Treatment of Citizens with Dual or Multiple Nationality and the Prohibition of Discrimination.'" CM2016. 2020. www.commissie-meijers.nl/comment/cm2016-policy-brief-on-differential-treatment-of-citizens-with-dual-or-multiple-nationality-and-the-prohibition-of-discrimination

Murphy, Alexander. "Political Rhetoric and Hate Speech in the Case of Shamima Begum." *Religions* 12, no. 10 (2021): 834. https://doi.org/10.3390/rel12100834

Spiro, Peter J. "A New International Law of Citizenship." *American Journal of International Law* 105, no. 4 (2011): 694–746. https://doi.org/10.5305/amerjintelaw.105.4.0694

Yeo, Colin. "The Rise of Modern Banishment: Deprivation and Nullification of British Citizenship." In *Citizenship in Times of Turmoil? Theory, Practice and Policy*, edited by Devyani Prabhat. 134–50. Cheltenham | Northampton: Edward Elgar Publishing, 2019.

## Case Law

*Begum, R. (on the application of) v. Special Immigration Appeals Commission & Anor*, UKSC 7, AC 765, HRLR 7, 2 WLR 556, 2 All ER 1063, INLR 316, WLR(D) 131 (2021). www.bailii.org/uk/cases/UKSC/2021/7.html, Imm AR 879

*Biao v. Denmark*, Application no 38590/10, Grand Chamber (24 May 2016).

*Genovese v. Malta,* Application no. 53124/09 (11 October 2011).

*Gouhmid and Others v. France,* Application no. 52273/16 and 4 others (16 November 2020).

*Karassev v. Finland,* Application no. 31414/96 (12 January 1999).

*Kurić and Others v. Slovenia*, Application no. 26828/06 (13 July 2010).

*Makuc and Others v. Slovenia*, Application no. 26828/06, decision on admissibility (31 May 2007).

*Ramadan v. Malta*, Application no. Application no. 76136/12 (21 June 2016).

Chapter 3

# The Banality of Statelessness and the Impossibility of Counting the Dispossessed

Nergis Canefe

Death gives us the minor key.

—Henry Purcell

## Introduction

Starting with the events of the Arab Spring leading to the dispossession of millions of Syrians, questions of dispossession, exile, and statelessness have become regular agenda items in the study of not just the MENA (Middle East and North Africa) region, but on a global scale. The most recent addition to the long tally of dispossession gone wrong is that of the Afghan stateless (Canefe 2022). In response, and no irony is intended here, exclusionary forms of political membership have become reinvented and reinvigorated, partly in relation to new waves of ethno-nationalism and partly due to the spread of temporary labor regimes and the incessant need for novel versions of precarious work. In addition, ingenious forms of the "status/non-status" binary have been operationalized, juridifying temporary permanence, which in turn intently limits participation and inclusion. The stateless peoples of the Middle East, Near East, South East Asia, North Africa, and South America have been particularly affected by these strategies of covert exclusion as they continue to face *en masse* dispossessions. In other words, contemporary statelessness is neither time-bound nor geographically distinct in origin—hence, the impossibility of addressing it from within the international refugee regime. As Bhupinder Chimni declared almost two decades ago, the focus on "returnee aid" (in whichever form it may take) to facilitate *en masse* repatriation as a solution to *en masse* dispossession remains the cherished ideal of the international refugee regime (Chimni 2004).[1] As such, it is understood that there is really no need to count statelessness, as ultimately, it is considered to be a transitional position.

This chapter addresses the limitations of regional and international advocacy that has endeavored to counteract statelessness and strived to determine solutions to the plight of stateless peoples in the postcolonial context. Central to the issue of statelessness is the presumption of an active and mutually beneficial relationship between the state and the individual, which in turn is regarded as essential for the protection and promotion of human rights. In cases of both *de facto* and *de jure* statelessness, however, this form of political membership is either perpetually elusive or entirely missing. Expanding on the idea of denizenship (Benton 2014), this chapter contends that membership exists along a spectrum, and statelessness, as a common form of dispossession, requires attention to the functionality of the triangular relationship among the state, society, and individual, rather than the myopic focus on the state–citizen duo. Although government-sponsored identities continue to be a prerequisite for rights protection in the grid-like structure of the modern state system, functional membership requires us to expand our understanding of collective human responsibility regardless of the citizenship status of those who are exposed to violence of precarity and denial of rights. As such, the chapter proposes that we critically examine the standard reading of Hannah Arendt's work dictating the ways individuals are recognized as worthy of rights or denied even the most basic protections on account of their absence from the roster of political membership (Arendt 1958, 1967, 2003).[2] We must push the discussion on dispossession beyond the thin notions of citizenship and reformulate the issue of membership to a political community true to the aporetic spirit of its Arendtian formulation.[3] The legal rationality imposed on nationality cannot be the only axis along which a person's worth is determined in terms of rights. Instead, we must attend to the multifarious, multiscalar, and contingent historical trajectories of the emergence and attribution of rights (Çağlar and Glick Schiller 2018).

In this specific context, the endemic nature of statelessness since the 1990s assumes a meaning far apart from one related to region-specific crises. This extreme form of vulnerability has been largely ignored by the academia, and the innate link between the concept of statelessness and contemporary forms of enslavement has often been reduced to a mere speculation. In what follows, I posit that statelessness is not an aberration or a radical exception. It is one of the discrete outcomes of processes of the gendered and racialized debasement of citizenship, and stateless people share the same predicament as those who are criminalized on account of their mobility, except that they are simultaneously rendered invisible by virtue of a lack of recognition of their sheer existence. From the extralegal expulsion of people who cannot be repatriated, to the concentrated erosion of the rights of once-citizens, the modes through which people experience statelessness, like citizenship, are not absolute but are experienced as a matter of degrees. The political value of seeing the connections among these seemingly discrete forms of dispossession (i.e., statelessness and precarity) is immense in terms of understanding the making and re-making of regional orders of dispossession, the erasure of subjecthood and, ultimately, the production and maintenance of bonded labor. In terms of its profitability, what and who statelessness involves have remained remarkably consistent (Gordon 2010, 2020). Contemporary conceptions of consent, hand in hand with the systemic obstruction of the "vulnerability of others," make statelessness one of the most lucrative forms of dispossession through the means of eradication of the right to life with dignity, normalization of premature death, and forcible transfers of capital. No wonder states and societies find it so difficult to name and count those whose losses are their gains.

## Narrating the Future? Disciplinary Illusions

Statelessness is to be recognized not only as a violation of the "right to a nationality" dictated by the post-WWII international human rights frameworks. It is the root cause of a cascade of rights abuses, threats, and violations that create novel forms of structural vulnerability. The pathways by which individuals become or remain stateless include denationalization, exclusionary citizenship laws, and inequalities that obstruct either registration or naturalization, and they often lead to regimes of discrimination against select populations (Kingston 2018; Canefe 2020). Structural barriers that emerge as a result of being stateless curtail the full protection these communities are assumed to have benefited from being under the purview of citizenship laws. Here, I will first argue that there is no such natural relationship between citizenship and the protection of rights. Furthermore, a critical analysis of the dynamics of the citizenship practices of states cannot be undertaken without identifying the stable and foundational relations among immigration, exclusion from citizenship, and selective attribution of rights that constitutes an essential component of border maintenance (Guild, Groenendijk, and Carrera 2016).

Despite the comprehensiveness and coordination of public responses concerning the inclusion of exiled populations within the curated framework of international law, the phenomenon of statelessness affects certain groups much more directly on a global scale (Vlieks and Van Waas 2022). In other words, statelessness is never random but often results from premeditated and politically endorsed action and social policy. This problematic poses a distinct set of definitional problems in need of reflection and reconsideration, first and foremost in the language of *limits of legalized belonging*. For instance, following the events of the Arab Spring, the security agenda of the states in Europe has been transformed and redefined with unique outcomes concerning the protection of specific categories of the dispossessed populations of the MENA region. Concomitantly, the question of political membership got subsumed under the theme of the governance of national insecurity (Wilmer 2018).

It's sufficient to say that this phenomenon is not unique to the relationship between the Middle East and Europe. Far from integration into the European citizenship regime, the "other" stateless of European societies, such as the Roma, remain both inside and outside, host and guest. In this regard, through the paradoxical paradigm of "stateless citizenship" (Molavi 2013), it is possible to examine not just the dynamics of exclusion of migrants, refugees, and *sans papiers*, but also unearth the mechanisms through which their statelessness is maintained. If we center our analytical gaze on what appears to be a paradox, again as Arendt's notion of the right to have rights dictates, the actual provisions of citizenship that render Europe's others stateless as a racialized and politically charged edifice become all the more visible (Canefe 1998).

"The passport is the most noble part of the human being. It also does not come into existence in such a simple fashion as a human being does. A human being can come into the world anywhere, in the most careless way and for no good reason, but a passport never can. When it is good, the passport is also recognized for this quality, whereas a human being, no matter how good, can go unrecognized." Thus wrote Bertolt Brecht in his Refugee Conversations in 1940, deeply affected by his own experience of exile. The vital importance that a seemingly simple administrative act—the issuance of personal identification papers—could acquire cannot be more pertinent in the age of statelessness. As the most obvious symbol of this belonging, offering proof and recognition of one's status, identity papers are something that the stateless person, who emerged as an inevitable by-product of the nationalization processes that began in the nineteenth century with the rise of European nationalisms followed by their postcolonial reiterations, continues to lack (Rürup 2011).

The tradition of exploring the relationship between statelessness and migration dictates that migration governance regimes ultimately set the parameters of the framework for international protection. Statelessness used to be associated with state succession, mass denationalization, and refugee flows in the twentieth century. However, irregular migration and forced migration were always the main sources of the production of new forms of statelessness. Contrary to the claims of international refugee regime expanded by organizations such as the UNHCR, neither customary international law, international conventions on statelessness, refugees, and migrant workers nor general human rights instruments provide effective protection for stateless persons on the move. And the majority of the stateless remain on the move.

As a case in point, since its creation, UNHCR has strived to provide an international protection regime and sought "durable solutions for statelessness."[4] Specifically, UNHCR actively participated in the drafting of the two global legal instruments concerning ending statelessness—the 1954 Convention relating to the Status of Stateless Persons and the 1961 Convention on the Reduction of Statelessness. Furthermore, in 1974 the UN General Assembly designated UNHCR as the organization to which persons claiming the benefit of the 1961 Convention may apply for examination of their claims and for assistance in presenting those claims to state authorities (Manly and Persaud 2009). And yet, UNHCR, or any other INGO with a clear international mandate, cannot produce solutions to problems created by states and normalized by societies chronically producing stateless populations and benefiting from their ordeal. If we are to rewrite the script, *contra* the dictum of durable solutions in international law, statelessness itself must be presented as a manmade solution to nation-state maintenance and global capitalism's fervent need for subhuman forms of extraction rather than being a burden to be alleviated.

Coming back to the prototypical treatment of statelessness, particularly since 1989, questions concerning the resolution of statelessness in Europe have once again gained traction. On the one hand, exclusionary forces have become reinvigorated, as a result of which new forms of status have been created, severely limiting participation and inclusion rights. On the other hand, Europe's own minorities have been systemically targeted for exclusion, with Roma and ethnic Russians being affected in particular. No doubt, there are developments in the areas of regional and international lawmaking to counteract these developments, as represented by the case law of the European Court of Human Rights and Council of Europe law. However, none of these jurisdictional interventions address the sources and kaleidoscopic proliferation of statelessness in Europe and elsewhere. Overall, these observations support the argument that debates on statelessness are above and go beyond the reexamination of citizenship, rights, and legal status. The continuous proliferation of statelessness worldwide confirms the need for a more nuanced understanding of contemporary forms of membership, attentive to the interplay among different rights regimes. Lack of citizenship does not constitute the bedrock of *bare life*. Instead, it reveals political subjectivity as an embodied and emplaced process where subjects actively negotiate their position in the world, despite the state-centered understanding of legitimate politics.

It is true that for Giorgio Agamben, refugees—and by extrapolation, the stateless—can be seen as the ultimate "biopolitical" subjects (Owens 2009). Presumably, they are regulated and governed in a permanent "state of exception" without the enjoyment of political freedom. But what if we think in terms of the formation of counter-publics and contestations of death by not just mere survival but also via formulations of alternative forms of political subjectivity and human dignity? What is at stake here is not more asylum rights, porous borders, or the right of all humans to be recognized as legal subjects, either. The problem is the beneficial nature of the production and management of stateless populations, and this cannot be adequately grasped within the matrix of a Kantian model of universal rights, falling back on the workings of institutions that are declared legitimate despite the essential role they play in the facilitation of an infinite expansion of dispossession. Further, the blurring of the distinction between biological and political lives to the degree of nullifying life that is not legally sanctioned as bare creates a very disconcerting residue: bare life easily slides into the civil death of Achille Mbembé (Mbembé 2003), thus further stripping stateless populations from even the potential of a future. The reduction of the stateless as a state of "superfluousness" and stateless people as "living corpses," their death becoming an instrument of biopolitical and necropolitical powers, covers over the extensive use of these lives (and not just bodies) for the societies embracing normalization of statelessness for their own benefit and affluence. Hence is my suggestion that the disciplinary illusions of forced migration studies, whether relying on Hannah Arendt, Bertrand Ogilvie, Giorgio Agamben, or Achille Mbembé as their ontological safe harbor, will ultimately fail to narrate the future of statelessness. These accounts tell us in detail how dispossession has been rendered an essential feature of the "modern polity," but they fail to think through the possibilities of radical survival.[5]

## The Canvas

According to the Institute of Statelessness and Inclusion's estimates (Van Eert 2021), in Asia and the Pacific, Malaysia is listed as one of the countries that have large populations of stateless persons (over 10,000). Malaysia's performance to date in relation to UNHCR's goal of ending statelessness in 2024, in particular through Action 1 (Resolving Major Situations of Statelessness); Action 2 (Ensure that No Child is Born Stateless); and Action 10 (Improve Quantitative and Qualitative Data on Stateless Persons), is seen as exemplar. This, of course, is despite the fact that the Rohingya crisis continues to unfold and the decades-long systemic persecution of the stateless Muslim Rohingyas in Myanmar (formerly Burma) remains generally unheeded by the world at large. Staggering numbers in human casualties, loss of property, gendered violence, and homelessness, with direct perpetrators behind many of the mass atrocities including members of Myanmar's military, police, and ultra-nationalist groups, and in the company of Buddhist monks who vow to rid the country of Muslims acting as instigators, introduces us to an altogether different picture (Canefe, Banerjee, and Chowdhory 2022). In addition, like many of the long-standing "statelessness" cases, the Rohingya crisis extends well beyond a localized humanitarian problem, affecting the whole of Southeast Asian region. The canvas is to be inclusive of all these dimensions before declaring Myanmar as a "success story" in terms of its "address of statelessness."

There are indeed formulations built into international law for the reduction of statelessness and the protection of stateless persons. However, as new forms of statelessness emerge, eradicating statelessness remains a siren call. Unless we problematize the very notions of nationality and citizenship, along with a careful study of regional integration of markets and capital, the transnationality of nonstate actors, the generic insistence upon an exclusionary communitarian citizenship model, the supranationality of migration, reaching out for salvation by the long arm of international law will leave us standing adrift in the face of the multiplication of stateless populations.

A key example to consider in terms of alternative approaches is the legal framework of statelessness developed and put into effect in Brazil with the country's new migratory law. Furthermore, with the adoption of the 2014 Brazilian Declaration and Plan of Action (BPA), twenty-eight Latin American countries and three Caribbean territories committed themselves to the transformation of statelessness in the Americas from a problem into a fact that can find legal redress. The precursor of this particular legal instrument was the 2010 Brasilia Declaration on the Protection of Refugees and Stateless Persons in Americas, along with decades-long jurisprudence and advisory opinions of the Inter-American Court of Human Rights and the Inter-American Commission on Human Rights. The answers will not come from Europe (Mondelli 2017, 2021; Assunção 2019). Indeed, a new approach to understanding statelessness must start with exploring the limits of Euro-centric modalities of international law on statelessness and the relationships between statelessness. It further must calls for an expanded definition of the "stateless" person: adding to the accepted *de jure* and *de facto* definitions a third category of "socially stateless" people who are often internally displaced. Ultimately, the lack of protection which the original Euro-centric framework of international law(s) offers around statelessness creates new forms of usurpation cloaked as nationalism and border sanctity.

## Half-Statelessness?

If we continue along the lines of the need for the formulation of a "third form of statelessness," a key example fortifying this call comes from Israel. In 2018, the state of Israel endorsed the passage of the Nation-State Law, leading to the formal and substantial reordering of the Israeli notion of citizenship. Redefining the Israeli state in exclusively ethnic terms, the new law placed the country's Palestinian citizenry in a remarkably precarious position, even more so than the Israeli state's previous practices since its foundation in 1948. The Israeli Palestinians have hitherto been declared neither fully stateless nor fully citizens in Israel. Again, drawing on the work of Arendt, but this time with reference to a conceptual category to which she alludes in *The Human Condition,* "half-statelessness" is what best describes the Palestinian citizens of Israel (Jamal and Kensicki 2020). The term is also applicable in numerous cases whereby the state unilaterally makes changes to citizenship laws, such as Myanmar and the Rohingya populations, creating millions of dispossessed people who habitually reside in the country discussed earlier, the Syrian refugees who have neither documentation nor claims-making rights pertaining to their country of origin, and Venezuelan refugees in Colombia, among others (Eliassi 2021). This unusual legislative apex of half-statelessness points to a phenomenon that transcends the typical prototypes of citizen and state. Its effective dehumanization of select groups is best observed in cases where there is no demotion but a persistent nonrecognition and thus normalization of political invisibility concomitant with the removal of agency and voice.

The notion of half-statelessness also makes it all the more transparent that both the collection of empirical evidence and the examination of policy developments pertaining to the migration, mobility, and statelessness nexus need to be subjected to critical political and legal theoretical inquiry. Statelessness cannot be regarded simply as a phenomenon, but as a concept in the making with changing content. What gives statelessness its shape and content draws on a set of ideas and practices starting with the conceptualization of the state itself, the citizen, and of course the nation, as well as those of the border, membership, polity, and rights. In this sense, it would be apt to suggest that we need a new theory of global statelessness that would enable evaluation and critique to emerge, rather than an accounting practice documenting legislative interventions and numerical posturing. This alternative route would also foster our ability to imagine alternatives to the current order of things. Current legal and political practices of exclusion from membership are contingent upon larger discourses. There is no substantive reason as to why these must be considered as constitutive of the limits of our thinking about migration, mobility, membership, and statelessness (Cole 2000). One question to consider, though, is whether practical concerns exist when it comes to imagining different possible political orders (Carens 2013). If, as Joseph Carens states, "[a]n exploration of what justice ideally entails with respect to immigration should take the whole world into account" (2013, 301), then we must start with a historical critique of the current world order. This has indeed been the call of TWAIL (Third World Approaches to International Law) scholars in their address on the legalization of dispossession in international law (Benslama-Dabdoub 2021). In search of a wider theoretical lens dealing with not just the postcolonial but also decolonial and anticolonial dimensions of dispossession, we can't propose what the right to membership of stateless persons would entail without addressing the justice-related demands historically overlooked by current political and legal practices.

This chapter strives to lay the groundwork for a radical vision by exposing the limitations of our sociopolitical and legal imagination that shape our current conceptualization of and expectations regarding statelessness. I would argue that theorizing itself amounts to praxis in this instance. As such, challenging the existing conceptual frame of reference on statelessness provides us the space to unpack citizenship into its relational components rather than reiterating it as a thing in itself with settled boundaries and a definite shape. Indeed, we might argue that the content of citizenship in turn defines the content of statelessness. If so, statelessness is marked by banality, just like nationalism and its corollary, national citizenship, is (Billig 1995).[6] Expanding on Billig's seminal study on the perpetual and everyday reproductions of nationalism, I invite us to attend to the importance of human agency and contextual interactions regarding the reproduction of statelessness as a relational concept and practice.

Furthermore, by bringing the voices of people in as active producers of contestations of what statelessness entails, I hope to offer a more complex picture of the banality of this particularly oppressive form of dispossession. Both the national "we" and the national "here" are construed as sociospatially differentiated and fragmented practices enacted on a plurality of scales, as opposed to statelessness being the opposite of singular, internally homogenous political entities. Stateless populations do not lack the properties necessary to enter the space of citizenship: the allegorical space of statelessness is a core element of what defines such presumed properties. What is more, the study of statelessness as an externality of citizenship models employed thus far also overlooks the properties stateless populations possess, which make it beneficial for them to be positively excluded from the realm of citizenship.

## Statelessness as the Residual Truth of the Postcolonial Condition

The residual view of neoliberalism with a postcolonial persuasion sees the global tally of dispossessed populations as a leftover that the Euro-modern state system is unable to absorb. This view pays no heed to the notion of economies that lie at the margins of the global economic order, constantly feeding its demand for cheaper, disposable, contractual labor. In contradistinction, the form of accumulation enabled by the production and circulation of stateless populations constitutes an important part of the global order. Dispossession is produced by how the system is structured, and the stateless, presumed to lie outside of the international system of sovereign states, are an integral part of it. They are not a structural failure but a product of that order, the residual truth of the postcolonial condition. As such, understanding statelessness means asking radical questions about the histories of the international political and legal order as well as the normative presuppositions of the nation-state system concerning full membership.

Caution must be exercised here regarding developing a line of argument about moral responsibility for the stateless. The primary focus here is not how people become stateless, but how the idea of statelessness is produced and normalized, to the point of being banal and yet always presented as part of some imagined crisis. The problem is that when we come to include the excluded, we are attempting to include them within a theory that has been actively structured around their purported exclusion. Historically, theories of migration and mobility have simply excluded the "stateless," whether they be physically present or in theoretical scope. Similarly, citizenship studies literature barely acknowledged their existence. Instead, it often presented a false universalism concerning the stateless populations being an anomaly. In other words, their persistent presence is deeply disruptive and disturbing for a theory of membership that has notoriously been structured on the assumption that we are dealing with voluntary inclusion and a fair delegation of political power to the state. However, immigration is not some marginal question to be added onto the core theory of membership, and neither is statelessness an addendum to our understanding of belonging.

The torrent of people in flight, not the least those who are stateless, presents a serious threat to the stability of the polities considered as the bedrock of stable identities. The scale and depth of postcolonial and decolonial migration indicate a dire need for a radical rethinking of both theory and practice of working with dispossession in the larger context of political, social, and economic justice. The gap between the legal practices of immigration reception, particularly vis-à-vis the categorical exclusion of the stateless populations, forces us to rethink these practices as a fractured facade that barricades the realities of the lived experiences of populations on the move.

The question of statelessness is a structural component of modern political theories of both citizenship and membership. Since the voice of the citizen/member is commonly acknowledged as the only legitimate voice in the polity, the stateless are a problem for the citizen/member but not with their silence. They are present despite their legal absence. Any solution that keeps the interests of the citizen/member at its center is produced by theorizing from the vantage point of a specific political topography. Here is how a postcolonial theory of migration comes to our rescue. Focusing on migration and rightful belonging centered on the interests not only of those who already have membership of a state, and not based on one particular historical lineage derived from a particular location in the world, the postcolonial condition emerges as a strategic concept (Samaddar 2010, 2017, 2020; Çağlar 2021). It allows for moving beyond the impasse presented by the Eurocentric juxtaposition of citizenship and membership within the confines of the nation-state. As Ranabir Samaddar repeatedly argues, the migrant is the quintessential subject of the postcolonial predicament. With migration comes the changing forms of labor, and the theoretical enterprise of understanding the continual crisis of historical capitalism through the lens of the structural qualities of dispossession is the urgent task laying ahead.

This alternative topography of theory-building dictates that even in its international legal form, work on statelessness cannot be habitually inclusive or egalitarian, as it embodies a long history of violence and exclusion. Further, the incarceration of the stateless populations, presumably remaining on the outside, excluded as participants in any negotiation of solutions, and confined to the periphery of politics, only further purports the integrity of the traditional political subject who depends on the exclusion or the confinement of the "other."

## Statelessness as a Reflection in the Labyrinth of Membership

The presence of the "other" in the theory of membership, the political subject against which the core identity of a polity is defined, reveals the particularistic aspirations and convictions of the very identity that is presented as universally valid. In *The World as Will and Representation*, Arthur Schopenhauer presents the human will as our sole window to the world (Schopenhauer 2010, 2020). The will, Schopenhauer maintains, is its own manifest character, evidenced in its objectifications. I am not to embrace a purified idealist position vis-à-vis the study of stateliness. However, suffice it to say that the objectification of the will of the European-self reveals its core identity in its formulation of statelessness. In the registers of the colonial project, the "flow" of natural and human resources spoke of "global interconnectedness" on the one hand, and the political subordination of those who move above and beyond the mandate of the states, on the other. The resultant process of the instrumental exclusion of the "stateless other" creates tensions and antagonisms that cannot be resolved without a radical, ground-up revision of the entire concept of membership to the polity.

In political terms, the abject are things that threaten our identity as members of the polity, such that we wish to expel them and keep them behind a border which will purportedly protect us from being exposed to such a condition of humanity. However, the abject are also an essential part of who we are, and the effort to maintain expulsions and distinctions has to be constant as the borders are always threatened and always porous. In response, the political rituals of expulsion become more detailed, juridified, complex, and intense (Cole 2006; Tyler 2013). For instance, as boats of humanity crossing the Mediterranean are constructed as abject and thus to be repelled, as a "swarm" of migrants is perceived to be threatening to "overwhelm Europe," as the fearful attitude toward the increasing "armies" of stateless pouring out of the Middle East continues to deepen, in the hierarchy of expulsions, stateless people have the questionable privilege of being the first in line not to be counted as political subjects.

If we assume that migrants have membership of some other state, and thus something to fall back onto, the very knowledge of the stateless "having no home" makes them the biggest threat to the sustenance of closed membership regimes. Their sheer existence destroys the border that guarantees the integrity of the core political subject of the modern state and challenges the boundary between the inside and outside of the polity. As a perfect example of the disproportionate reaction to the arrival of the stateless, the European Union's ten-point program for dealing with the unfolding tragedy in the Mediterranean was aimed not just at strengthening the border but also addressed the stateless as abject in the extreme, never to be included in the discussions on potential membership and pushed back at all cost, including near certain obliteration in the waters of a sea otherwise known as the cradle of Civilization. If so, there is nothing that can be fixed by the old topologies of political membership since it is our very idea of membership in the polity that constitutes and constructs the idea and practice of statelessness.

## Conclusion

Statelessness provides us the very grounds from which established discourses of membership and mobility must not only be challenged but also transformed. This amounts to taking the call of the Arendtian reading of *the right to have rights* one step further while remaining true to its aporetic call. What membership in a polity means, and the association of rights with membership must be fought over, rather than taken as our settled point. However, the fight here is not about membership *per se*, but about the substantive meaning it entails. What is also needed is a bridging act between theories, recordings, observations, and the lived experience in our work on statelessness. The political and everyday struggles of the stateless people radically surviving and sustaining their own lives and the lives of those around them, often in conditions of utter political, social, and economic oppression and exclusion, must be incorporated into theories of statelessness, providing space for the voices and experiences of the stateless people themselves.[7]

We already know of the myriad ways in which the privileging of the voice of the insider is deeply ingrained in political theory, as articulately shown by Seyla Benhabib's take on the human right to membership (Benhabib 2004) and Susan Sontag's interventions concerning the pain of others (Sontag 2003; Möller and Sontag 2010). As Sontag comments in her essay series *On Photography* penned during the 1970s (Sontag 1977), while trying to understand the aesthetic and ethical implications of the omnipresence of photographic images in our lives, a disproportionate part of "our knowledge of things" comes not from direct experience. In compensation, the information generated by the image is regularly taken as equivalent to that of experience. This is otherwise known as the politics of gaze. On the issue of proximity and distance, Sontag cites Robert Schwartz: "when we look closely at those things that are distant, we see them close, but without responsibility" (Sontag 1977). Statelessness generally suffers from this aforementioned optical illusion of a problem we see and we know, but never from the position of being part of the hell that marks the very experience. In Francisco Goya's words, "*No se puede mirar* [One cannot look at this]. *Yo lo vi* [I saw it]. *Esto es lo verdadero* [This is the Truth]." These are the captions for the etchings in his series *Los Destasres de la Guerra*. Counting the number of stateless people is the equivalent of looking but not seeing. It is not the truth of it. Rather, it is an exercise from the safe distance of observing without responsibility.

Acknowledging that stateless people's stand in a political relationship vis-à-vis the state of either intended or accidental destination for migration and resettlement requires acknowledging that both the original state and the polity are obligated to offer justifications as to why this categorical rejection of membership emerged in the first place. This, however, calls for the stateless to be treated as equals in terms of their political agency (Watson 2008). For the stateless political subject to be regarded as an equal in such an exchange, we must think outside of the conventional political frameworks of immigration and refugee law as well as precepts concerning citizenship as the ultimate and absolute form of membership. In conclusion, I would dare to posit that statelessness is not the "problem" in this relationship. Neither are the stateless who are the problem. Rather, they are the epitome of the relationship between the state and citizens itself, a relationship that privileges the "insider" on account of membership, and renders the stateless political subject silent as if they are outsiders (Cole 2015). This pretension becomes farcical in the face of the chronic failure of the attempts to count the stateless.

In closing, I agree with Gordon that statelessness and contemporary forms of enslavement have become increasingly intertwined since the 1990s (Gordon 2020). Neither statelessness nor enslavement and contemporary forms of human trafficking are radical exceptions. They have been and are endemic to the Euro-modern state system, its Global South version being the postcolonial state. Stateless subjects of the global polity are discrete outcomes of processes of the racialized and gendered debasement of citizenship. In this regard, extralegal expulsion of people who cannot be repatriated, and the concentrated erosion of the rights of full-fledged citizens must also be counted as primary modes through which people experience both degrees of statelessness and a spectrum of citizenship rights. The centuries-long practice of enslavement has taken on some new guises necessary to its profitability in the current global economy, with its specificities being those of dispossessed wage laborers, guest workers, and indentured labor, making vulnerability of others so lucrative for the system overall.

## Notes

1. According to Chimni, the "durable solutions rhetoric" must be analyzed in a staggered fashion: the period between 1945 and 1985 marking resettlement and repatriation as the optimal solution to dispossession, and the period from 1985 onward introducing the "options" of safe return, accompanied by the global embrace of temporary protection on the one hand and extreme forms of the juridification of refugee crises on the other.

2. The difficulties and reversals that mark interpretations of Hannah Arendt's idea of a "right to have rights" (1967, 177–78), and in particular the foundational understanding of politics that the standard interpretation of her work on rights presupposes are worthy of a brief note here. The most conventional interpretation considers the right to have rights in terms of the use of power to implement rights in

institutional terms. However, Arendt's broadly Kantian interpretation understands it in terms of the positionality of rights-claimants or rights-holders themselves (O'Neill 2001; Benhabib 2004). In its most demanding and expansive rendition, it could fully honor the emphasis on autonomy and thus does not have to be anchored in the nation-state per se and is not bound by the conventional universalist frame of rights. Throughout this work, this is the reading I adhere to. For a similar debate, see Oman 2010.

3. Arendt's critique centers on the paradoxes of human rights and analyzes them in line with a mode of inquiry that she associates with Socrates's teachings. Aporia in this context is not a heralder of a paralyzing impasse, as declared by Jacques Rancière in his reading of Arendt (Rancière 1992, 2004). Rather, it can create possibilities for rethinking key concepts, especially in times of crises (Gündoğdu 2011). Rereading Arendt, we can see the stateless person as someone whose status exposes the contradiction of state-centered citizenship and the discourse of human rights hinging upon it, rather than merely as an institutionalist track.

4. As summarized by Manly and Persaud, "[i]n the end it is action by states that is required to prevent and reduce statelessness. UNHCR cannot substitute for states. What UNHCR can do, however, is document gaps in legislative and administrative frameworks and provide assistance to address them." Mark Manly and Santhosh Persaud, "UNHCR and Responses to Statelessness," *Forced Migration Review* 32 (2009): 7.

5. For instance, in his work *L'Homme jetable, Essai sur l'exterminisme et la violence extrême*, Bertrand Ogilvie (2012, 73–74) makes a case for contemporary political order being based on an "indirect logic of extermination," morally allowing governments to abandon their "surplus populations" to their own fate. These "disposable people" purportedly cannot function as part of the economic and public sphere and become the l'homme jetable (disposable man). It is quite a jump, and in this case an utterly mistaken one, to declare that the stateless people become disposable.

6. Billig's work on nationalism, in particular his application of banality, is truly inspirational. Throughout the 1990s, Billig's *Banal Nationalism* set a new way to study nationhood. Moving our gaze away from the traditional concerns with its historical origins and its substantial features, *Banal Nationalism* offered a systematic analysis of nationalism's reproduction. Specifically, Billig pointed out the role played by familiar, unremarkable "little words" (*deixis*) to explain the persistence and pervasiveness of the idea of a world divided into nations.

7. Bronwen Manby's (2018) particular study for UNHCR is a case in point. It provides a comparative analysis of nationality laws and their implementation in Partner States of the East African Community (EAC). The idea is to highlight the gaps that allow statelessness with the aim of finding legal and political solutions. The overall trend is to identify the populations that are stateless or at risk of becoming stateless in the region and to make recommendations for the remedies that address the problem both at the national and regional levels. In these accounts, there are

states, institutions, NGOs, and INGOs, but not the people themselves, other than as a counting exercise, which ultimately fails due to the very nature of the beast.

## References


Arendt, Hannah. *The Human Condition*. Chicago: University of Chicago Press, 1958.

———. *The Origins of Totalitarianism*. London: George Allen & Unwin, 1968.

———. *Responsibility and Judgment*. New York: Schocken Books, 2003.

Assunção, Thiago. "Apatridia No Brasil: Da Invisibilidade Ao Convite Para Se Tornar Cidadão." *Revista de Estudos e Pesquisas Sobre as Américas* 13, no. 1 (2019): 279–307. https://doi.org/10.21057/10.21057/repamv13n1.2019.24301

Benhabib, Seyla. *The Rights of Others: Aliens, Residents, and Citizens*. Cambridge: Cambridge University Press, 2004. https://doi.org/10.1017/CBO9780511790799

Benslama-Dabdoub, Malak. "Colonial Legacies in Syrian Nationality Law and the Risk of Statelessness." *The Statelessness & Citizenship Review* 3, no. 1 (2021): 6–32.

Benton, Meghan. "The Problem of Denizenship: A Non-Domination Framework." *Critical Review of International Social and Political Philosophy* 17, no. 1 (2014): 49–69. https://doi.org/10.1080/13698230.2013.851479

Billig, Michael. *Banal Nationalism*. London & Thousand Oaks, CA: Sage, 1995.

Çağlar, Ayşe. "The Multiple Tenses of a Postcolonial Age of Migration: A Commentary on Samaddar, R. The Postcolonial Age of Migration." *Dialectical Anthropology* 45, no. 3 (2021): 317–20. https://doi.org/10.1007/s10624-021-09619-4

Çağlar, Ayse, and Nina Glick Schiller. *Migrants and City-Making: Dispossession, Displacement, and Urban Regeneration*. Durham, NC: Duke University Press, 2018.

Canefe, Nergis. "Citizens versus Permanent Guests: Cultural Memory and Citizenship Laws in a Reunified Germany." *Citizenship Studies* 2, no. 3 (1998): 519–44. https://doi.org/10.1080/13621029808420696

———. "New Faces of Statelessness: The Rohingya Exodus and Remapping of Rights." In *Citizenship, Nationalism and Refugeehood of Rohingyas in Southern Asia*, edited by Nasreen Chowdhory and Biswajit Mohanty, 197–215. Singapore: Springer, 2020. https://doi.org/10.1007/978-981-15-2168-3_11

———. "Afghanistan and Its Futures." *International Migration* 60, no. 1 (2022): 262–67. https://doi.org/10.1111/imig.12961

Canefe, Nergis, Paula Banerjee, and Nasreen Chowdhory. "Gender, Identity and Displacement: Nexus Requirements for a Critical Epistemology." In *Gender, Identity and Migration in India*, edited by Nasreen Chowdhory and Paula Banerjee, 1–14. Singapore: Springer, 2022. https://doi.org/10.1007/978-981-16-5598-2_1

Carens, Joseph. *The Ethics of Immigration*. Oxford Political Theory. Oxford & New York: Oxford University Press, 2013.

Chimni, B. S. "From Resettlement to Involuntary Repatriation: Towards a Critical History of Durable Solutions to Refugee Problems." *Refugee Survey Quarterly* 23, no. 3 (2004): 55–73. https://doi.org/10.1093/rsq/23.3.55

Cole, Philip. "At the Borders of Political Theory: Carens and the Ethics of Immigration." *European Journal of Political Theory* 14, no. 4 (2015): 501–10. https://doi.org/10.1177/1474885115594283

———. "Towards a Symmetrical World: Migration and International Law." *Éthique et Économique = Ethics and Economics* 4, no. 1 (2006): 1–7. https://papyrus.bib.umontreal.ca/xmlui/handle/1866/3371

———. *Philosophies of Exclusion: Liberal Political Theory and Immigration*. Edinburgh: Edinburgh University Press, 2000.

Eliassi, Barzoo. *Narratives of Statelessness and Political Otherness : Kurdish and Palestinian Experiences*. Cham: Palgrave Macmillan, 2021. http://urn.kb.se/resolve?urn=urn:nbn:se:lnu:diva-102456

Gordon, Jane Anna. "Degrees of Statelessness: Vulnerability and Political Capital." *Journal of Contemporary Thought*, no. 32 (2010): 17–39.

———. *Statelessness and Contemporary Enslavement*. London & New York: Routledge, 2020.

Guild, Elspeth, Kees Groenendijk, and Sergio Carrera, eds., *Illiberal Liberal States: Immigration, Citizenship and Integration in the EU*. London & New York: Routledge, 2016.

Gündoğdu, Ayten. "Arendt on Culture and Imperialism: Response to Klausen." *Political Theory* 39, no. 5 (2011): 661–67. https://doi.org/10.1177/0090591711413548

Jamal, Amal, and Anna Kensicki. "Theorizing Half-Statelessness: A Case Study of the Nation-State Law in Israel." *Citizenship Studies* 24, no. 6 (2020): 769–85. https://doi.org/10.1080/13621025.2020.1745152

Kingston, Lindsey. "Worthy of Rights: Statelessness as a Cause and Symptom of Marginalisation." In *Understanding Statelessness*, edited by Tendayi Bloom, Phillip Cole, and Katherine Tonkiss, 17–34. London & New York: Routledge, 2018.

Manby, Bronwen. "Statelessness and Citizenship in the East African Community." UNHCR, 2018. https://data2.unhcr.org/en/documents/download/66807

Manly, Mark, and Santhosh Persaud. "UNHCR and Responses to Statelessness | Forced Migration Review." *Forced Migration Review*, no. 32 (2009). www.fmreview.org/statelessness/manly-persaud

Mbembé, J. A. "Necropolitics." Translated by Libby Meintjes. *Public Culture* 15, no. 1 (2003): 11–40.

Molavi, Shourideh C., *Stateless Citizenship: The Palestinian-Arab Citizens of Israel*. Studies in Critical Social Sciences 54. Leiden & Boston: Brill, 2013.

Möller, Frank, and Susan Sontag. "Rwanda Revisualized: Genocide, Photography, and the Era of the Witness." *Alternatives: Global, Local, Political* 35, no. 2 (2010): 113–36. https://doi.org/10.1177/030437541003500202

Mondelli, Juan Ignacio. "Eradicating Statelessness in the Americas." *Forced Migration Review* 56 (2017): 44–46.

———. "From the Brasilia Declaration to the Brazil Plan of Action." In *Latin America and Refugee Protection: Regimes, Logics and Challenges*, edited by Liliana Lyra Jubilut, Marcia Vera Espinoza, and Gabriela Mezzanotti. Forced Migration 41. New York: Berghahn, 2021.

Ogilvie, Bertrand. *L'Homme Jetable: Essai Sur l'exterminisme et La Violence Extrême.* Paris: Éditions Amsterdam, 2012.

O'Neill, Onora. "Agents of Justice." *Metaphilosophy* 32, no. 1–2 (2001): 180–95. https://doi.org/10.1111/1467-9973.00181

Owens, Patricia. "Reclaiming 'Bare Life'?: Against Agamben on Refugees." *International Relations* 23, no. 4 (2009): 567–82. https://doi.org/10.1177/0047117809350545

Rancière, Jacques. "Politics, Identification, and Subjectivization." *October* 61 (1992): 58. https://doi.org/10.2307/778785

Rancière, Jacques. "Who Is the Subject of the Rights of Man?" *South Atlantic Quarterly* 103 no. 2–3 (2004): 297–310. https://doi.org/10.1215/00382876-103-2-3-297

Rürup, Miriam. "Lives in Limbo: Statelessness after Two World Wars." *Bulletin of the GHI Washington* 49 (Fall 2011): 113–34.

Samaddar, Ranabir. *Emergence of the Political Subject.* New Delhi: Sage, 2010. https://doi.org/10.4135/9788132108108

———. *Karl Marx and the Postcolonial Age.* New York: Springer, 2017.

———. *The Postcolonial Age of Migration.* London & New York: Routledge, Taylor & Francis Group, 2020.

Schopenhauer, Arthur. *The Essential Schopenhauer: Key Selections from The World as Will and Representation and Other Writings.* New York: Harper Collins, 2010.

Sontag, Susan. "In Plato's Cave." In *On Photography.* New York: Farrar, Straus and Giroux, 1977.

———. "Regarding the pain of others." *Diogene* 201, no. 1 (2003): 127–39.

Tyler, Imogen. "Revolting Subjects: Social Abjection and Resistance in Neoliberal Political Equality." *San Diego Law Review* 45 (2013): 981–88.

Van Eert. "Stitching Institute on Statelessness and Inclusion: Annual Accounts for the Year 2020." Stitching Institute on Statelessness and Inclusion, 2021. https://files.institutesi.org/year_report_2020.pdf

Vlieks, Caia, and Laura Van Waas. "Stateless Persons." In *Elgar Encyclopedia of Human Rights.* Edward Elgar Publishing Limited, 2022. www.elgaronline.com/view/nlm-book/9781789903614/b-9781789903621.fm1.xml

Watson, Lori. "Equal Justice Comment on Michael Blake's Immigration and Political Equality." *San Diego Law Review* 45, no. 4 (2008): 981.

Wilmer, S. E. *Performing Statelessness in Europe.* Cham: Springer, 2018. https://doi.org/10.1007/978-3-319-69173-2.

# Part II

# City as a Site of Statelessness

Chapter 4

# The Conundrum of Trafficking and Statelessness in West Bengal

Paula Banerjee and Sangbida Lahiri

Statelessness is a problem that has been plaguing states, human rights activists, the UNHCR, other international organizations, and the vulnerable and displaced populations around the world. Statelessness does not respect borders; it robs the stateless of their rights and dignity, including rights over their bodies and the dignity of life. It deprives them of the ability to protest rampant exploitations. It also robs the states and its representatives of the right to act humanely. Stateless men, women, and children become insecure because they can be displaced any time that the state or the majority community so desires. Even those who are representatives of states are themselves unable to fathom what to do with stateless people, where to place them, and how to treat them. Citizenship is central to the statist imagination. Therefore, stateless people are not the opposite of citizens. Rather, they do not exist within the statist imaginary. But, ironically, statelessness can often be produced through hyperstatism. Often, a narrow and rigid definition of who is a citizen can lead to large groups being left out. Those left out then join the ranks of the stateless. This shift from citizen to stateless is often the result of multiple transitions. Initially, it might be a case of deprivation of rights, which then leads to displacement. Or sometimes, displacement can lead to erosion of rights that renders people de facto stateless. However, what is clear from the experiences of population groups that face situations of protracted displacement is that they often become stateless. Here, one can consider the situation of the Chakmas in India, the Lhotshampas living in Bhutan, or the Sri Lankan refugees of Indian origin. The most spectacular of such cases are the Rohingyas in South and Southeast Asia. One group that is habitually neglected in these discussions are the trafficked people who live in near-bondage situations in different parts of the world. It is surprising that they do not frontally come up in discussions of statelessness. Is it because large sections of these people, whether trafficked for labor or love (read: sex) are women? In the context of South Asia, they share a precarious relationship with the state. They are subjects of the state, but often they face situations of endemic deprivation and lack of rights. It is their vulnerability that makes them accessible to traffickers. At least in the context of South Asia, the difference between smuggling and trafficking is mere semantics. In this chapter we will discuss particularly the situation of trafficked women spatially in West Bengal during COVID times, but a major contention is to portray the conjunctions between trafficking and statelessness that existed before the pandemic and are continuing even today.

Patricia Tuitt argues, "space in its physical and mental form is organized between race, class and gender among other factors" (1999, 107). When women are displaced, they are destabilized from their moorings, and such destabilization is often made an occasion for their sexual exploitation, making them ready prey for traffickers. Both trafficked men and women are marked as aliens in all the countries of South Asia, but it is largely the women and children whose alienness translates into sexual vulnerability. By marking such women as sexually available, their sexual exploitation becomes facilitated. In fact, trafficked people lose most of the rights and entitlements that accrue as a result of citizenship. Statelessness and trafficking are thus related, if not two sides of the same phenomenon. No amount of legislation on any one of these can ameliorate the conundrum. Also, one must understand the specific gender dimension of the problem. To address the problem of statelessness, one must address the problem of trafficking and the gender dimensions of that problem. Trafficking is also very much an urban phenomenon, as trafficked people are usually brought to urban centers for various forms of labor extraction.

Cities are never formed without the presence of a trafficked population. Those who are trafficked are brought in for their labor, sexual or otherwise. They provide cheap services for jobs that the natives often shun. Once trafficked, they join the ranks of the *sans papier* population. This is a small step away from becoming de facto stateless. This chapter is based on ethnographic and long-term interactions with people who were trafficked into the city of Kolkata, reports on trafficking, data culled from first-person interviews, newspaper reports, and interactions with human rights groups, security personnel, and policymakers who deal with such population groups.

## Where We Stand

Human trafficking remains among the top organized crimes in India. Although trafficking in persons is legally banned, it is carried on with impunity. According to one *Reuters* report from 2017, which created a stir: "Of an estimated 20 million commercial prostitutes in India, 16 million women and girls are victims of sex trafficking, according to campaigners" (Nagaraj 2017). According to the Government of India (GoI) data, as quoted in the media: "[L]ess than half of the more than 8,000 human trafficking cases reported in 2016 were filed in court by the police and the conviction rate in cases that did go to trial was 28 percent" (Nagaraj 2018). In a spectacular case from 2018, two Indian brothel owners, a husband–wife team from Gaya in eastern India, were jailed for life after four of their victims, rescued by a police raid in 2015, took the stand against them. However, this case was the first of its kind, as traffickers are rarely prosecuted, and even fewer are punished. In fieldwork carried out by the authors in 2015 in six jails in West Bengal, among the one hundred Bangladeshi women interviewed who had violated the 1946 Foreigners Act, only one of them complained against her trafficker. As per the National Crime Records Bureau's 2016 crime statistics, there were 1,100 cases of trafficking (National Crime and Records Bureau 2016). These numbers stood at 2,278 in 2018, 2,208 cases were reported in 2019, and 1,714 in 2020 (Crime in India 2018, 2019, 2020).

The Government of India has a number of provisions against trafficking. These include the following:

- Article 23 (1) of the Constitution of India prohibits human trafficking: "Traffic in human beings and beggar and other similar forms of forced labor are prohibited and any contravention of this provision shall be an offence punishable in accordance with law" (Government of India 1950).
- The Immoral Traffic (Prevention) Act, 1956 (ITPA): Extending to the whole of India, this is the premier legislation for the prevention of trafficking for commercial sexual exploitation.

- Section 370 and 370A of the Indian Penal Code (IPC): Established through the Criminal Law (Amendment) Act 2013. Section 370 prohibits buying or disposing of any person as a slave: "Whoever imports, exports, removes, buys, sells or disposes of any person as a slave, or accepts, receives or detains against his will any person as a slave, shall be punished with imprisonment of either description for a term which may extend to seven years, and shall also be liable to fine" (*Criminal Law (Amendment) Act 2013*). Section 370A penalizes the exploitation of trafficked persons and children: "A) Whoever, knowingly or having reason to believe that a minor has been trafficked, engages such minor for sexual exploitation in any manner, shall be punished with rigorous imprisonment for a term which shall not be less than five years, but which may extend to seven years, and shall also be liable to fine. B) Whoever, knowingly by or having reason to believe that a person has been trafficked, engages such person for sexual exploitation in any manner, shall be punished with rigorous imprisonment for a term which shall not be less than three years, but which may extend to five years, and shall also be liable to fine" (*Criminal Law (Amendment) Act 2013*). Section 370, however, requires force or coercion on the part of the trafficker, which, if unable to be proved, renders the measure quite ineffective for prosecution.

- Protection of Children from Sexual Offences (POCSO) Act, 2012: Having come into effect on 14th November, 2012, the POCSO Act is a law to protect children from abuse and exploitation, especially of the sexual kind. This law may be brought into court in cases of child sex trafficking. In terms of shortcomings, the POCSO Act provides highly precise definitions for different forms of sexual abuse, including penetrative and non-penetrative sexual assault, sexual harassment, and many law courts often refuse to use it when circumstances are dubious or lacking in "tangible" proof.

- Prohibition of Child Marriage Act, 2006: While not directly connected to trafficking, this law may be brought into prosecution in cases of trafficking of young people, especially girls, under the rouse of marriage. Many cases of trafficking involve temple marriages of victims to hide the fact that they are being used as sex slaves by older men of often higher caste.

- Bonded Labour System (Abolition) Act, 1976: Deploying people as bonded, free labor after kidnapping, coercing, or manipulating them is a common phenomenon in India. While the association between bonded labor and trafficking is often overlooked, this law prohibits bonded labor, and thereby may be used to rescue trafficked workers placed in industry and agriculture over generations.
- Juvenile Justice (Care and Protection) of Children Act, 2000: This law made it a criminal offense with imprisonment for anyone to purchase or employ a child in any hazardous employment or in bondage.
- Child Labour (Prohibition and Regulation) Act, 1986: This law, prohibiting child labor, is impactful in curbing child labor, also a common bane for trafficked children and children in trafficked families, who are often placed in factories.
- Transplantation of Human Organs Act, 1994: This law calls for the "prevention of commercial dealings in human organs and for matters connected therewith or incidental thereto." Thus, it is a legal preventive measure for the human experimentation and commercial dealings of human organs, which is a significant aspect of human trafficking.
- Sections 372 and 373 of the IPC: These sections of the IPC prohibit prostitution. Section 372 prohibits the prostitution of minor females: "Whoever sells, lets to hire, or otherwise disposes of any person under the age of eighteen years with intent that such person shall at any age be employed or used for the purpose of prostitution or illicit intercourse with any person or for any unlawful and immoral purpose, or knowing it to be likely that such person will at any age be employed or used for any such purpose, shall be punished with imprisonment of either description for a term which may extend to ten years, and shall be liable to fine" (*Criminal Law [Amendment] Act 2013*). Section 373 prohibits and penalizes the buying, hiring, or otherwise possessing a minor for the purpose of prostitution. This may be important as a measure against sex trafficking, especially of minors.
- Scheduled Castes and Scheduled Tribes (Prevention of Atrocities) Act: This act prohibits the exploitation of members

of Scheduled Castes and Scheduled Tribes, and criminalizes bonded labor from any member of these communities.

- Articles 24, 39(e) and 39(f) of the Constitution of India: While article 24 prohibits child labor, articles 39(e) and 39(f) ordain that the health and strength of individuals are not abused and that no one is forced by the economic necessity to do work unsuited to their age or strength, and that childhood and youth should be protected against exploitation, and are thus indirectly related to bonded labor and trafficking through manipulative means.

India has ratified the 2000 *UN Protocol to Prevent, Suppress and Punish Trafficking in Persons* in 2011. But in a report by the US State Department in 2021 (2021 Trafficking), it is stated that although the GoI has made some progress to stop trafficking, the actions remain inadequate. Among other issues, the report stated the following:

- Section 370 of the IPC, criminalizing trafficking that includes any physical or sexual exploitation, does not directly address trafficking in labor.
- Sections 372 and 373 of the IPC criminalized the exploitation of children through prostitution without requiring a demonstration of force, unlike Section 370.
- Bonded labor was criminalized in the Scheduled Castes and Scheduled Tribes (Prevention of Atrocities) Act and the Bonded Labour System (Abolition) Act (BLSA), but without sufficiently stringent penalties, and that has adversely affected the legal system.
- Trafficking cases were filed under the Juvenile Justice Act and other sections of the IPC, but these were unevenly enforced and with short penalties.
- The government also prosecuted sex trafficking crimes under the Protection of Children from Sexual Offences Act (POCSO) and the Immoral Traffic Prevention Act (ITPA).

Although government reports on trafficking showed a high number of people being trafficked, these were not regularly updated and were not sufficiently addressed for redress. Online court trials were utilized to hear trafficking cases during the pandemic. But the procedures for filing trafficking cases are uneven and lengthy, allowing easy bails for the alleged traffickers. Also, uneven and irregular court proceedings during the pandemic led to victims and prosecutors being unable to present counterarguments in bail hearings and raised the chances of victims being threatened (2021 Trafficking).

## The Media Response

It is estimated that in the post-pandemic period, poverty will drive many more young girls and women into the hands of traffickers. A Salvation Army report of 2021, quoting Kathy Betteridge, director of anti-trafficking and modern slavery for the Salvation Army, states " 'The perpetrators often target the most vulnerable in our society those in poverty, people who are homeless, those with mental health problems and those with addictions . . . And we fear that the economic fallout from the pandemic will put even more people at risk of falling prey to modern slavery.' . . . [Betteridge] added that despite the number rescued this year, 'many more' are 'still trapped in slavery, unable to escape' " (Atkinson and Turner 2021). Other international media houses, such as CNN, agreed that the pandemic has put women at greater risk:

> The pandemic also caused governments to divert resources away from anti-traficking efforts, the State Department found, "resulting in decreased protection measures and service provision for victims, reduction of preventative efforts, and hindrances to investigations and prosecutions of traffickers . . . If there is one thing we have learned in the last year, it is that human trafficking does not stop during a pandemic," acting Director of the Office to Monitor and Combat Trafficking in Persons Kari Johnstone wrote in her introduction to the annual Trafficking in Persons (TIP) report. (Hansler 2019)

The Indian media also echoes the international media houses. One such media report states:

> The pandemic exposed and exacerbated the systemic and deeply entrenched socio-economic inequities in Indian society, thus

> increasing manifold the consequential vulnerability and marginality. The disruption in economic activities across sectors, massive rise in unemployment and sources of livelihood have put a sizable population of India under desperate circumstances. A study by Azim Premji University estimates that nearly 230 million Indians have fallen below the poverty line since the pandemic. The vulnerable populace reeling under such desperation makes the perfect recipe for exploitation. One such form of exploitation that we need to be vigilant about is human trafficking. As many as 27 lakh distress calls were made to the Ministry of Women and Child Development between March and August 2020. Between April 2020 and June 2021, over 9,000 children were rescued from traffickers. (Patnaik 2021)

Another report discusses the personal experience of a victim:

> On June 4, Pooja (name changed) was rescued from her employer's house in Patna. At 10, Pooja had been working as a domestic help for about a year. She was taken by child traffickers in June 2020, when the country was exiting from a nationwide coronavirus lockdown. After a year of child labor, she was rescued by Dhawa Dal-a task force constituted by the Bihar's Department of Labour Resources Department with the help of Suresh Kumar, Executive Director of Centre DIRECT, an NGO working for the empowerment of women, youth and children. Pooja told her rescuers that she was maltreated by her employers, who used to beat her thrice a day as a matter of routine on one pretext or the other. She had bruises on her body when she was rescued on June 4, the NGO said. The alleged child traffickers had taken Pooja after luring her parents—living in East Champaran district of Bihar—in the name of giving their daughter a good education and a bright future. (Sushmita Ghosh 2021)

In the context of Bengal, too, the reports are similar to those of both national and international media. *The Hindu* reported that strict lockdowns followed by a massive cyclonic devastation in the coastal areas of Bengal in 2020 have made girls extremely vulnerable to traffickers. In one report, the newspaper said that the two massive devastations, COVID-19 and the cyclone Amphan, on the lives of the poor have increased child marriages in the Sundarban areas of Bengal where the devastation was maximum. These districts with extreme poverty have also become hotspots for trafficking in women and girls. The paucity of legal aid in many areas of these districts due to loss of connectivity has resulted in an alarming situation for human trafficking (Singh 2020).

The other areas that are extremely vulnerable to human trafficking are the tea plantation areas of West Bengal, such as New Jalpaiguri and Darjeeling. On January 30, 2022, the law enforcement officers in the plantation area held consultation with the plantation workers to reduce trafficking of minors. Due to the pandemic lockdowns, the workers in the plantations are helpless and practically living without food. In this situation, they are sending their minor girls and boys to work outside as cheap labor. One of the Bengali television channels reported that the district police have noticed that most of the minor girls trafficked from the tea gardens in the last two years have been found in red light districts of Bengal. The police officers are said to be holding awareness camps among the tea garden workers so they get an idea about where they are sending their children for work and also what kind of subhuman work these children are getting in the cities (Bangla 2022).

Another newspaper reported news that the government of West Bengal started a scheme for compensating victims of trafficking with the idea that if they wanted to get out of their lives in brothels or other repressive areas, they could do so. A newspaper reported that two minor girls from South 24 Parganas district were trafficked between the years 2014 and 2015. They were rescued after a few months of being trafficked. Since 2016, they have been staying in their village and applied for the compensation grant for trafficking victims so they could start a new life. This report suggested they applied for the grant in 2016. They received the money in 2021, after nearly five years. The reporter argues that the lengthy process of applying for grants/compensation often confuses people, and they lose hope and stop pursuing such compensation. On the other hand, the report argues that most of the remote village girls are unaware of being eligible for compensation when trafficked. They are also unaware of the government facilities they may access; the lack of information makes them afraid to step outside of the red light areas, so they can rarely garner support for receiving any such compensatory grants or other assistance (Bandyopadhyay 2021).

The media report clearly points out the fact that any critical situation may drive the people who are already precariously placed into devastation and crisis. When an entire family faces starvation, they employ whatever tactic might have any extractable social capital to survive. A woman's or a child's body can be an extractable commodity that may sustain a family. In such a situation, the primary object is to survive, and it is never about any other kind of right but the right to survive. A citizen has claims to a spectrum of rights. For the stateless, it is always about the right to survive.

## Voices: The Young Adults

Piya, a girl of seventeen, is at present staying at a juvenile home in south Bengal. Her mother is a sex worker who works at one of the famous red light districts of Kolkata and stays in the north suburban areas of the city. Piya never stayed with her mother. Her mother kept her in boarding school so she could have a better life than her own. Piya is a studious and meritorious girl who has secured 92 percent in the Madhyamik examination in the year 2021. Unfortunately, the pandemic lockdown forced her to leave the hostel and to stay with her mother. In October 2021, her mother sent Piya to Kolkata to buy new clothes for the festive season. Her mother gave her a little cash in her hand. She was accompanied by an uncle who was her mother's new baboo (boyfriend) and was currently staying at their home. Piya says that her uncle bought a lot of expensive clothes and jewels for her from a Hatibagan market and convinced her to take a hotel room for a few hours at a hotel in Sealdah region so that, ostensibly, she could get some rest and food. She says that when they arrived in the hotel room, her uncle started flirting with her. As she resisted him from doing so, he slapped her hard and locked the room from outside. She says that night he returned and brought dinner for her. After dinner, he raped her several times. Late into the night, he started persuading her that her mother struggled a lot for her studies, and that she should start earning now, as she was capable, so that her mother could get relief. The uncle never stayed in the hotel during the daytime. She was locked in whenever he was not in the hotel. He came to Piya's room only when he felt the urge to have sex at night or in the late afternoon. Piya said that on the first day she tried to run away. But on the second day, she realized that it was impossible. So, she tried to connect with her school friends who can report to the child line, and she may be rescued from the physical and mental torture. On the third evening, when her uncle arrived with food and beverages, suddenly police officers and rescue workers appeared in the room. They arrested her uncle, and she was brought to a juvenile home, where she now resides. Piya wants to get back to her school and study. But she wants neither to see her mother or return to her home. She is seventeen years and four months old. She has the provision to stay in the juvenile home for another eight months. After that, she worries where can she go? Nobody has an answer to this question (personal interview with Piya, 2022).

One of Piya's companions, Jaseema, is twenty years old and Bangladeshi by nationality. She was rescued four years ago from Bihar and sent to the same home. Jaseema is psychologically unstable, and could not return to her country. Her case has been pending for four years. As she is the major witness of an Indo-Bangladesh trafficking network, the government is not allowing her to return to her family. At the age of thirteen, she came to Kolkata as domestic labor. Her mother stays in the Khulna district, where she is also a domestic worker. One of her neighbors—she called her *bua* (aunt)—allured her and her mother by saying that in Kolkata the rates of domestic workers are higher than in Bangladesh. So, if they reached Kolkata, their lives would be sorted. Initially, Jaseema thought she would come to Kolkata on her own, and later she would bring her mother. But crossing the India–Bangladesh border was difficult for them because they had no identity document, such as a passport or visa. Jaseema's aunt took her to the bordering areas of Satkhira, and then through Jessore they came to the international border region. Her aunt did not accompany Jaseema to cross the border. She handed over Jaseema to a local resident, who was called "master" by everyone in the locality. Jaseema said that "master" was renowned for bribing border forces on both sides. He started for India along with her late at night. In the early dawn, when they reached India, the "master" handed Jaseema over to another young man and returned. Jaseema and that man boarded a train that arrived at Sealdah station, from where she went to Delhi with yet another person. Jaseema says she worked as a sex worker in Delhi for two years. Later, she traveled to Bihar and stayed near Patna. In Bihar, she also worked in this sector for another two and a half years on her own. On a festive night, police caught her in a hotel with a client. After some legal procedures, she was sent to a Bengali home at the age of sixteen. When she started sex working, Jaseema says, she was only eleven years and two months old (personal interview with Jaseema, 2022).

Like Jaseema, another girl and her sister, both Bangladeshi nationals, became trapped in a similar situation. Both sisters were caught under India's Foreigners Act (1946) and are the victims of a trafficking chain. They must attend court per summons and have no permission to go home. These two sisters are from Dhaka Zila. They were trafficked by their own maternal uncle, with the consent of their parents. Therefore, although they want to go back to Bangladesh, they do not want to go home because they know their parents will re-sell them to traffickers. Otherwise, perhaps it would be difficult to get rid of them, as they are not just two more mouths to feed but two young girls who might bring shame to their family. Both girls served as bonded labor in a red light district near Kolkata. They were caught by police in a tourist's hotel. The hotel owners and the attendants are the pimps of sex rackets. The hotel owner himself recruits girls for sex work and runs a hostel for girls in this trade.

The Bangladeshi girls are prohibited from talking to anyone in this country. They are not allowed to visit the marketplace or religious places where they are staying now. They are not allowed to have cell phones. While the other girls can enroll in schools and get an education, they are not allowed to register for schools in India. They cannot visit hospitals unless they fall seriously ill. Even at the time of severe illness, the home authority must ask for the government's permission to admit them. Hospital care is often delayed, and the girls suffer significantly as a consequence. The home authorities informally train them in dance and handicraft.

Sangeeta Ghosh, a psychological counselor, said that most girls in homes tend to suffer mental trouble—sometimes so severe that they are a danger to both themselves and others. They tend to frequently seek attention from the home supervisors, and to feel insecure for minor reasons. Over time, they lose their sense of self-worth. Another psychological counselor, Anisha Chandra, told us that the minor girls are often ashamed of what happened to them, especially if they are rescued from red light areas. They suffer perpetually from self-guilt and find their own fault in everything. In most of the cases, girls below the age of fifteen are depressed and cannot understand what is happening to them. They cry frequently and refuse entertainment. Sometimes they lack the attention span for learning and lose any sense of rights or entitlements. When they grow up, they have no sense of their own worth, or the inherent rights and privileges that they deserve as citizens (personal interview with Sangeeta Ghosh and Anisha Chanda, 2022).

The problem with many girls staying in government homes or homes run by NGOs is the uncertainty, which is always with them. Some may ask, what is the reason behind this uncertainty? The answer is that in most cases the girls do not know where they will go from the government homes. Their families may not want them, and their countries may not take them back. They don't want to use the address of their families. During the lockdown, most NGOs spoke of the increasing number of girls who were sold by their own families or relatives, with the consent of their parents. In times of extreme deprivation, many parents sent their daughters to the recruiters of the flesh-trade market. Girls of Sneha Shelter Home spoke of how their parents wanted to be rid of them. Deprived of their families and their country, these girls are permanent exceptions to the status of citizens. Even if they are not de jure stateless, they are in fact de facto stateless, as they do not have a home of their own or a country to which they belong.

## Voices: The Adult Women

Mily Laskar was trafficked from Joynagar to Kolkata when she was thirteen years old. Mily came from the Sunderban area and, according to her, "the profession of my family was to collect natural resources from natural forest nearby and to sell those things in the local town markets. Precisely, my parents used to collect honey and crabs from the forest-water and used to sell those to the local dealers" (personal interview with Mily Laskar, 2022). Reminiscing about her earlier life, Mily shared,

> When my youngest brother was born, my mother was severely ill. Unfortunately, at that time, my father also faced an accident in the jungle, which caused paralysis to his limbs. I became the eldest member of my family at that young age and had to earn money to keep my parents and siblings alive. You know, I have seen how my mother was left totally uncared for, without medicines or food in her post-natal days. Her newly born son was screaming every moment, but her breasts were unable to produce a single drop of milk. We, the other three children of hers, were clueless at that time. We used to beg for meals at the neighbors' houses. And we never had a single full-belly meal in those days. (Laskar interview, 2022)

It was around this time that she came to know of a woman she called *didi*, or older sister. This woman would come to their village once a month to recruit girls to work in Kolkata.

> One day, Didi came to our house, talked to my mother and told me to be prepared for domestic work in Kolkata. The next day, at three o'clock in the morning, wearing a torn frock and

> barefoot, I came to Joynagar station with her. We got on a train and reached Sealdah station when the sun had begun to rise. It was early winter, and I felt my stomach burning with hunger. I remembered that I had my last meal in the late afternoon the previous day. Outside the station there were many tea shops. Didi took me into one of those. We sat on the bench. She ordered two cups of milk tea for both of us and two pieces of bread stuffed with omelets. That meager meal created magic for me. I started to follow that woman silently thereafter. She seemed the closest thing that I had in my life. (Laskar interview, 2022)

Although she was underage, when *didi* brought her to the red light areas, Mily could do nothing. She did not know she could take recourse in the law. She felt she was bereft of all rights and must abide by whatever *didi* said if she wanted to survive. In the brothel, she met two other girls she knew. At night, they would speak to each other and persuade one another that being a sex slave was not all bad. At least they had proper food and could send money home for their family (Laskar interview, 2022).

Kumkum Halder, a resident of Nilmoni Mitra Street, spoke of her life in Kolkata. She got married at an early age. This is how she described her life:

> After two years of having the first baby, I gave birth to another one. We did not have food at home, but we had no idea how to stop ourselves from conceiving. In a village society, of which I was a part nearly 25–27 years ago, it was considered that a woman should bear children within short intervals to make her place strong in her husband's household. Initially, I followed the same rule. But later when I saw that my children were starving like me, I was afraid of life. My first child was a daughter. I was afraid of her life, thinking that she had to face the same hardship and ignominy that I was facing then. I made up my mind that I would come to Kolkata every morning. I will work so that my children can get food every day. I told my mother about my wish. My mother has worked in Kolkata since we were children. She told me that it is really hard to find a decent job in Kolkata unless you had a particular skill. I requested her to help me find a suitable job in Kolkata, as my situation was intolerable. We had no idea what my mother did in Kolkata. We knew my mother works in a hospital as an attendant and stays in Kolkata for her work.

> I came to Sonagachi with my mother. I understood what she did to bring us up. My mother was not available to many people. She had a particular man, a *baboo* who was a government official and kept my mother as a mistress in this region. Initially, I was very afraid of this trade. I started staying with my mother and children. My husband and in-laws said many filthy words to me and my mother. I did not listen to them. I worked as a sex laborer here. My mother used to keep my children at home when I used to get customers. As I became known to the customers and a few of them became fond of my work, I started earning a good sum of money. Then, I hired a room for my work and my children were kept far from this atmosphere. When my daughter was six and my son was five, I went back to my husband's place. I told him to keep my children with him and I would send money for their schools and daily expenses. I kept an old woman as a caregiver to look after my children, who hailed from my mother's village. My husband and the members of in-laws were stunned and did not say a single word against me because now I could not only pay for my children but could also pay them to look after my children. (personal interview with Kumkum Halder, 2021)

Although Kumkum Halder could buy some respect for herself and her way of life, she also discussed the ignominy that she faced. She describes her situation as one of perpetual filth. When questioned about what she thought of her rights as a citizen, she was completely baffled. Neither Mily nor Kumkum thought they had any rights in their lives. They never voted, never complained against any mistreatment, and never demanded that they be treated with respect. The entire discourse of rights was completely alien to them, and to many others who were living a similar life.

## Conclusion

It is not as if there are no changes on the horizon. Durbar, one of the first trade unions of sex workers in West Bengal, is trying to popularize the concept of emancipation among the formerly trafficked people. Soumen Mitra, a veteran police officer, said that under Indian rules, the trafficked girls can also have certain rights. After eighteen years of age, they can have a voter card and assert their voting rights. They can marry, have a family, and have children. Many of them have done this. In Sonagachi, the trafficked girls who have crossed the age of eighteen are casting votes. It is evident from Soumen Mitra's interview that trafficked victims are not prohibited from exercising their rights (Mitra interview, 2021). But the question remains: how many of these women are aware of their rights? The situation becomes even more dire when women are trafficked across an international border. That is, when they truly become stateless. In 2015, when we were doing our fieldwork on cross-border women in Bengal jails, we came across thirteen women in the Dum Dum jail. The welfare officer informed us that thirteen women were intercepted at the Bengal–Bangladesh border who had violated the Foreigners Act of 1946. They did not speak Bengali, but a dialect similar to the people from the CHT (Chittagong Hill Tracts) area. We identified their language as Arakanese. They had already served two years of their jail sentence, but they could not be released or sent back to their country simply because they could not prove their citizenship. Therefore, they were languishing in jails even after they had served their sentence. The law had no recourse for them because they were stateless. Statelessness is thus a lose-all phenomenon.

Poverty, deprivation, hunger, and environmental disasters all lead to the erosion of rights. Often, such erosion of rights leads to such desperation that people fall prey to traffickers. Perhaps the phrase "falling prey" is also incorrect. They submit themselves to traffickers in the hope of a better life. Once trafficked, their rights are even further eroded, so that one day they discover they are without a country and belong to the ever-increasing number of the stateless population. But in a city's eco system, they are important both as sex workers and as bonded labor. The increasing demand for such population groups is a testimony to their necessity. They perform essential services for the city. The highest extraction of their labor occurs when they are deprived of their rights as citizens. Large interest groups are thus invested in keeping them stateless. Statelessness and trafficking therefore often work as a dyad. Yet there are hardly any studies on statelessness in which trafficked people find space of their own.

## References

"2021 Trafficking in Persons Report: India." Office to Monitor and Combat Trafficking in Persons, U.S. State Department, 2021.

Atkinson, Carolyn, and Lauren Turner. "Covid Pandemic May Increase People Trafficking Says Charity." *BBC News*, October 18, 2021. www.bbc.com/news/uk-58920152

Bandyopadhyay, Anwesha. "Char laksha kore kshatipuran pabe pacharer par uddhar dui kanya." *Ei Samay*, February 28, 2021. https://eisamay.com/west-bengal-news/24pargana-news/trafficked-girls-will-get-4-lakhs-each-as-a-victim-compensation/articleshow/81256337.cms

*Constitution of India, 1950*. www.constitutionofindia.net/constitution_of_india/fundamental_rights/articles/Article%2023

"Crime in India 2016: Statistics." National Crime and Records Bureau. Ministry of Home Affairs, 2016. https://ncrb.gov.in/sites/default/files/Crime%20in%20India%20-%202016%20Complete%20PDF%20291117.pdf

"Crime in India 2018: Statistics." National Crime and Records Bureau. Ministry of Home Affairs, 2018. https://ncrb.gov.in/sites/default/files/Crime%20in%20India%20-%202016%20Complete%20PDF%20291117.pdf

"Crime in India 2019: Statistics." National Crime and Records Bureau. Ministry of Home Affairs, 2019.

"Crime in India 2020: Statistics." National Crime and Records Bureau. Ministry of Home Affairs, 2020.

*Criminal Law (Amendment) Act 2013*. Indian Penal Code.

Ghosh, Sushmita. "Covid-19 Made Poor More Vulnerable to Child Trafficking, Say NGOs—Coronavirus Outbreak News." *India Today*, June 8, 2021. www.indiatoday.in/coronavirus-outbreak/story/covid-19-poor-marginalised-vulnerability-child-trafficking-ngos-1812519-2021-06-08

Hansler, Jennifer. "Covid-19 Pandemic Increased Number of People at Risk of Human Trafficking, State Department Report Says." CNN, 2019. www.cnn.com/2021/07/01/politics/2021-trafficking-in-persons-report-covid/index.html

"Human Trafficking at Tea Gardens: Coronay bandha kaj, pachar rukhte tatpar prashasan." *Zee 24 Ghanta*, January 30, 2022. https://zeenews.india.com/bengali/state/government-of-west-bengal-has-taken-a-new-initiative-to-stop-human-trafficking-from-the-closed-tea-gardens_420210.html

Nagaraj, Anurandha. "Rescued Child Sex Workers in India Reveal Hidden Cells in Brothels." *Reuters*, December 13, 2017. www.reuters.com/article/us-india-trafficking-brothels-idUSKBN1E71R1

———. "Indian Brothel Owners Get First Life Sentence for Trafficking Children." *Reuters*, March 28, 2018. www.reuters.com/article/us-india-trafficking-women-idUSKBN1H419U

Patnaik, Amar. "Why a Strong Law against Human Trafficking Is Necessary in Post-Covid Times." *The Indian Express*, September 8, 2021. https://indianexpress.com/article/opinion/web-edits/strong-law-human-trafficking-post-covid-times-7497207

Singh, Shiv Sahay. "Lockdown, Amphan Render Girls Vulnerable in West Bengal." *The Hindu*, July 30, 2020. www.thehindu.com/news/national/other-states/lockdown-amphan-render-girls-vulnerable-in-bengal/article32233610.ece

Tuitt, Patricia. "Rethinking the Refugee Concept." In *Refugee Rights and Realities Evolving International Concepts and Regimes*, edited by Frances Nicholson and Patrick Twomey, 106–18. Cambridge: Cambridge University Press, 1999.

Chapter 5

# Can Undesirables Inhabit the World?

## From Camps to *Instant Cities*

Michel Agier (translated by Helen Morrison)

### Introduction

In the contemporary world, the production, consumption, and political organization of states and regions, which exemplify economic modernization, constantly generate waste products, either close at hand or at a distance. These can be in the form of industrial waste, or nuclear waste, but also of human waste or "wasted lives" according to the expression used by Zygmunt Bauman (2004). Bauman describes, under the heading of "a culture of waste," the vast global and planetary management of these waste products, including the disposal not only of surplus products but also of supernumerary human beings. In this vision of the world, the "undesirables" seem to form another world, one kept at a distance through various political and logistical means on local, national, and global levels. This is why, in my work on refugees, internally displaced people (IDPs), and irregular migrants, particularly in the context of the camps, I emphasized the concept of undesirability (Agier 2011), and it seems to me useful to return to this subject once again.

The figure of the undesirable has a long history, linked to certain aspects of slavery-based and/or colonial societies, and to the racism of separation and segregation these gave rise to. The attitudes and knowledge, prevalent in a dominant Europe toward and about these "other" territories and populations, were shaped over the course of centuries of conquest, colonization, exploitation, and exclusion. In the context of territorial governance, the

Bantustans (a creation of apartheid in South Africa), and the Senzala (slave quarters in rural Brazil), epitomized such a combination of strict physical and social distancing and economic exploitation, in the same way that the status of "native" in a colony epitomized subordination in terms of both the economic and social governance of local populations (Spivak 1994). In past dominations, this epistemology created the most radical form of otherness, one almost inferior to humanity, and it continues to do so in current dominations. First, as a slave and colonial subject, then as the racial subject of apartheid and the postcolonial refugee, and today, the portrayal of the undesirable has spread and is now generic.

Undesirables can be treated as subalterns in various ways. It might indeed be thought that the two representations of the undesirable are born at the same time and develop in parallel. In fact, undesirables are the result of the same "epistemic violence" as that through which, according to Gayatri Spivak, Europe imagined the extreme radicality of "the other" in the guise of the "colonial subject" (Spivak 1994, 37). The two images are heterogeneous in terms of social and economic condition. Their definition is political and relative and depends on the contexts and circumstances that generate these categories in the popular imagination and in public policies. Yet, undesirability has an additional and distinct meaning, one that is absent from the definitions proposed by both Spivak and Bauman. It is this meaning that makes the concept of undesirability essential to recognizing other realities of domination and to explore other questions, since a separated space, and therefore potentially a separated social life, exactly corresponds to this ideological and political (dis)qualification. Put differently, undesirability has a spatial form that can be observed and analyzed in depth.

It is from this perspective that, in this chapter, I reexamine, albeit briefly, a series of ethnographic investigations carried out in different places that correspond to various forms of exclusion and also to the reinvention of a fragile yet lasting urbanity. In doing so, I shall revisit some of the sites of my urban research in Brazil (in Salvador de Bahia) and those of the camps and encampments of sub-Saharan Africa and Europe, focusing in particular on the question: can those who, at a given moment and in a given place, as a result of their social position, their origin or their appearance, find themselves considered and governed as undesirables, still inhabit the world? How do they succeed in this apparently impossible task? What form of energy is needed in order to live in, transform, and even become attached to spaces that are essentially defined as places of relegation, exclusion, and confinement for the undesirable? Such forms of resistance and adaptation have an even more far-reaching significance when it becomes clear that they have a role to play in re-envisaging the model of "instant cities," a concept that embodies a future way of living in a more unstable, more mobile, and a more insecure world.[1]

## Texaco, Liberdade and *l'En-ville* (the In-City)[2]

In 1992, I had been living in Salvador de Bahia in Brazil for six years. During this period, I had lived for almost two years in the Liberdade district where I was conducting urban and anthropological research. During my time there, I studied racism, poverty, social mobility, the Black movement, and the history of the Afro Carnival. At that time, a powerful movement around Black pride and the Afrocultural movement injected fresh energy and brought new fame to the neighborhood that originated around a network of lanes opened up at the end of the 1940s by migrants coming from Recôncavo, the vast region surrounding Salvador. In Liberdade, I came across bleak, cheerless lives and discovered the labyrinth of the side streets, dead ends, and alleyways. I met Maria das Cinzas (Mary of the Ashes), an elderly woman who described her life as "a novel" and her family as "a disgrace." She was of indeterminate age. Her skin no longer had any color. She was ashen, gray, like her clothes, with always the same skirt and the same shirt, faded to the color of worn cotton. And it was there in Liberdade that I discovered Texaco! More precisely, it was *from there* that I watched Marie-Sophie Laborieux found the Texaco district in Fort-de-France, as described by Patrick Chamoiseau in the novel of the same name[3] (Chamoiseau 1998). I read the book with wide-eyed attention, fascinated and enchanted by so many resonances.

First, there was the similarity between the Brazilian and the Caribbean stories: slavery—abolished just one century earlier in Brazil and one and a half centuries earlier in Martinique; the racialized dimension of identities and relationships in a multiracial society; pragmatism, fatalism, and the power of spirits in popular Black urban culture born out of slavery and perpetuated in post-slavery society; the "gentle languor" of the Caribbean and of the *saudade* in Brazil; the zombies and spirits in Martinique and here, in Bahia, the *Preto Velho* (the Old Black Man, emblem of resistance to life as a slave), the *Saci Péréré* (a folktale character in the form of a little imp who hops about on his single leg smoking a pipe), as well as a host of other imaginary characters representing an entire parallel life. I wondered if

Chamoiseau, the "Word Scratcher" (as the character of the author is referred to in the book) was not in fact describing my district of Liberdade, which we will call Liberty, in the City of Saint Sauveur on the Bay of All Saints in the country of Brazilwood (Brazil). And if old Marie-Sophie Laborieux of Texaco was not perhaps the sister of my old friend Maria das Cinzas of Liberdade . . .

Then perhaps it was simply a case of empathetic writing. All ethnologists know that describing something is all about the writing. A perfect example of *descriptive* writing would be one that succeeds in finding the words and the syntax where both content and form are in perfect harmony. That is the role of the Word Scratcher *Marqueur de Paroles*. At the beginning, the reader knows nothing and then gradually he learns the tone, the true voice, the grammar, and the rhythm, and finally the meanings of the words, which become as familiar to him as the characters and the settings.

Or perhaps . . . in reality, if Texaco struck a chord in me, an anthropologist of the invention of the city and of *favelas, invasiones*, abandoned neighborhoods, slums, camps, shelters, it is because of the concept of *l'Enville* (the *In-City*).

This *In-City* is a story without an end that links the center and its fringes, the thing itself and its outer limits. Everything is played out on the borders. And so, my Esternome (the father of Marie-Sophie) said, "Tell-me about this *In-City* . . . what did you feel when you first arrived there?" Nothing at all. There's nothing really there, just the object of a desire, just being there and being part of it. The *In-City* is the place you run to, but it is just "somewhere you pass through," old Esternome added. Nothing remained in his memory; the story that has survived is always that of movement, of arriving in the town from behind the Texaco filling station.

Almost thirty years after first discovering it in the book, I find myself searching feverishly for the moment where Marie-Sophie Laborieux first found the Texaco district with "the rage of a warrior." It comes a few pages from the end, the moment she drives her four bamboo sticks into the ground and drapes canvas over them: ". . . then I carefully weeded my space, flattened down the earth within my chosen area, chopped down the surrounding undergrowth over a radius of four meters." And it was done, "it was nothing, just a shade to keep off the sun, but it was my anchor within the *In-city*." Setting up home is the most basic and fundamental human gesture. It is directly opposed to the concept of roots or origins. Setting up home means coming from somewhere else, crossing a threshold, establishing a space at a border, and marking out, with a line drawn on the soil, the place that is my own, the place to which everyone has a right, a shelter, a corner, a nook, a home, a warm feeling.

The *campêche*, this area where the Texaco district of Fort-de-France was born, is the name of a bush, of bushland in general, and bushland is the best possible translation of the word *favela*, which was also the name of a small shrubby tree found in certain hilly areas. At the beginning of the twentieth century, in the area around Rio de Janeiro, the occupation by soldiers of the *morro da favela* was the very first . . . favela. Pushing back the bushland, the scrub, the *campêche*, means marking out the delicate limit between the *in-city* and its fringes, its external spaces, between nature and culture. A limit that is uncertain, removeable, and constantly evolving . . .

The Liberdade neighborhood, birthplace of Maria das Cinzas, has its origins in a favela story. I encountered Maria in a tiny pedestrian alleyway called an *avenida* (literally and ironically an "avenue"). We would need to study the ethnography of each alleyway in order to understand the various "invasions" of this city.[4] Between 1940 and 1970, a key period of migration to the city, families from the arid regions of the Nordeste and from the south coast of Bahia ended up settling in an area behind the existing houses in the district—Liberdade was the name of a road leading into the town—in a zone that, at the time, was still peripheral and semi-rural. Contemporary accounts describe the moment when the occupant of a *casa da frente* (the "front-facing" house, or in other words, those houses giving on to and visible from the street) relinquished the space behind the house (*quintal*, garden, backyard) to the homeless migrants, authorizing their illegal settlement against the promise of rent or services. Shacks of wood and dried mud rapidly spread behind the house along a dirt track that extended over tens of meters. The area extended to the boundary between the next cluster of huts and shacks at the back of another "front-facing house." When linked together, these alleyways and lanes formed the labyrinthine landscape of the *favelas*.

In this way, the area owed its origins to a process that involved the sharing and marking out of the preexisting urban space (the already occupied front house and road) and of the still uninhabited land (behind the houses). Its existence as a place in its own right required this initial separation from others and from nature, and later the illegality of the set-up made it necessary to refer back to this initial process and its borders. With the passage of time, and even before it was legally permitted, the inhabitants of the *avenidas* added an entrance (sometimes featuring a door or even a porch) and set aside an area (*fundo da Avenida)* where they carried out domestic or artisanal activities. Sometimes they created an exit, which marked the outer limit and the way out toward the surrounding area and beyond, accessible via another alleyway, another door, etc.

In the meantime, throughout most of the neighborhood, although to a different extent depending on the alleyways, the spaces themselves were transformed. Houses were added to and enhanced, sometimes with upper floors, or linked, either legally or illegally, to the town's service networks (water, electricity, sewers, transport). With all kinds of nuances and local specificities, the same story was repeated in many Latin American countries between 1940 and 2000. Initially (between 1940–1960), the migrants' urban "invasions" and "occupations" were followed by violent expulsions from the official, inner area of the city. It itself was in a period of demographic growth, toward the external periphery, a process that often signified social rejection and a political desire to keep out poor and undesirable migrants (1960–1970). Then, in the 1990s, as a result of the failure and the economic and political cost of strategies aimed at bringing order to urban life, combined with the resistance of the *favelados* (1980–1990), a political change occurred that meant from then onward, the existing and ongoing transformation of these fragile urban zones was to be negotiated. Even if she described her family as a disgrace, Maria das Cinzas was surrounded by the little "world" of her *avenida*, in the form of a hundred or so inhabitants housed in shacks and wooden houses, open to the outside. In this familiar context, she was able to feed herself, her daughter, and her grandson each day and maintain contact with the world.

What the internal, long-term, and empathetic study of fragile social environments reveals is the reconstruction of a familiar city in the form of networks of people and places, however disadvantaged their physical and architectural context.[5] When confronted with spectacle of demolition, the tearful reaction of the inhabitants of apartment blocks in French suburban housing projects is evidence of the capacity to make even the most hostile space familiar. Similarly, thousands of kilometers away, a further example of this phenomenon is found in the movements of the associations of *favelados*, campaigning for the transformation and improvement of their living accommodation, as opposed to demolition with very often the alternative of being rehoused in still more peripheral areas, even further from the city. Renovating a temporary shelter—in other words, rendering habitable a self-constructed lodging rather than destroying it—is the pragmatic solution advocated by popular urbanism. It is the very opposite of an industrial, anonymous solution inspired by a rigid vision of the city and limiting any innovation to an aesthetic context, an approach that remains the preferred solution, usually by default, for a still dominant number of planners, urbanists, or architects. Today, however, this approach is being challenged.

## Making a Community, Making a City

The observation is still a fragile one, but it would seem that, over recent years, certain specialists in the urban environment and those reflecting on urban issues have increasingly begun to challenge the urban functionalism of the twentieth century, the effects of which are being retrospectively measured in terms of authoritarianism and violence. Its "plans" and "programs," and even its most recent "projects," the last avatar of the 1990s, epitomized voluntarist and vertical urban policies that saw themselves endowed with an almost magical power to bring order and happiness by assuming transparency between an urban form that was decided from above and a social life that went on somewhere from below. Today, a radical inversion of this technicist and spontaneously authoritative approach is possible.

Recently, words and ideas that are simpler and more flexible, more liquid, to use the terminology of sociologist Zygmunt Bauman (creator of the concept of liquid society—an unstable and uncertain world), have crept into the debate. Acknowledging in particular the role of mobility in shaping the form of the city, architects and urbanists now advocate a resilient, inclusive city, a "welcoming city" (Hanappe 2018). They envisage the possibility of an "unfinished city" and of a "temporary urbanism" (Bouchain 2006) or of a "situational urbanism" (Fromonot 2011).

For sociologist and urbanist Richard Sennet, and before him, for urbanist and activist Jane Jacobs, in order to be effective, we need to return to the level of the micro-urban and to informality as opposed to the authoritarianism of the overplanned. We should even aim toward "an architecture without architects," "an urbanism without urbanists" (Sennett 2018). Such an approach sets the pragmatism of the inhabitants against the formal and idealized vision of planners.

In the course of research carried out in refugee camps in Sierra Leone during the 2000s, I encountered Liberian refugees who were desperate to return home. Not quite "home," however. Their villages in North Liberia had been destroyed and needed to be completely rebuilt. They were in the process of drawing up a plan for reconstruction, while at the same time demonstrating in front of the offices of the HCR to demand repatriation.

Two aspects of their project particularly struck me. First, in spite of having little or no expertise in planning or putting together projects, they were nevertheless engaged in preparing a request that was to be presented to various international NGOs who, they knew, would easily provide them with the financial aid they needed to return to their country. For them, the refugee camp had been a space that had allowed them to make contact with the "global" world, an opportunity to find out about and study models existing within the international community. Second, I was struck by the fact that their project was for a "city project," because, as they told me, returning to live in villages was too risky—such communities were too small; the inhabitants would be isolated and vulnerable to any possible return of armed groups. Grouping together in an efficient manner meant, in the first place, creating a city, a concept that they associated with notions of security and development.

It is not simply a matter of demographics or of the size of the urbanized space, but rather of the city as a state of mind, as a social organization, and a culturally diverse community, and equally important, as a city constructed from a practical point of view and where provision is made for spaces in which to live, to move around freely, and to encounter other people. The reason urban anthropology with its universalist goals is required, it seems to me, is precisely as a means of *reflecting on this link between space and the community*: how do we go about creating relationships in and with the place, a sense of local identity, memories, and also behavior—in other words, everything involved in *inhabiting* a place, in living in it. This approach therefore closely associates two French terms recently used and discussed by Richard Sennet, notably *la cité* (indicating a mentality associated with a form of collective life, a shared mindset and perception) and *la ville* (a physical reality in terms of its spatial and material existence) (Sennett 2018).

## Strange Futuristic Settlements

This is why fragile spaces, hastily put together with little or no formal construction, have considerable experimental and heuristic value, provided that we take the trouble to look at them from a scientific point of view, involving observation and analysis, rather than from a political or moral point of view based on judgments that may be compassionate, accusatory, or aesthetic. It is easy to underestimate the paradoxical effect that indignation over "shameful" shanty towns and camps can have, in particular when this is double-edged. The same words can just as easily prompt social and community-based actions calling for the recognition of those most disadvantaged members of society or seek justification for mass eviction and demolition. The occupants may, for their part, see these same places as a stage marking their arrival in the city as part of a nonlinear journey of integration.[6] The entire history of the *favelas* echoes this urban odyssey over a period of several decades, up until the so-called *favelo-bairro* policy (from shantytown to neighborhood) in the 1990s. The policy, introduced initially in the city of Rio de Janeiro and subsequently applauded and adopted by numerous other capital cities in Latin America, involved stabilizing temporary structures rather than getting rid of them, and transforming them into enduring neighborhoods.

It is in such fringes, wastelands, and non-cities that I found an already existing future. It was a somewhat anachronistic one, very far from the historic, and particularly European, notion of the city, which still too often tends to dominate our thinking in terms of the universality of cities. I have become acquainted with everyday life in such marginal zones or frontiers, the borderlands, and with people who live there or who pass through them. Far from being a one-off phenomenon, this research seems experimental and indicative of a certain urban future. It is reminiscent of urbanists who, like Jane Jacobs or Richard Sennett, envisage an urbanism that is practical, or pragmatic, and according to Sennett, who has long based his thinking on the notion of *homo faber*, on *what humans do*. It was, he wrote, essential to place "*Homo faber* in the city" (Sennett 2018).

The human settlements that formed the landscape of my field of research were indeed strange. They featured flexible frameworks which were endlessly malleable, transparent walls, reversible or transposable cubes. Curiously, at first sight, such places bear some initial resemblance to a city, but one which is temporary and easily dismantled. Some are temporary agglomerations with walls of plasticized fabric, supported on a frame made up of wooden planks, metal tubes, or branches, with water tanks made of rubber, drains, and toilets always ready-to-install, ready-to-remove, and ready-to-transport somewhere else. The lighting is intermittent and feeble, supplied by generators set up with each new wave of arrivals (who come as a result of some form of turmoil or catastrophe). They have become as predictable as their associated technical consequences—interruptions in the supply and stocks of energy, food, or services. In this all-too-real landscape, white lorries covered in tarpaulin come and go constantly, transporting huge quantities of rice and bulgur, but also bringing in displaced people. Sometimes, on a patch of wasteland in the refugee camps, children play football, or else, as happened on the perimeter of the so-called Calais "jungle," adults set up a cricket pitch.

Using the raw natural materials readily available (dirt, water, wood from the forest) or waste materials from available manufactured goods (wooden boards, pallets, plastic sheets, sacking, metal sheeting, polystyrene), the inhabitants tinker and improvise as best they can to create an adaptive and reactive architecture, using whatever comes to hand, just like the architecture of the favelas and shantytowns elsewhere and in the past. Houses of mudbrick sit alongside other constructions made out of fabric, cardboard, and metal sheeting. All of this is in a state of constant flux.

## Instant Cities

Inspired by these residual spaces, and by the "wasted lives" that they shelter, inevitably destined to become increasingly widespread as mobility of all kinds (temporary or more permanent, local, regional, or on a worldwide scale) becomes more common, an urban ecology and anthropology will need to be developed to meet the demands of tomorrow's world. For the moment, we can scarcely conceive what shape these will take except that they will be underscored by a culture of urgency, of the present, and of uncertainty, and will involve organizing and equipping these empty, cleared or abandoned spaces for unknown periods of time. What is striking is not only the repeated theme of emptiness that is evident from the very first day of these fragile settlements, but also the rapid resurgence of social life, of technical ingenuity, of political organization, and of the search for meaning. These instant cities today exist on the fringes of modernity, and yet they test out and even anticipate innovative forms of urban communities, which reach beyond that same modernity. Futuristic, alternatively dystopian or utopian, they are to be found all over the world and already seem to illustrate a new urban model. This is why, it seems to me, the theme of instant cities ("instantaneous" cities, constructed "from one day to the next") has once again found its way into the discussions of today's urbanists and architects. It is a theme that can be approached more broadly from the perspective of the anthropological development of cities.

This theme is not a new one, first appearing in the 1960s and 1970s, initially through the history of the cities in the American far west, created in the space of a single day and that grew and developed at a rapid rate, as evident from the descriptions of San Francisco or Denver,[7] in which migrants arrived and carved out their new lives by taking over empty spaces. In the same period, English architects (Peter Cook and the Archigram group) drew inspiration from mass gatherings and temporary festivals, such as Woodstock, to imagine cities that were themselves mobile—a utopia of a city constructed out of transposable objects, images, and sounds rather than fixed physical elements. The third form of these so-called instant cities, one very different in appearance, is the one that went from instant cities to "ghost cities," as in the case of the reified graphic utopias of cities constructed without reference to reality, primarily in Asia, in the Persian Gulf, and in the Middle East, on the model of Dubai. Today, we are witnessing another manifestation of this model. In 2015, the Cité de l'architecture et du patrimoine in Paris put on an exhibition entitled *Habiter le campement* (Living in the Camps), which vividly portrays this concept in the context of festival gatherings (the three-day "city" of the Burning Man festival in the United States), but also of the yurt camps of migrant workers in Mongolia, the campsites and mobile homes for European or North American tourists and travelers, or the tent cities for refugees in Africa or in south-east Asia.[8]

The common element of all these instant city experiments is their ambition to reduce or even eliminate the gap between time and space. The temporal parameter therefore becomes one of the factors used for classifying space: how many days, weeks, or months will it take for a particular place, neighborhood, or city to be built or developed? It is also interesting to reflect on the utopian or dystopian nature of urban concepts inspired as a result of the observation of today's instant cities and of their capacity to endure in spite of repeated destruction. Should we object to the occupation of a Zone d'Amenagement Différé (ZAD) (designated development area), the invasion of a shanty town, or a settlement of homeless migrants transformed into a jungle, on the basis of why they came to exist, which is always specific? Should we not instead look at them from the perspective of how they came into existence, always somewhere between resistance and adaptation, and in the context of the possibilities they open up? If these human habitats can be considered, over and above their immediate justification, as the very first gestures of an urban process, of city-making in its universal sense, then we should instead be looking at them from the point of view of what they might lead to, and exploring them through a range of possible scenarios.

## "The Very Spirit of the City"

How do we progress from this marginality with its negative associations to the city itself and to a potential model for being-in-the-world? A practical approach, an architecture stripped of aestheticism, a minimal habitat constantly capable of adaptation, can bring justice to these situations and enable them to inspire other experiments and other ways of making a city. This reflects the approach and some of the terminology used by the Franco-Greek architect Georges Candilis (1913–1995). In the early 1970s, Candilis was shocked by directly observing, on the outskirts of Lima, Peru, the process of establishing and constructing an *invasión*. His Peruvian colleague described to him how during that night "thousands of people" invaded an area of wasteland "in order to construct a new city" (Candilis 1977, 304).

It is less the invasion itself that interests me here than the reaction of the European architect. Candilis worked closely with Corbusier for an extended period, and then spent years, mostly in Europe, working on low-cost, large-scale constructions for the "most deprived." For him, the urban invasion in Lima was "a tidal wave of popular opinion which forced the authorities to give way and resulted in the construction of a house, a city, without materials or architects, simply on the strength of superior numbers and a determination to survive" (Candilis 1977). On the second day of the invasion, under the gaze of the architect, now reduced to the role of a simple bystander, houses began to be built out of recycled materials, neighborhoods were created, and the inhabitants ("including children") voted to select those who would take on specific responsibilities. "I witnessed in amazement," Candilis wrote, a few years later, "the birth of a genuine 'urban community,' and he described, with enthusiasm, what for him was "the very spirit of the city" (1977).

With these words, he was expressing the intense sense of discovery that this event had represented for him, and in particular the fact that the making of a city represented an *event*, which took the form of the sudden arrival of a simple citizen who embodied the spirit of the city and set about creating an urban community. It is this simple citizen and this urban community that together make the city, and which enable us to reflect afresh on the model of instant cities, and to reject the idea that such a model can exist in the abstract, with no relations to reality.

If this sharing of experiences is to become systematic and efficient and to avoid imitation or the random rearrangement of existing forms, it must involve a genuine understanding of the theoretical equality of all urban forms. Without exoticism or populism, but with regard to what is most universal in this mode of city-making, that is to say, the energy to bring together and to share. It is the absence of this which, conversely, results in the sprawling settlements and ghettos that we see today throughout the world. The recognition, on both an intellectual and a political level, of this universality and this capacity to act is just as much the concern of those living in such places, and who are confined there in the first place as the consequence of their undesirability and of the exclusion associated with that state.

## Notes

1. The following text was first published in France in the review *Esprit* in September 2021.

2. Translator's note: '*L'En-ville*' is a phrase used in the novel *Texaco* by Patrick Chamoiseau, which is discussed in this section. The term comes from the creole word *an-vil* (town or city). I have chosen to translate it here as the *In-City*.

3. An amended version of these, sourced from the published English translation, will be referenced at a later stage.

4. In Salvador de Bahia, the areas that in Rio de Janeiro or in Brazil are generically referred to as "favellas" are called "invasions" or, more recently, "occupations."

5. An anthropological approach characteristically focuses first on the micro-local description of the processes to arrive at an understanding of the places. See my publication *Anthropologie de la Ville* (2015) for a description of this approach.

6. The possibility of an *arrival city* as described, for example, by journalist Doug Sanders. Sanders, *Arrival City: How the Largest Migration in History is Reshaping our World* (New York: Vintage Books, 2012).

7. See Gunther Barth's study of these cities in G. Barth, *Instant Cities: Urbanization and the Rise of San Francisco and Denver* (Oxford: Oxford University Press, 1975).

8. See the exhibition catalog: Fiona Meadows (curator), *Habiter le campement*, Paris/Arles: Cité de l'architecture et du patrimoine/Actes Sud, 2016. Placing all these contemporary forms of short-term settlements side by side, shocking as it might seem, helps us to understand the emergence of a model of instant city beyond the moral, aesthetic, positive, or negative dimensions associated with such places.

## References

Agier, Michel. *Managing the Undesirables: Refugee Camps and Humanitarian Government*. Cambridge: Polity Press, 2011.

———. *Anthropologie de la Ville*. Paris: PUF, 2015.

Barth, Gunther. *Instant Cities: Urbanization and the Rise of San Francisco and Denver*. Oxford: Oxford University Press, 1975.

Bauman, Zygmunt. *Wasted Lives: Modernity and Its Outcasts*. Reprint. Cambridge: Polity, 2004.

Bouchain, Patrick. *Construire Autrement: Comment Faire? L'impensé*. Arles: Actes sud, 2006.

Candilis, Georges. *Bâtir la vie: un architecte témoin de son temps*. Collection Archigraphy. Gollion (Suisse) [Paris]: Infolio, 1977.

Chamoiseau, Patrick. *Texaco*. 1st Vintage International ed. New York: Vintage International, 1998.

Fromonot, François. "Manières de Classer l'urbanisme.'" *Criticat*, no. 8 (2011): 40–61. https://issuu.com/criticat/docs/criticat08

Hanappe, Cyrille, et al. *La Ville Accueillante: Accueillir à Grande-Synthe, Questions Théoriques et Pratiques Sur Les Exilés, l'architecture et La Ville*. Collection Recherche, no 236. La Défense: Plan urbanisme construction architecture PUCA, 2018.

Meadows, Fiona. *Habiter le campement*. Paris/Arles: Cité de l'architecture et du patrimoine/Actes Sud, 2016.

Sanders, Doug. *Arrival City: How the Largest Migration in History is Reshaping our World*, New York: Vintage Books, 2012.

Sennett, Richard. *Building and Dwelling: Ethics for the City*. London: Allen Lane, an imprint of Penguin Books, 2018.

Spivak, Gayatri Chakravorty. "Can the Subaltern Speak?" In *Colonial Discourse and Post-Colonial Theory*, edited by Patrick Williams and Laura Chrisman, 66–111. London: Routledge, 1994.

Chapter 6

# Stateless in Informal Settlements

Efadul Huq and Faranak Miraftab

## Introduction

Remembering the 2002 demolition and eviction in an informal settlement located adjacent to Dhaka's most affluent neighborhoods, Rokeya, a mother of four, shared, "there was no one to help us . . . We lived in an open field and burned wood for fire. No electricity, no water . . . No government came to help" (Huq and Miraftab 2020, 8). She went on to relate how the evictions happened over and over, the details of which we've covered elsewhere. When we grapple with how the lack of substantial rights goes hand in hand with symbolic inclusion into citizenship in such contemporary urban spaces as Dhaka's informal settlements, any clear separation in the binary of citizen/stateless appears to be untenable. In close examination of the two groups, the spatially and experientially overlapping dimensions of de facto and de jure statelessness become visible. Particularly, informal settlement dwellers (ISD) such as Rokeya live with little to no protection that citizenship is supposed to guarantee. In light of the massive displacements under way across and within nation-states, statelessness must be understood beyond its conventional attachment with (to) legality.

Conventionally, statelessness can result from various geopolitical realignments among states, as well as racialized and ethnicized persecutions. Statelessness leads to a lack of all the rights that nation-states promise. Statelessness implies that people lose their basic social and economic rights, such as education, housing, healthcare, as well as civil and political rights, such as freedom of movement and political participation. Yet, this more common attachment of statelessness to the discursive field of rights and laws forecloses a deeper engagement with the ambiguous, precarious, and contested terrains where citizenship and statelessness overlap. The structurally precarious position of informal settlement dwellers, who may be citizens, is one such form of statelessness. Informal settlement dwellers do not experience the promised rights that come with citizenship and engage in life-making collective practices comparable to camp dwellers. Statelessness in such cases is spatially produced and experienced through rightlessness in the informal settlements. In this chapter, building on two critical bodies of literature—one on informal and insurgent grassroots practices and another on spatial practices and the governance of refugees—we relationally theorize informal settlements and camps as an expanding and overlapping reality in the era of intensified global displacement. We read about the inhabitants' experiences in Korail, an informal settlement in Dhaka, through literature grounded in the experiences of refugees and highlight the comparable spatial practices of the so-called citizens and the so-called stateless. Although citizenship status is supposed to be the defining feature distinguishing the two groups, the converging spatialities and technologies of governance of the two suggest otherwise. Both groups result from global displacements but are framed through distinct relationships with the national state: ISDs as rights-bearing citizens, and camp dwellers as temporary and, in some cases, stateless. Within the purview of institutional and discursive instruments of state and humanitarian governance, ISDs and camp dwellers occupy geopolitically contingent statuses of "deserving" and "undeserving" peoples. Refugee camp dwellers, for instance, are presented in the hierarchy of humanitarian needs as those with purity of claim and innocence (Fassin 2011), thus deserving protection by humanitarian agencies above and beyond the state. ISDs fall under the supposed ambit of de jure citizenship but can be criminalized, evicted, and persecuted because of their "informal" (read: illegal) housing status.

Inspired by Gillian Hart's (2006) relational comparison as a means to interrogate the similarities and differences in the production and governance of urban space, we pay attention to key processes, relations, and practices that produce and govern informal settlements and camps. Relational comparison avoids the trap of direct comparison, by allowing us to understand phenomena (a place, a community, a city), not in and of itself but in relation to other processes and places through relations with wider arenas. Clarifying these connections and mutual processes of constitution helps to generate new understandings of possibilities for social change, a deep understanding that animates the work of activists and dwellers trying to build solidarities across historically manufactured divisions among the destitute and the displaced. Such an understanding can also guide planning practitioners in moving beyond the separate categories of citizen vs. non-citizen or state vs. non-state actors, and, in appreciating the agential planning role of subordinate communities within the overlapping complexities of global displacements, planning practitioners set out to mitigate and negotiate.

The analytical insights of this relational conversation highlight two crucial aspects of statelessness in informal settlements: *institutional* to highlight the humanitarian matrices of care that provide governmental structures in both contexts, and *micropolitical* to characterize dwellers' contestations with state and humanitarian governance that constitute the processes of life-making in informal settlements, much as in the camps. Contemporary cities are sites that receive displaced populations as well as engender displacement through urban development, on scales of intensity that are comparable to international displacements. We argue that in spaces where urban humanitarian crises are concretely manifest, the lines between citizen and refugee, and between informal settlement and camp, blur. In this case, within informal settlements, impoverished and stigmatized dwellers are held in a limbo of citizenship-in-wait and in-situ displacement, where NGOs, not the state, produce participatory matrices within and against which slum dwellers contest and realize their needs and wants. Framing the spatial practices and governance of these two groups vis-à-vis the state can be instructive in looking beyond citizenship. More specifically, such a framing allows us to see how people articulate their claims and guide their actions, not because of but despite their citizenship status and relationship vis-à-vis the state. These insights, we hope, will contribute to dismantling the false but prevalent assumptions about the state-planning-citizenship relationships that buttress planning theory and provide rationale in support of activists' efforts to overcome divisions and build solidarities among displaced people.

This chapter proceeds as follows: we begin with a brief introduction to Korail, an informal settlement in Dhaka, Bangladesh, whose inhabitants' experiences we read through concepts derived from camp literature. We then present the insights we gain from this analytical conversation on statelessness under two sections: institutional (humanitarian governance) and micropolitical (interstitial power). In section 2, we focus on the governance of informal settlements and camps to highlight the commonalities between the non-state governmental matrices that provide institutional structures in both contexts. We show how humanitarian governance entrenches itself as a durable form in Korail and operates at a calculated distance from the state. In section 3, we document micropolitical practices among Korail's dwellers to engage both state forces and humanitarian governance. Indeed, it is these interstitial practices that constitute the social reproduction of ISDs in Korail, much like the cases of camps studied elsewhere. In conclusion, we reflect on the conceptual and political implications of the insights gained by exposing the similarities between refugees' and ISDs' experiences of statelessness and spatial strategies for planning and for grassroots placemaking.

## The Informal Settlement of Korail

Korail is home to more than 100,000 residents and is situated in Dhaka's Mohakhali area, surrounded by the capital's upper-class residential and commercial districts. Before 1980, people started migrating to Korail from rural Bangladesh in search of work, but from 1990 onward, the settlement visibly accelerated in size. Residents have built varied structures on ninety acres of government land and also filled up the edges of a nearby lake, much like the larger residential encroachments of upscale apartments and houses on the other side of the lake. More recently, the government designated the area for the construction of an Information and Communication Technology (ICT) Village. The project promotes the relocation of Korail residents, who have challenged any intention to evict them from this prime real estate where many were born and have lived for over three decades and made their homes. One resident said, "this is silver land; everyone wants it for their greed." The state ran major eviction drives in 2011 and 2012. There were also fires in 2004, 2010, 2016, 2017, 2020, and 2021. Some claim the fires were arson. Given Korail's proximity to the lake and since much of it is constructed over the water, Korail is vulnerable to seasonal urban flooding and associated hazards. Korail residents are a representative slice of the over 2 million informal settlement inhabitants in Bangladesh (Bangladesh Bureau of Statistics 2015).

Korail residents themselves have experienced multiple displacements—some from rural to urban, some within Dhaka—but in the narratives of Korail residents, one often hears the distinction they wish to make from refugees and transnationally displaced people in Dhaka. Impoverished settlement dwellers, many of whom are internally displaced migrants, speak with some pride about being Bangladeshis and look down upon the Rohingya refugees who "don't belong here." Not all dwellers echo such exclusionary rhetoric. One community organizer, arguing with others at a tea stall, pointed out, "They [refugees] are people too, and like us, nobody cares about them." For this Korail resident, the lived experiences of Korail dwellers and Rohingya refugees are similar. Cautiously probing such intuitions, without erasing the many ways in which refugees are discriminated against and excluded (Bornman and Oatway 2020), and cross-hatching the similarities between statelessness in informal settlements and camps, can further the ongoing political project of solidarity across manufactured social divides. We advance our argument by weaving back and forth between the camp literature and Korail's reality.

## Governing Informal Settlements

In their situation of de facto statelessness, ISDs can continue to wait for citizenship and survive everyday displacement, partially because of the humanitarian institutions that make informal settlements durable. In camp literature, the notion of humanitarian governance looms large. Humanitarianism, in common parlance, is advocated as a yardstick for the humanity of states. Humanitarian care, it is argued, alleviates suffering, saves vulnerable lives, and lays the groundwork for a sustainable and secure life. But humanitarianism is also understood as an ideology that "mobilizes a range of meanings and practices to establish and sustain global relations of domination" (Chimni 2000, 244) without seeking "political solutions addressing root causes" behind global crises (Peteet 2005, 144). Agier, for example, calls humanitarianism "the left hand of empire," which contributes to the "end of politics" as humanitarianism sidesteps questions of global inequalities in the immediacy to "care" for globalization's victims (Agier 2010, 29–30). Within the scope of this chapter, we are interested in the infrastructural and logistical materiality of humanitarian governance that index statelessness in both camps and informal settlements. Parallel to the evolving discourses of humanitarianism, camp researchers point to the unique material reality of humanitarianism, what Potvin calls the post-1960 "material turn" of humanitarian organizations, representing "a radical shift from a legal protection regime towards a material regime where assistance was the new organizing principle for humanitarian action" (Potvin 2019, 10). Building on his decades-long ethnography of camps on the African continent, Agier argues that humanitarianism is a "globalized apparatus: a set of organizations, networks, agents, and financial means distributed across different countries and crisscrossing the world," circulating and building upon its own knowledge base (Agier 2010, 32). Questions of service provision, from roads to sanitation to water, are solved through implementing templates of urbanism (Agier 2010). Similarly, Jansen reflects that "camps have been cast as experiments, as places where humanitarian governance is tested, and where new and innovative measures and technological novelties are trialed and errored" to be later mainstreamed at other sites of humanitarian intervention (Jansen 2016). Observing the materiality of humanitarianism, Agier conceptualizes "city-camps" as a "novel sociospatial form" created during emergencies such as wars and disasters, but far outlasting the moment of emergency as hostilities continue and, more importantly, as humanitarian intervention entrenches itself as a durable form (Agier 2002, 320).

The infrastructural and logistical materiality of humanitarianism can be so vast and deeply embedded that at times the economies of entire towns rely on the jobs and resources in the humanitarian economy (Branch 2013). For instance, the humanitarian agencies providing resources to Rohingyas in southern Bangladesh are also providing the same resources to the surrounding urban poor in informal settlements in order to avoid conflicts between refugee and host communities (Kazi 2018b). The magnitude of humanitarian care in the context of Bangladesh, a country smaller in size than the US state of Georgia, may be understood through the size and extent of NGO operations. According to the government, there are close to 2,500 NGOs. The larger NGOs operate with massive budgets and staffs; for example, BRAC, one of the largest NGOs in the world, operates in all sixty-four districts of Bangladesh on a 300 USD million budget and employs over 108,000 staff, leading to some calling BRAC a "parallel state" (Muhammad 2018). BRAC runs operations in Rohingya refugee camps and in informal settlements around the country.

The prominent and globalized apparatus of physical and institutional structures of humanitarian intervention can be read as a marker of statelessness across informal settlements such as Korail and camps. In Korail, various NGOs provide basic infrastructure, services, and employment. NGOs operating in informal settlements and camps cross-pollinate knowledge and strategies of humanitarian governance, and they sometimes directly transfer modular practices and programs. BLAST, a long-running NGO that works in Korail, is building on its existing procedures in informal settlements to develop women's health rights–related advocacy work in the Rohingya refugee camps in southern Bangladesh. The physical and institutional materiality of humanitarian governance in informal settlements points to policies that give comparable socio-spatial dimensions to informal settlements and camps. Moreover, the operations of NGOs in informal settlements are decided through situated political calculations. In Korail, BRAC has made major infrastructure investments, but it avoids taking a strong position regarding the eviction of Korail dwellers. For instance, it avoids creating a tenure map of Korail that would bust the myth that Korail is the stronghold of a few big and corrupt landlords. One interpretation is that BRAC does not want to jeopardize its relationship with the state, which wants to use prevalent stereotypes to justify going forward with the redevelopment scheme. We argue that the replicated presence of certain NGOs, along with their relation to the state, produces specific informal settlements and camps as new global governmental spaces of statelessness operating at a calculated distance from states.

Amin, in his mid-thirties, was born in Korail. His father moved to Dhaka as a government employee in 1963, under the government of Pakistan. In his tin-shed house, where Amin has lived since 1989, he remembers the slow increase of NGOs in Korail, as detailed elsewhere (Huq and Miraftab 2020). Amin's recollection is a common tale among other long-time Korail residents. Their recollections of how NGOs incrementally worked on water meters, drainage, roads, house upgrades, and toilets over decades help explain the infrastructural unevenness of Korail. For example, Unit 1 and Unit 2 areas consist primarily of tin-shed houses with functioning drainage, water, and maintained alleyways. Baubazar Kapor Potti is mostly small shops and broken, with muddy paths and poor drainage. Godown Bosti is composed of makeshift houses along the lakeside and houses on stilts or constructed over the trash-filled lake. Comilla Potti has two-story, tin-roof houses made of concrete; their green CI sheets are evidence of the last NGO-driven reconstruction effort after the 2017 fire (Shafique 2020). A mix of NGOs has worked for different durations and with different aims across these areas. The heterogeneous internal spatial features of Korail reflect the operational aims of NGOs, indexing what the camp literature conceptualizes as humanitarian urbanism (Jansen 2016). Amin explained that "an NGO might get a project for fifty water meters, but you can't give that to everybody, so you select specific blocks to give the meters" (Huq and Miraftab 2020, 12). The resource and time parameters of NGO projects produced the spatially segmented blocks with uneven infrastructural features in Korail.

NGOs provide a wide array of amenities and services: road construction, drainage, water, toilets, schools, job training centers, clinics, financial support for businesses, and more. The activities of NGOs in Korail reflect the operations of humanitarian regimes in camps, as shown in Jansen's research in Kakuma camp, where humanitarian actors govern and empower refugees "with entitlements and other forms of inclusion and public service delivery based on human and refugee rights, and aspirations of democracy, development, education and empowerment" (Jansen 2016). Much like camp dwellers, ISDs are not, however, passive recipients of global charity. Their everyday experience of symbolic and material precarity leads ISDs to make demands on humanitarian organizations and vocalize alternative pathways for land development. While NGOs file petitions against evictions in court, Korail dwellers demand that the state and private owners sell the land to them at an affordable price so that they can develop the land themselves. At the decision-making table during resettlement negotiations, Korail dwellers state their demand for on-site resettlement. One interviewee, a community representative in the resettlement negotiation process, asked, "What sense does it make to demolish so much service, housing, and support infrastructure that NGOs have already created for us? In fact, resettlement is a rather easy process if the state simply legitimizes the infrastructures NGOs have already built and creates a plan so that we can build the rest ourselves" (Huq and Miraftab 2020, 12). Humanitarian institutional matrices and materiality, in effect, become sites as well as discursive tools for ISDs engaged in contesting their de facto statelessness. Within these new governmental spaces, as we shall see in the next section, novel forms of political contestations take place, and dwellers as political actors craft a space of power between the state and humanitarian governance in the terrain of statelessness.

## Micropolitics

Sites of statelessness are not merely sites of despair at the mercy of humanitarianism and the goodwill of charities and nonprofit organizations. Drawing on case studies of Palestinian refugee camps in Beirut, Sanyal argues that refugees enact agency through "their micro politics of squatting and occupying land, building shelters against the dictates of the state and the like" (Sanyal 2016). Observing how camp dwellers were able to claim shelter through squatting, Sanyal concludes that camps are not merely "sites of containment and management" but also "sites of contestation" (2016). Similarly, observing Kenya's Kakuma refugee camp where camp dwellers engaged in informal livelihood strategies and transformed the camp into a cosmopolitan place, Jansen suggests that "humanitarian urbanism" is the result of dwellers organizing "themselves in such ways that they create room for maneuver to build their lives and livelihoods inside" humanitarian regimes (2016). Camps are sites of "people's routines, strategies and actions over time that contest, alter, and change these initial bureaucratic spaces into lived spaces" (2016). Camp dwellers sometimes find themselves dueling against both the state and the humanitarian regimes, and at times they deploy the resources of one regime against another to reach their political goals, which are not always benevolent. Reading the lived experiences of ISDs through camp contestations, we see how ISDs, like camp dwellers, articulate demands and engage in political contestations within the new institutional matrix of humanitarian governance. Sometimes they organize or invent spaces of action and maneuver in the tiny spaces that open up for their action; sometimes they act in opposition to governmental agencies; sometimes they act in agreement, accepting the "invited spaces" of action extended to them by governmental, non-governmental, and humanitarian agencies (Cornwall 2002); and sometimes they pit one against the other to achieve their ends. Building on Cornwall's "invited spaces," Miraftab articulates invented spaces and their non-binary dynamics with invited spaces of action as interstitial practices of power in poor communities, and as practice of citizenship from below when the formal citizenship supposedly granted by the state is irrelevant to people's realities (Miraftab 2004). The following stories from Korail highlight the material implications of such micropolitical contestations in conditions of rightlessness rendering ISDs stateless within the city.

In Korail, multiple residents pointed to accessing post-primary education as a major challenge they had to overcome. The early NGOs provided only primary education. Once the first generation of children had completed primary schooling, however, residents demanded further education from the NGOs. Under the pressure of dwellers' organized demands, NGOs expanded their programs to include middle- and high-school education. Amin's unit received 6,300 taka per year for every child's education up to high school completion, though these fees came with conditions. As dwellers like Amin continue advancing claims to access condition-free post-primary education, their past and present practices show how informal settlement dwellers appropriate the terrain of NGO-led development programs, not state-led schemes, as the site of their claim-making to reach their ends.

Instances of informal settlement dwellers maneuvering the space between the state and state-like actors, between and among the governmental and global humanitarian organizations, are numerous—not only in Korail but also in the vast number of informal settlements and low-income neighborhoods cited by informality-insurgency literature from around the world (examples are too many to cite, but see, for instance, contributions to the special issue of *Planning Theory* [2009 vol. 8, no. 1] on informality and insurgency or Pithouse 2014). In the case of Korail, dwellers use collective power to deploy NGO operations against state forces. During the 2012 evictions, for example, when the bulldozers showed up in front of the slum, Rokeya related the story of how everyone brought out all their objects (pillows, utensils, mattresses, etc.) and, along with their children, blocked the bulldozers' path. A few residents approached the magistrate and forty to fifty police officers who were in charge of operations. They convinced the magistrate to "slow down" the operation, while another group of residents ran to NGO offices and got lawyers (including BLAST) to urgently file a case in the High Court. The High Court ordered a stay order of the eviction procedure.

Korail dwellers collectively organized a committee, composed of several resident leaders, that took on the responsibility of negotiating disputes and conflicts without getting the local police involved (dwellers perceive the police as agents of stigmatization and criminalization). The committee now hears cases ranging from shop robberies to family disputes to tenant-landlord disputes to interpersonal conflicts, including conflicts between residents and drug dealers. Although organized local committees in informal settlements are not always benign or without controversy (Meth 2010; Miraftab 2018), the messy "political society" of ISDs has to be engaged in a grounded way where insurgent planning practices actualize the transformative potentials of collective action (Huq 2020). In 2016 and 2017, the committee in Korail "liberated" multiple drug houses and turned them into elder and disabled residences and childcare centers. In 2018, another daycare center was created from another drug house.

The interstitial space of power is not, however, always used for securing the collective needs of the underclass (Chatterjee 2004; Meth 2010). The space between state and humanitarian apparatuses can also be deployed for the goals of corrupt individuals through a politics of connections and taxes. Korail's resident community leaders compete with each other over NGO connections for development. They also demand taxes (i.e., bribes) from interested NGOs that want to provide services in the area. For instance, when an NGO wanted to start a school in one Korail area, a resident leader demanded money from the NGO. When the NGO offered only a partial amount of the "tax," the leader showed his power by using his political party connections to halt the project.

After the 2017 fire, NGOs gave green tin roofs for reconstruction. Residents related how they saw community leaders selling the tin roofs. The presence of green tin roofs outside fire-impacted areas is physical evidence of this misplacement of resources. Using humanitarian resources as a means for capital accumulation echoes similar processes seen in camps—for instance, with refugees selling food rations outside Kenya's Dadaab and Kakuma camps or Rohingya subgroups clashing over camp-land appropriations (Kazi 2018a; Montclos and Kagwanja 2000). The complicated portrait of contestations establishes that slum dwellers are crafting a political space against the state as well as against humanitarian governance. In some cases, they are deploying humanitarian interventions and state forces against each other. The unpredictable, sometimes emancipatory, and sometimes accumulative, pathways that contestations take in the interstitial space between states and humanitarian governance show the similarities in how dwellers—whether formally stateless or citizens—embody and suffer a similar micropolitics between the machinations of state and humanitarian apparatus in the context of scarce resources.

## Conclusion

Conceptualizing the lived experiences of Korail dwellers in relation to camp literature reveals emerging spaces of global governance and political contestations where dwellers in both sites live under a regime of imposed precarity and citizenship-in-wait. In both cases, the state and state agencies are of course present, but their presence is not as direct as in the conventional state-centered theorization of citizenship. The state's presence, in both the refugee camps and informal settlements, is often accomplished by other means, often through other global and supposedly nongovernmental organizations. Statelessness, whether de facto or de jure, structurally shapes the social and political relations in these spaces. In informal settlements, statelessness is urbanized spatially and experientially through the rightlessness of dwellers. Seeing the ontological blurring between informal settlement and camps in specific instances, like that of Korail, is crucial for a new grassroots politics that organizes the globally dispossessed across citizen and refugee divides. It is also crucial conceptually: it deepens the Southern turn in planning scholarship theorizing, not based on Eurocentric binary models of planning as mediator between state and citizens (Miraftab 2012), but based on the messy realities of the dispossessed (Korail informal settlement dwellers) and displaced (refugees) groups, constructing their localized categories of belonging (beyond citizenship) from below, through innovative negotiations with a multitude of agencies and organizations.

## References


Agier, Michel. "Between War and City: Towards an Urban Anthropology of Refugee Camps." *Ethnography* 3, no. 3 (2002): 317–41. https://doi.org/10.1177/146613802401092779.

Bangladesh Bureau of Statistics. "Census of Slum Areas and Floating Population 2014." Ministry of Planning, 2015.

Bornman, J., and J. Oatway. "South Africa: Migrants Excluded from Government Food Aid. *All Africa*, 2020. https://allafrica.com/stories/202005130663.html

Bornman, Jan. "Migrants Excluded from Government Food Aid." *New Frame.* May 13, 2020. www.newframe.com/migrants-excluded-from-government-food-aid

Branch, Adam. "Gulu in War . . . and Peace? The Town as Camp in Northern Uganda." *Urban Studies* 50, no. 15 (2013): 3152–67. https://doi.org/10.1177/0042098013487777

Chatterjee, Partha. *The Politics of the Governed: Reflections on Popular Politics in Most of the World.* Leonard Hastings Schoff Memorial Lectures. New York: Columbia University Press, 2004.

Chimni, B. S. "Globalization, Humanitarianism and the Erosion of Refugee Protection." *Journal of Refugee Studies* 13, no. 3 (2000): 243–63. https://doi.org/10.1093/jrs/13.3.243

Cornwall, Andrea. "Locating Citizen Participation." *IDS Bulletin* 33, no. 2 (2002): i–x. https://doi.org/10.1111/j.1759-5436.2002.tb00016.x

Fassin, Didier. *Humanitarian Reason: A Moral History of the Present Times*. Berkeley: University of California Press, 2011.

Hart, Gillian. "Denaturalizing Dispossession: Critical Ethnography in the Age of Resurgent Imperialism." *Antipode* 38, no. 5 (2006): 977–1004. https://doi.org/10.1111/j.1467-8330.2006.00489.x

Huq, Efadul. "Seeing the *Insurgent* in Transformative Planning Practices." *Planning Theory* 19, no. 4 (2020): 371–91. https://doi.org/10.1177/1473095219901290

Huq, Efadul, and Faranak Miraftab. " 'We Are All Refugees': Camps and Informal Settlements as Converging Spaces of Global Displacements." *Planning Theory & Practice* 21, no. 3 (2020): 351–70. https://doi.org/10.1080/14649357.2020.1776376

Jansen, Bram. "The Protracted Refugee Camp and the Consolidation of a 'Humanitarian Urbanism.' " *IJURR* (blog), 2016. www.ijurr.org/spotlight-on/the-urban-refugee-crisis-reflections-on-cities-citizenship-and-the-displaced/the-protracted-refugee-camp-and-the-consolidation-of-a-humanitarian-urbanism

Kazi, Anis Ahmed. "10 Injured in Clash between Two Rohingya Groups." *Dhaka Tribune*, June 19, 2018a, sec. Nation. https://archive.dhakatribune.com/bangladesh/nation/2018/06/19/10-injured-in-clash-between-two-rohingya-groups

———. "UN Launches Environmental Project for Rohingyas and Bangladeshis." *Dhaka Tribune*, September 23, 2018b, sec. Nation. https://archive.dhakatribune.com/bangladesh/nation/2018/09/23/un-launches-environmental-project-for-rohingyas-and-bangladeshis

Meth, Paula. "Unsettling Insurgency: Reflections on Women's Insurgent Practices in South Africa." *Planning Theory & Practice* 11, no. 2 (2010): 241–63. https://doi.org/10.1080/14649351003759714

Michel, Agier. "Humanity as an Identity and Its Political Effects (A Note on Camps and Humanitarian Government)." *Humanity: An International Journal of Human Rights, Humanitarianism, and Development* 1, no. 1 (2010): 29–45. https://doi.org/10.1353/hum.2010.0005

Miraftab, Faranak. "Invited and Invented Spaces of Participation: Neoliberal Citizenship and Feminists' Expanded Notion of Politics." *Wagadu: Journal of Transnational Women's and Gender Studies* 1, *no.* 1 (2004): 1–7. https://digitalcommons.cortland.edu/wagadu/vol1/iss1/3

———. "Planning and Citizenship." In *The Oxford Handbook of Urban Planning*, edited by Randall Crane and Rachel Weber, 786–802. New York: Oxford University Press, 2012. https://doi.org/10.1093/oxfordhb/9780195374995.013.0038

———. "Insurgent Practices and Decolonization of Future(s)." In *The Routledge Handbook of Planning Theory*, edited by Michael Gunder, Ali Madanipour, and Vanessa Watson. New York: Routledge, 2018. https://doi.org/10.4324/9781315696072

Montclos, M.-A.P.D., and P. M. Kagwanja. "Refugee Camps or Cities? The Socio-Economic Dynamics of the Dadaab and Kakuma Camps in Northern Kenya." *Journal of Refugee Studies* 13, no. 2 (2000): 205–22. https://doi.org/10.1093/jrs/13.2.205

Muhammad, Anu. "Rise of the Corporate NGO in Bangladesh." *Economic and Political Weekly* 53, no. 39 (2018): 45–52.

Peteet, Julie. *Landscape of Hope and Despair: Palestinian Refugee Camps*. The Ethnography of Political Violence. Philadelphia: University of Pennsylvania Press, 2005.

Pithouse, Richard. "The Shack Settlement as a Site of Politics: Reflections from South Africa." *Agrarian South: Journal of Political Economy: A Triannual Journal of Agrarian South Network and CARES* 3, no. 2 (2014): 179–201. https://doi.org/10.1177/2277976014551490

Potvin, Marianne. "Humanitarian Urbanism: Cities, Technology, and the Hybrid Practices of Humanitarian Planners." Dissertation, Harvard University, Cambridge, Massachusetts, 2019. https://dash.harvard.edu/handle/1/42013101

Sanyal, Romola. "From Camps to Urban Refugees: Reflections on Research Agenda." *IJURR* (blog). 2016. www.ijurr.org/spotlight-on/the-urban-refugee-crisis-reflections-on-cities-citizenship-and-the-displaced/the-protracted-refugee-camp-and-the-consolidation-of-a-humanitarian-urbanism

Shafique, Tanzil. "300,000 People in a Tenth-of-a-Square-Mile: Analysing the Morphological Evolution of the Largest Self-Organized Settlement in Dhaka." Presented at the International Seminar on Urban Form, Salt Lake City, Utah, September 1, 2020.

Chapter 7

# Statelessness and Camp Settlements

## The Curious Case of South Asia

Nasreen Chowdhory and Shamna Thacham Poyil

## Introduction

Statelessness, in popular parlance, is a construct that is antithetical to citizenship, an "other" of a citizen (Kerber 2007; Macklin 2014), and is rightless, as suggested by Arendt. Despite the burgeoning literature on statelessness that portrays varied meanings, statelessness has been introspected from the sociological domain of rights, belonging, and citizenship (Isin 2002; Isin and Nielsen 2008; Barrett and Sigona 2014). Everyday statelessness and rightlessness as experienced by the refugees and the vulnerable have emphasized camps as a site where the impacts of such abrogation of rights are experienced and negotiated (Sigona 2015; Redclift 2013a, 2013b). This everyday experience of statelessness of the refugees in camps is constituted by the denial of the status of legal personhood in their country of origin and later by the absence of recognition and membership in the host state. Between the varied alignments of territorial sovereignty and assertions of nation-state, the ambiguity of categorical definitions that makes up the global protection regime and conspicuous bias that universal human rights have toward the state order of things, statelessness as rightless indicates the "precarious legal, political and human standing" (Gündogdu 2015, 298) of individuals who have been denied the protection, rights, and privileges of citizenship. The caricatures of refugees and stateless as "bare life," who are considered "scum of earth" and "undesirables," can be considered to be in sync with the Arendtian notion that on being ousted from the political community of the state through denial of citizenship, an individual forfeits the "right to have rights" (Arendt 1968). But while conceptualizing statelessness in the framework of rights, it has to be asserted that the denial of citizenship is not tantamount to the denial of "fundamental human capacity to act" (Krause 2008, 335). Rightlessness emanating from lack of citizenship does not necessarily signify "total exclusion from polity" (Sigona 2015, 267); rather, it showcases the distortions within the nuanced pattern of political membership (Bosniak 2006; Sigona 2015). Hence, even within the segregated confinements of camp structures, with adequate political will and institutional support, a spectrum of membership and inclusion can be constituted and sustained through allocating distinctive rights and privileges to refugees. Rather than homogenizing camps merely as "spaces of exception," there is a political and moral contingency to acknowledge and recognize the varying claims of belonging made by refugees and stateless people. The instances where "territorialization of entitlements is increasingly made in spaces beyond the state" (Ong 2005, 697), camps can emerge as "abject spaces" (Isin and Rygiel 2007) where membership can be realized and "acts of citizenship" can be performed (Isin and Nielsen 2008; Sigona 2015). It is by precluding their chances of political agency by confining them to demeaning conditions of life and prolonged exile in camp settlements as unrecognized refugees that their rightlessness is perpetuated, and their statelessness is reconstituted.

Refugee camps, in essence, become spatial units of refugee protection that do not entail "expectations of citizenship" (L. H. Malkki 2002, 355). Defying the perception of being just passive beneficiaries of aids and provisions, Palestinian refugees started actively partaking in the establishment of an "autonomous political space" (Abourahme and Hilal 2012). They also exert their political agency in negotiating or renegotiating the various sociopolitical aspects of their daily lives in the camp. Without normalizing the political state of life in exile, the Palestinian refugees have altered camps like Dehesheh, near Bethlehem, from a transient space of liminality to a zone that signifies political representations of agency (P. Misselwitz and Hanafi 2009; Petti 2013). The dichotomy and comparison between organized institutional camps on one side and cities on the other cause a "right to camp" in line with the "right to city" (Grbac 2013). This chapter argues that a strict separation within the spatial structures of refugee protection that places camps and cities at the two ends of the spectrum is infeasible, especially in the empirical context of South Asia. Rather, refugee settlements in South Asia should be seen as camp settlements, which primarily involve camps but also include spillovers and informal settlements in rural and urban areas. Arguably, camp settlements in South Asia represent a city or space that is transformed from a temporary site to a vivid and permanent structure, involving camp economies, infrastructure, and public service adapting to a humanitarian context, wherein a new kind of rightlessness is configured. In analyzing the refugee settlements, the most prevalent categorization is that of organized camp settlements and unorganized non-camp settlements. The latter can take a variety of forms, such as unorganized settlements in rural areas or urban areas like cities. Using the empirical cases, this chapter showcases how camp settlements emerge as sites where statelessness is perpetuated and reconstituted.

Camps, for the purpose of the chapter, can be considered as "spatial practices" that encompass both the "field and event" within a definitive framework of time (Hailey 2009). The "spatial and temporal indeterminacy" in the conceptualization of camps is also conditioned by the fact that many encampments have served as precursors in the evolution of cities like Barcelona or Vienna (Abourahme 2020). The temporary settlements that emerge on the brink of, and are often huddled within, cities and states, including camps, reception, detention, or expulsion centers, and camp-like spaces such as shanty towns and "arrival cities" (Saunders 2010), are collectively referred to as "camp spaces" (Rygiel 2012). Such camp spaces exemplify the structural inequality and exclusion brought about by the forces and processes of securitization and globalization (2012). In bringing an urban approach to the introspection of refugee camps, Agier argues that camps exemplify "unfinished cities" (Agier 2002, 337). While looking at refugee settlements, we need to take into consideration this expanded yet overlapping framework of spatiality that comprises both institutional camps and other unorganized settlements. The refugee settlements in South Asia similarly see a situation of shared ethnicity and kinship between the host population and refugees as a significant factor as a default response mechanism of the host state.

## The Curious Case of Camp Settlements in South Asia

Despite the increased rendezvous of migration scholarship with post-coloniality and an overt hyphenation of forced migration in the global south with its colonial past, there is still a dearth of critical engagement on how precisely post-coloniality has shaped the debate on camps. Çağlar suggests that rather than merely "shifting the temporal and geographical scope to the times of colonialism," what is required is to develop an "analytical lens beyond established repertoires of traditional and migration studies" (Çağlar 2021, 318). In other words, the "colonial gradient" (318) in forced migration can be understood by laying emphasis on intricacies of various governance mechanisms, border control, exclusion, and politics of belonging that shapes the process. Samaddar, in *The Postcolonial Age of Migration* (2020), unravels the intricacies of this colonial inclination, and the various patterns of population flow inherent in migration. Examining the tangibility of colonial history and imperial practices, Samaddar explains how the nature of the colonial state, decolonization, and partition have laid the groundwork for the process and response in the postcolonial states of South Asia. The causative analysis of forced migration in South Asia (among other factors such as natural disasters, climate change, and development induced) significantly showcases the negative impacts of postcolonial state building that attempts to carve homogenous populations by relegating different cultural/ethnic/religious minorities to the margins of the state, forcing them to migrate (Chowdhory 2018). The centrality of refugee camps as spatial sites to shelter the undesirable emerges in South Asia too, albeit with a shared postcolonial history that has conjured a distinct sociocultural milieu in which forced migration needs to be analyzed.

The focus of much of the Euro-centric scholarship has been disproportionately inclined toward introspecting the efficacy of various policies of accommodation so as to ameliorate the burden of migration (Morris 2000; De Genova 2017). The prevalent methods of sheltering the forced migrants have led to the larger observation that the accommodation practices of refugees in the global south are hyphenated with "refugee camps," whereas those of the global north are along the lines of "asylum centers" (Kreichauf 2018). Urban ethnographers increasingly perceive this as "camp urbanization," a process that showcases a pattern of urbanization of the camp settlements that necessarily doesn't correspond to the material needs of the encompassing population but rather showcases "congested, impoverished, slum-like settings" of the camp settlements (Misselwitz 2009, 16). Scholarship has invariably referred to this as "virtual-cities" (Montclos and Kagwanja 2000) or camp cities (Agier 2002). An analysis of the introspection of the rights or lack of rights of the refugees should consider the apparent normalization of the nuanced patterns of these camp settlements.

Irrespective of the causative factors or the variable circumstances and nature in which statelessness is created, *de jure* or *de facto*, individual or collective (Sigona 2015), primary or secondary (Blitz 2006), statelessness should be seen as a situation where an individual is deprived of the basic protection that the state guarantees by virtue of their citizenship rights. Statelessness elucidates the forms of exclusion from the political community of the nation-state and its membership. In doing so, a stateless person becomes the definitive contrary of a citizen (Kerber 2007). The "paradox" prevalent in the case of stateless refugees is that the veil of protection provided by virtue of their "inalienable" human rights is effective only when they are citizens of the state (Arendt 1968, 279). The perpetual conditionality of rightlessness cannot be glossed over by normalizing it as a by-product of the constitution of exceptionality in the camps. It brings to the forefront the dichotomies of inclusion and exclusion that are deeply situated in the concept of political membership (Bosniak 2006) and the interlinkages between citizenship and hierarchies of belonging that determine the contours of inclusion/exclusion (Chowdhory and Poyil 2021). The chapter argues that the everyday experience of statelessness cannot be categorically distinguished and neatly mapped onto their differentiation as self-settled refugees outside the physical structure of the camp or collectively settled refugees availing the institutionalized protection of the camp. At the same time, the introspection of refugees in camp settlements ought to take into account four factors: (1) the sociopolitical and unique cultural milieu of camp settlements emanating from their common postcolonial history with the host state; (2) their sense of belonging in the host state; (3) the false sense of security that emerges on receiving the refugee status (RSD) from humanitarian agencies like UNHCR; and (4) the recognition (or lack thereof) in the host state that accordingly ameliorates or accentuates their situation of rightlessness. Together, these factors determine not just the reconstitution of statelessness but also the relative extent of statelessness.

Despite not being a part of the 1951 Refugee Convention and not having a concerted regional framework for refugee protection, countries in the region, like India, let the vulnerable forced migrants enter their territory. This tacit consent for admission and basic protection offered to the refugees on entering the borders is based on the performative practices of hospitality grounded on the principle of humanitarianism (Chowdhory, Poyil, and Meghna 2019). The closed refugee encampments in South Asia spatially materialize two concepts at their cores: segregation and exclusionary protection. But refugee camps become effective instruments for the nation-state to enforce a "segregated protection" that prevents the refugees from being integrated into the host society. In a nation-state global order arbitrated through borders and territories, the camp excludes the refugee by admitting him into the space it occupies. The prevalence of closed encampment structures in the south can be traced back to the imperial administration practice of the government in British India. As a tool to further their vested interests, "the barbed-wire aesthetic of camps" constituted by the Imperial British administration imposed "heavy labor and penal rations under dire economic restraints" so as to restrain and guard the "problem populations" (Forth 2015). The policy of spatial segregation was laid by the British Empire by promoting administrators to institute the material conditions necessary for the forceful internment of potentially threatening groups of people in colonies, based on their racial and cultural attributes, thus constructing the category of "other." The postcolonial countries of South Asia structurally organize and administer camps in a manner that exemplifies Zygmunt Bauman's observation on camps, that is, "camps are built using the techniques of enclosure and isolation developed by the managers and supervisors of Auschwitz and Gulag" (Bauman 1989, 17). This colonial temperament of segregating and amassing a large number of vulnerable "others" in camps remains the characteristic trait of South Asia's refugee protection approach.

This situation in South Asia differs remarkably from that of the global north, which currently sees the urbanization of refugee settlements manifesting as camp-cities, camp spaces, or even virtual cities from their earlier version of closed institutional encampments. Evolving from the concept of containment, the partition refugee camps had become sites of short-term emergency aid and assistance centers that addressed the forced migration in the aftermath of partition. For South Asia, the history of refugee camps is entwined with the account of forced migration across the borders at the instance of the mutation of the colonial space into two distinct nation-states based on the religious identity. Arguably, the narratives of this migration were not homogenous in nature. The inherent variations in gender, caste, and class occasioned diverse experiences of partition for each person who migrated across the border to their new homeland. The relatively affluent migrant population self-settled in residential areas with proper housing and adequate facilities, whereas the socioeconomically deprived sections settled in the tents and camps erected in different parts of the city. There was also a spatially variant pattern of migration such that mobility was continuous across Eastern Pakistan and the West Bengal region of India, whereas that across the north-western borders of India and West Pakistan was an instantaneous response to the partition (Bagchi and Dasgupta 2003). Both the countries established many camps in the nature of transit camps or relief camps, mainly in the territories of the border states of Bengal and Punjab. The enormous number of partition refugees involved caused the government to reconsider their initial plan to directly rehabilitate them at the outset. Instead, they were segregated into three categories of refugee camps: Transit Camps/Relief Camps, Colony Camps/Work site Camps, and Permanent Liability camps (Datta 2013). But the bulk of these partition refugees, irrespective of their pattern of refugee settlement (camps or outside camps), were effectively integrated into the nation-state through recognition and citizenship, which signifies the guilt of the nation-state in creating them.

The second factor is the sense of belonging that the refugees inculcate in the host state. The nature of protection offered through refugee camps to various groups of people has varied in both approach and impact since then, owing to the vested political priorities of the countries in South Asia. They have not just been humanitarian spaces that offer care and compassion to the refugees, or "spaces of control" that systematically institutionalize the segregation and separation of "others" from the host population, or yet again mere "spaces of destitution" that perceive the inhabiting population as victims devoid of agency (Herz 2012). Caught between the contentious spectrum of control, order, and protection, refugee juxtaposes his space of exiled life in the camp with his space of homeland. The heterotopic space, being those zones that ascertain their difference through underscoring the unity that encloses it (Foucault 1997), becomes pertinent in the context of porous borders and forced migration in South Asia (Chowdhory and Poyil 2022). The refugee camps that shelter these forced migrants become a heterotopic space that mirrors the utopias of host societies that surround it (2022). The attempts to carve culturally homogeneous states created tangible friction that in turn caused separatist movements, minority persecution, and explicit state-orchestrated violence against targeted minority populations in the countries of South Asia.[1] This created conditions for the forced migration and refugee flows to the neighboring countries. The notion of building a homogenous state causes the host state to segregate the refugees from its population. By demarcating the refugee camp to the outskirts, the state carves intangible boundaries of segregation and separation within its tangible borders. In order to understand the necessity of the state segregating the refugees, we should take into account the shared sense of belonging nurtured by the refugees. This sense of belonging to the host state emanates from the shared ethnic/cultural/linguistic affinity with the host society, owing to their common colonial past. The ethnic kinship between people in the host state and the refugees causes the refugee groups to "seek asylum in a society that shares a similar language, culture and kinship structures" (Chowdhory 2018, 30). This can be exemplified in the case of Sri Lankan Tamil refugees in India, Afghan refugees in Pakistan, and Rohingya refugees in Bangladesh. Drawing on Malkki's observation and based on the fieldwork among Sri Lankan Tamil refugees in the camps in Tamil Nadu, Chowdhory asserts that the camp refugees perceive themselves as "de-territorialized people with deep associations with the physical location of campsite" and "seek to re-territorialize in exile in camp" (Chowdhory 2018, 35). Even for the self-settled refugees like Chakmas or Rohingyas in India, this sense of belonging is instrumental in rooting their stay in the host state. As argued elsewhere by Chowdhory and Poyil (2021), the camp settlements in India effectually challenge the notion of being a "non-place" for refugees in exile distinguished by a lack of history, relations, or identity. The idea of belonging is entwined with the notion of attachment that an individual develops with their identity and the territory in which they are located. The forced migration of minorities from their country of origin that is instigated due to their differential ethnic/cultural traits reaffirms the contours of territorialized belonging. For non-citizens, such as refugees who do not enjoy the legal rights and privileges provided by the state of asylum, this necessity to "belong" is instrumental to assert the Arendtian concept of "right to have rights."

Across both Europe and Asia, despite the variations in camp formations or camp settlements, they become primary sites that inhabit the "urban outcasts" (Wacquant 2008). But beyond this commonality, a comparative analysis would shed light on the ways in which the experiences of membership and belonging of these populations are shaped by varying aspects of ethnicity, culture, or nationhood. The South Asian experience differs primarily on account of the nature of nationalism that shaped the identity formulation and articulation of these groups. Another factor would be the absence of a colonial state whose presence in the case of South Asia occasioned the development of multilayered and overlapping identities among various groups. James Scott refers to "jelly fish" communities that display "fissioning, disaggregation, [and] physical mobility" as characteristic features that help them to navigate their response to multiple forms of state authority and assert their freedom (Scott 2009, 17). At one level, this reference seems to find an allegory in the cultural traits of Romas, which is most prevalent in their exonym as "gypsy" communities. At another level, it also points out the "diasporic identity," indicating the cultural and material heterogeneity that emanates from their geographical dispersion throughout, causing them to self-identify as Hungarian, Bulgarian, or Italian Roma groups apart from the distinction of Muslim Romas or Christian Romas. Therefore, the assertion of a common Roma ethnic identity has inadvertently caused them to emphasize their differences when compared to the host society (Vermeersch 2006, 182). This precipitates a situation of self-exclusion as they inevitably become the "ethnic other" who do not belong and are "non-constitutive" of the nations they reside in (McGarry 2011, 294). In comparison, the uniqueness in the case of South Asia is that the stateless groups like the Rohingyas or Sri-Lankan Tamils have been ousted from their country of origin owing to their ethnic affiliation with India and Bangladesh, apart from the specificities of nation-building attempts in their respective countries (Chowdhory 2018). On being stateless, they seek refuge in the same countries to which their statist and territorialized belonging is attributed by their countries of origin, causing them to develop this sense of belonging based on ethnic and kinship affinities to the host societies in which their camp settlements are located. This is not the same for the "multidimensional identity" of Roma, which rests primarily on a "community-society axis" of identity formation and crystallization (Marushiakova and Popov 1997, 56–58), complicating their notion of belonging toward the host states.

In relation to the third and fourth, the refugee protection framework is a hybrid structure that involves states, international humanitarian organizations and non-state actors. Though UNHCR-managed camps can be normatively considered to be a humanitarian obligation fulfilled by the host countries or asylum states toward the vulnerable refugees, they are implemented as top-down structures of alternate governance are carried out. Admission and sheltering of refugees within the camps could be seen as a way in which refugee "subjects are gradually, progressively, really and materially constituted through a multiplicity of organisms, forces, energies, materials, desires, thoughts etc." (Foucault 1980, 97). Essentially stripping the inmates of their capacity to exercise their rights and choice, the administration of these camps was being transmuted to sites where not just aid but discipline is administered as well.

Despite designating responsibilities and delegating duties to various departments, the respective state governments do not conjure a sovereign structure similar to that which is being exercised in the rest of their territory in the administration of the refugee camps. These camps signify an "in-between place" (Bulley 2014) where the territory on which the camps are built is conceded or provided on lease by the host country to the temporary jurisdiction of international humanitarian organizations such as

UNHCR. UNHCR occupies a significant role in refugee administration as a primary affiliate of state governments in offering both assistance and protection to refugees in camps, solemnized formally through a Memorandum of Understanding (MoU). Refugee status Determination (RSD) done by the UNHCR is instrumental in securing access to aid and provisions for these vulnerable refugees. Even in the case of self-settled refugees outside the camps, UNHCR plays a significant role in providing verifiable refugee status and refugee identity cards to the population. Yet, the role and stake of individual governments are not limited to being hosts to refugee crises. Without governments and governmental organizations' support as donors, there would be no global protection regime, including UNHCR itself.

Unlike countries of the global south like Botswana or Tanzania, which provide citizenship to refugees that facilitate their integration, many of the states in South Asia have carefully calibrated varying policies in their approach toward various groups of refugees. The Indian government's treatment of refugees follows an ad hoc approach based on various pieces of domestic legislation, such as the Passport (Entry of India) Act 1920, the Passport Act 1967, the Registration of Foreigners Act 1939, the Foreigners Act 1946, and the Foreigners Order 1948. The allocation of refugee status by the Indian state is not based on an individual per se or collectively on a group based on their affiliation. Instead, it is determined by the ambit of bilateral relations and understanding prevalent between the Indian government and the country of origin of the refugee (Chowdhory 2016). Apart from the principle of non-refoulement that the state adheres to in spirit, the Indian judiciary understands that the fundamental rights guaranteed by the constitution to citizens and non-citizens alike, such as Article 14—right to equality, Article 21—right to personal life and liberty, Article 25—freedom to practice and propagate one's own religion, can be availed of by the refugees as well. The treatment meted out to the "Partition refugees" by the Indian government, for example, using methods such as the "Rehabilitation Finance Administration Act 1948," showcased how India's responsibility to care metamorphosed into a "regime of charity" rather than being an ideal "regime of rights" for refugees. As mentioned before, this was indicative of the guilt of the nation-state in creating the refugees and the need to integrate the population that the state deemed to belong to its territory. Similarly, the Tibetan refugees were supported using various rehabilitation and resettlement plans, along with the provision of registration certificates (RC) and even permission to establish the "Tibetan Government in exile" under the regulatory supervision of the Indian government. It is important to note that the Tibetan refugees were self-settled outside institutionalized camps with the assistance from the state. They were given recognition and rights that enabled them to navigate the everyday struggle of statelessness in a relatively better manner. In comparison, the protection that the Tamil refugees from Sri Lanka received in India could be attributed to their cultural proximity with the Tamils in India, which weakened the fault line between "us" and "them." Though settled in institutional camps, much of the aid and assistance for Tamil refugees came from the state government of Tamil Nadu in India, providing them with basic access to education and shelter and validating the role of the host state in refugee protection.

## Sri Lankan Tamils, Rohingyas, and Reconstitution of Statelessness in Camp Settlements

Having lived in India as refugees for over thirty years and having an ethnic affinity to the host society, most of these refugees wish to be integrated into India through citizenship. But their exclusion from the category of individuals who were to be eligible for fast-tracking the citizenship procedures as per the Citizenship Amendment Act of 2020 has thwarted their hopes for the attainment of Indian citizenship. Hence, despite the end of the conflict that induced displacement, Sri Lankan Tamil refugees in India live a life of perpetual exile. While camp inmates were eligible for the assistance provided by the state such as shelter, health care, sanitation, basic education, food ration, and cash doles—all for which non-camp refugees are ineligible (Chowdhory 2018). The refugee camps in Tamil Nadu that were established temporarily to provide protection to these refugees have now attained a state of transient permanence. Yet, instead of reducing their life of refuge in camps to that of a victim who is merely sustaining a "bare life," most of the refugee women have exercised their agency in navigating their everyday camp life. Without attempting to homogenize the differential experiences of displacement among refugees, this chapter argues that Sri Lankan Tamil refugees living in the camps of Tamil Nadu, where the authors have undertaken extensive fieldwork, challenge the Agambenian notion of camps being a space of exception that shelters bare life. The primary fieldwork conducted by the authors and similar observations from other scholarship ascertain that the majority of Sri Lankan Tamil refugees in India do not wish to be repatriated to Sri Lanka even with the end of conflict, and prefer local assimilation through the attainment of Indian citizenship. Using minimal state assistance, aid provisions, various livelihood strategies, and resource utilization, these refugees devise coping mechanisms to re-negotiate their lives in camps. The Sri Lankan conflict, in emphasizing the difference between "us" and "them," had engrained and re-ascertained the notion of Tamil identity among the Sri Lankan Tamils and projected them as custodians of this Tamil identity. The ethnic, religious, linguistic, and cultural affinity of the host society of Tamil Nadu with this reaffirmed Tamil identity of camp refugees had inculcated in them a sense of belonging within the host state that has been instrumental in helping them navigate the "bare life." They have transformed the space of camps into an active political space that has facilitated the creation of opportunities to engage with the state, thereby enabling them to assert their "right to have rights."

In comparison to Sri Lankan Tamils in India who were largely settled in camps, Rohingyas who managed to cross the borders to India were accommodated in makeshift camps, and a significant number of them settled as refugees in the peripheries of cities such as Delhi and Hyderabad, or even in the rural areas of Jammu and Kashmir. Viewed collectively, Rohingya refugees in camp settlements in India are subjected to a perennial condition of statelessness. The non-citizen status and structural exclusion that forced them to flee Myanmar are perpetuated in their everyday struggle as refugees. Although the linkage between people and the places they occupy constitutes the base for a territorialized notion of identity (Malkki 1992), there is considerable significance of kinship structures and cultural proximity (through ethnic, linguistic or religious affinity) in crystallization of such identities. Rohingyas can be traced back to the Arakan region of present-day Burma since the ninth century and are considered to be descendants of Arab Muslim traders, apart from the influence brought about by Moorish, Arab, Persian, and Bengali traders, and other migrants in this port city. The Chittagong region in present-day Bangladesh remained a part of the Kingdom of Arakan until 1784, following which Arakan came under Burmese monarchy (Ahmed 2009; Ullah 2011; Kipgen 2013). Two-thirds of the Arakanese Muslims fled the region toward Chittagong in 1796 after a failed attempt to overthrow Burmese Buddhist rule in Arakan. The British acquired Arakan as part of the empire in 1886, following which many of the earlier displaced Arakanese Muslims returned. Instances of back-and-forth movement happened between the Arakan region and East Bengal during the colonial period, the most prominent being the out-migration that happened in 1941 during the Japanese invasion of British Burma. These Rohingya Muslims were integrated into the host Bengali community owing to their religious, cultural, and linguistic proximity (Pittaway 2016). Despite the distinctively exclusive features of both Rohingya Muslims and Bengali Muslims, they share a certain set of culturally identical religious practices that create a tangible ground for mutual affinity. Except for undertaking Hajj, Rohingya refugees would not be prohibited from or persecuted for following their religion, making their struggle in everyday life a little less harsh than in Myanmar. Precolonial and colonial historiography of the region shows the voluntary or labor-oriented migration that happened between India, Bangladesh, and Burma, which were all part of the British Empire, causing similarities to emerge in terms of culture, language or religion. Although the Rohingya dialect is distinct from the Chittagonian dialect of Bengali language, both have many similarities in their oral form, though they differ entirely in script. Arguably, the shared sense of belonging of Rohingyas with the host state does not correspond to the territorial borders instituted by the postcolonial states; rather, it is shaped by cultural kinship and a common religion or language (Chowdhory and Poyil 2021).

While the Rohingyas in institutional camps in Cox's Bazar in Bangladesh, which is their first country of asylum, are to a large degree provided formal refugee identity cards using the biometric aided RSD process of UNHCR. The quasi-identity (Chowdhory and Poyil 2020) imparted by biometric registration creates an ambiguous empowerment devoid of the active agency of these refugees. In the context of living a bare life in camp, the Rohingyas perceive the aid and rations ascertained through their biometric refugee identity as their only means of survival. These refugees only ascertain their conditional provision and protection in camp through this identification process but are unable to challenge the underlying structural conditions that precipitate the need for this conditional protection. In its concerted effort to make the invisible stateless asylum seekers and refugees visible through the provision of an institutional refugee identity, it gives these powerless, vulnerable refugees a false hope for potential membership with the political community. The situation in India for these refugees is no better. Though over 45,000 Rohingya refugees are spread across various parts of India in the camp settlements, only about 6,000 of them have registered with UNHCR. This effectively leads to a situation where the rest are deemed as "illegal immigrants" by the country rather than refugees, while the national rhetoric on the matter portrays them as a security threat to the country. As seen in the case of partition refugees or Tibetan refugees who are integrated well into the nation-state, recognition or any semblance of formal membership is not provided by the Indian state for the

Rohingyas. In India, when compared to the Sri Lankan Tamil refugees who could negotiate a better situation of state-mediated protection due to their ethnic and cultural proximity to the host state, Rohingyas are stigmatized as the quintessential "other" who do not belong to the idea of a religiously homogeneous nation. Even in the organized institutionalized settlements of refugee camps in Cox's Bazar, refugee groups undergo a constant deprivation of their fundamental rights, just as much as in the settlements outside the walls of the makeshift camps in India. Apart from the inability to ensure basic rights, refugees are incapable of challenging the violations of their fundamental human rights due to the absence of formal rights provided by the state. Equating humanitarian protection, which is often conditional and minimal, cannot be equated to a scenario of recognition provided by the state. But in Bangladesh, the aspect of religious, cultural, and linguistic proximity with the majoritarian Bengali Muslim community, apart from having a shared history with the region, causes Rohingyas to develop a sense of belonging to the host state.

## Conclusion

Although based on humanitarianism, the protection provided by the states of South Asia is often mediated by the vested interests of the state. The territorially rooted conception of belonging precipitates a statist response to the state-orchestrated exclusion that created refugees in the first place. Such a solution is based on the sovereign recognition of the host state, which otherwise pushes refugees into a liminal existence. Any non-statist response, such as the efforts of international agencies like UNHCR, in ameliorating the plight of refugees in their places of asylum is merely moderating the hostility or facilitating the protection offered by the asylum state. An emerging body of scholarship argues for "camp abolition," by underscoring the fact that camps constitute a system of "carceral humanitarianism" (Brankamp 2022; Pfister-Ammende 1973). In the case of resource-scarce countries of South Asia where camps emerge as a de facto solution, theirs abolition will precipitate a new level of chaos that might compromise even the minimal protection that refugees avail themselves of through institutional support. Camps and camp-cities have coexisted from the beginning in most of the independent nation-states of South Asia, which requires a revised conceptualization not catering to the binary of camps and non-camp cities. Hence, whether inside closed institutional encampments or outside them, the imperative here is to understand that the recognition provided by the state is instrumental in determining the ambit of rightlessness that the refugees are subjected to on a day-to-day basis. Underscoring the centrality of the state in refugee protection, the need of the hour is to ensure better systemic protection in camp settlements fortified by at least basic rights that ensure human dignity for these refugees.

## Note

1. For a more detailed discussion on historical understanding on camps, see N. Chowdhory and S. T. Poyil. "Interrogating Camps in Forced Migration Studies: The Exceptionality of South Asia," in *Gender, Identity and Migration in India*, eds. N. Chowdhory and P. Banerjee (Singapore: Palgrave Macmillan, 2022).

## References

Abourahme, Nasser. "The Camp." *Comparative Studies of South Asia, Africa and the Middle East* 40, no. 1 (2020): 35–42. https://doi.org/10.1215/1089201X-8186016

Abourahme, Nasser, and Sandi Hilal. "Political Subjectification, the Production of Space and the Folding of Polarity: The Case of De-Heishe Camp, Palestine." In *Peripheries: Decentering Urban Theory*, edited by James Holston and Teresa Caldeira, 142–66. Berekely: University of California Press, 2012. https://bobjessop.org/2014/01/16/spatial-fixes-temporal-fixes-and-spatio-temporal-fixes

Agier, Michel. "Between War and City: Towards an Urban Anthropology of Refugee Camps." *Ethnography* 3, no. 3 (2002): 317–41. https://doi.org/10.1177/146613802401092779

Ahmed, I. "The Rohingyas : From Stateless to Refugee." 2009. www.semanticscholar.org/paper/The-Rohingyas-%3A-From-Stateless-to-Refugee-Ahmed/078b2fc5ec5dc8bae1e03cb699ae7387a704943b

Arendt, Hannah. *The Origins of Totalitarianism*. London: George Allen & Unwin, 1968.

Bagchi, Jasodhara, and Subhoranjan Dasgupta. *The Trauma and the Triumph: Gender and Partition in Eastern India*. Kolkata: Stree, 2003.

Barrett, Jenny, Nando Sigona. "The Citizen and the Other: New Directions in Research on the Migration and Citizenship Nexus." *Migration Studies* 2, no. 2 (July 2014): 286–94. https://doi.org/10.1093/migration/mnu039

Bauman, Zygmunt. "Sociological Responses to Postmodernity." *Thesis Eleven* 23, no. 1 (1989): 35–63. https://doi.org/10.1177/072551368902300103

Blitz, Brad K. "Statelessness and the Social (De)Construction of Citizenship: Political Restructuring and Ethnic Discrimination in Slovenia." *Journal of Human Rights* 5, no. 4 (2006): 453–79. https://doi.org/10.1080/14754830600978257

Bosniak, Linda. *The Citizen and the Alien: Dilemmas of Contemporary Membership*. Princeton, NJ: Princeton University Press, 2006.

Brankamp, Hanno. "Camp Abolition: Ending Carceral Humanitarianism in Kenya (and Beyond)." *Antipode* 54, no. 1 (2022): 106–29. https://doi.org/10.1111/anti.12762

Bulley, Dan. "Inside the Tent: Community and Government in Refugee Camps." *Security Dialogue* 45, no. 1 (2014): 63–80. https://doi.org/10.1177/0967010613514788

Çağlar, Ayşe. 2021. "The Multiple Tenses of a Postcolonial Age of Migration: A Commentary on Samaddar, R. (2020), *The Postcolonial Age of Migration*." *Dialectical Anthropology* 45, no. 3: 317–20. https://doi.org/10.1007/s10624-021-09619-4

Chowdhory, Nasreen. "Marginality and the 'state of Exception' in Camps in Tamil Nadu." *International Journal of Migration and Border Studies* 2, no. 2 (2016): 132. https://doi.org/10.1504/IJMBS.2016.075582

———. "State Formation, Marginality and Belonging: Contextualising Rights of Refugees in India, Bangladesh and Sri Lanka." In *Refugees, Citizenship and Belonging in South Asia: Contested Terrains*, 43–71. Singapore: Springer, 2018. https://search.ebscohost.com/login.aspx?direct=true&scope=site&db=nlebk&db=nlabk&AN=1832056

Chowdhory, Nasreen, and Shamna Thacham Poyil. "Biometrics, Notion of Governmentality and Gender Relations in Rohingya Refugee Camps, Policies and Practices." *Policies and Practices* 114. Kolkata: Mahanirban Calcutta Research Group and Rosa Luxembourg Stiftung, 2020. www.mcrg.ac.in/PP117.pdf

———. "Speaking the Language of the 'Other': Negotiating Cultural Boundaries through Language in Chitmahals in Indo-Bangladesh Borders." *Citizenship Studies* 25, no. 6 (2021): 791–807. https://doi.org/10.1080/13621025.2021.1968716

———. "Interrogating Camps in Forced Migration Studies: The Exceptionality of South Asia." In *Gender, Identity and Migration in India*, edited by Nasreen Chowdhory and Paula Banerjee, 153–79. Singapore: Springer Nature 2022. https://doi.org/10.1007/978-981-16-5598-2_4

Chowdhory, Nasreen, Shamna Thacham Poyil, and Kajla Meghna. "The Idea of Protection; Norms and Practice of Refugee Management in India." *Refugee Watch* 53, no. 1 (2019): 36–54.

Datta, Antara. *Refugees and Borders in South Asia: The Great Exodus of 1971*. Routledge Studies in South Asian Politics. New York: Routledge, 2013.

De Genova, Nicholas. "Introduction. The Borders of 'Europe' and the European Question." In *The Borders of "Europe": Autonomy of Migration, Tactics of Bordering*, edited by Nicholas De Genova, 1–36. Durham, NC: Duke University Press, 2017.

Forth, Aidan. "Britain's Archipelago of Camps: Labor and Detention in a Liberal Empire, 1871–1903." *Kritika: Explorations in Russian and Eurasian History* 16, no. 3 (2015): 651–80. https://doi.org/10.1353/kri.2015.0042

Foucault, Michel. *Power/Knowledge: Selected Interviews and Other Writings, 1972–1977.* 1st American ed. New York: Pantheon Books, 1980.

Grbac, Peter. "Civitas, Polis, and Urbs: Reimagining the Refugee Camp as the City." Working Paper Series, no. 96. Refugee Studies Centre, University of Oxford, 2013. www.refworld.org/docid/55c9f3504.html

Gündogdu, Ayten. *Rightlessness in an Age of Rights : Hannah Arendt and the Contemporary Struggles of Migrants*, 90–116. Oxford & New York: Oxford University Press, 2015. https://doi.org/10.1093/acprof:oso/9780199370412.001.0001

Hailey, Charlie. *Camps: A Guide to 21st-Century Space.* Cambridge, MA: MIT Press, 2009.

Herz, Manuel, ed. *From Camp to City: Refugee Camps of the Western Sahara.* Baden: Lars Müller, 2012.

Isin, Engin F. *Being Political: Genealogies of Citizenship.* Minneapolis: University of Minnesota Press, 2002.

Isin, Engin F., and Greg Marc Nielsen, eds. *Acts of Citizenship.* London & New York: Zed Books, 2008.

Isin, Engin F., and Kim Rygiel. "Abject Spaces: Frontiers, Zones, Camps." In *The Logics of Biopower and The War on Terror: Living Dying, Surviving*, edited by Elizabeth Dauphinee and Masters Cristina, 181–203. New York: Palgrave Macmillan, 2007. www.palgrave.com/products/title.aspx?PID=276802

Kerber, Linda K. "The Stateless as the Citizen's Other: A View from the United States." *The American Historical Review* 112, no. 1 (2007): 1–34. https://doi.org/10.1086/ahr.112.1.1

Kipgen, Nehginpao. "Conflict in Rakhine State in Myanmar: Rohingya Muslims' Conundrum." *Journal of Muslim Minority Affairs* 33, no. 2 (2013): 298–310. https://doi.org/10.1080/13602004.2013.810117

Krause, Monika. "Undocumented Migrants: An Arendtian Perspective." *European Journal of Political Theory* 7, no. 3 (2008): 331–48. https://doi.org/10.1177/1474885108089175.

Kreichauf, René. "From Forced Migration to Forced Arrival: The Campization of Refugee Accommodation in European Cities." *Comparative Migration Studies* 6, no. 1 (2018): 7. https://doi.org/10.1186/s40878-017-0069-8

Macklin, Audrey. "Citizenship Revocation and the Privilege to Have Rights." *Queen's Law Journal* 40, no. 1 (2014): 1–54. https://doi.org/10.2139/ssrn.2507786

Malkki, Liisa. "National Geographic: The Rooting of Peoples and the Territorialization of National Identity among Scholars and Refugees." *Cultural Anthropology* 7, no. 1 (1992): 24–44.

Malkki, Liisa H. "News From Nowhere: Mass Displacement and Globalized 'Problems of Organization.'" *Ethnography* 3, no. 3 (2002): 351–60. https://doi.org/10.1177/146613802401092797

Marushiakova, Elena, and Vesselin Popov. *Gypsies (Roma) in Bulgaria*. Studien Zur Tsiganologie Und Folkloristik 18. Frankfurt & New York: P. Lang, 1997.

McGarry, Aidan. "The Roma Voice in the European Union: Between National Belonging and Transnational Identity." *Social Movement Studies* 10, no. 3 (2011): 283–97. https://doi.org/10.1080/14742837.2011.590030

Misselwitz, P., and S. Hanafi. "Testing a New Paradigm: UNRWA's Camp Improvement Programme." *Refugee Survey Quarterly* 28, nos. 2–3 (2009): 360–88. https://doi.org/10.1093/rsq/hdp039

Misselwitz, Philipp. "Rehabilitating Camp Cities : Community Driven Planning for Urbanised Refugee Camps." University of Stuttgart, 2009. http://elib.uni-stuttgart.de/handle/11682/82

Montclos, M.-A.P.D., and P. M. Kagwanja. "Refugee Camps or Cities? The Socio-Economic Dynamics of the Dadaab and Kakuma Camps in Northern Kenya." *Journal of Refugee Studies* 13, no. 2 (2000): 205–22. https://doi.org/10.1093/jrs/13.2.205

Morris, Lydia. "Rights and Controls in the Management of Migration: The Case of Germany." *The Sociological Review* 48, no. 2 (2000): 224–40. https://doi.org/10.1111/1467-954X.00213

Ong, Aihwa. "(Re)Articulations of Citizenship." *PS: Political Science and Politics* 38, no. 4 (2005): 697–99.

Petti, Alessandro. "Spatial Ordering of Exile. The Architecture of Palestinian Refugee Camps." Crios 1 (2013): 62–70. www.decolonizing.ps/site/wp-content/uploads/2009/03/Spatial-Ordering-of-Exile.-18-March_Petti.pdf

Pfister-Ammende, Maria. "Mental Hygiene in Refugee Camps." In *Uprooting and After . . .* , edited by Charles Zwingmann and Maria Pfister-Ammende, 241–51. Berlin, Heidelberg: Springer, 1973. https://doi.org/10.1007/978-3-642-95213-5_20

Pittaway, Eileen. "The Rohingya Refugees in Bangladesh: A Failure of the International Protectin System." In *Protracted Displacement in Asia: No Place to Call Home*, edited by Howard Adelman, 83–106. London & New York: Routledge, 2016. www.taylorfrancis.com/books/e/9781315602752

Redclift, Victoria. "Abjects or Agents? Camps, Contests and the Creation of 'Political Space.'" *Citizenship Studies* 17, no. 3–4 (2013a): 308–21. https://doi.org/10.1080/13621025.2013.791534

———. *Statelessness and Citizenship: Camps and the Creation of Political Space*. London & New York. Routledge, 2013b. https://doi.org/10.4324/9780203096871

Rygiel, Kim. "Politicizing Camps: Forging Transgressive Citizenships in and through Transit." *Citizenship Studies* 16, no. 5–6 (2012): 807–25. https://doi.org/10.1080/13621025.2012.698511

Samaddar, Ranabir. *The Postcolonial Age of Migration*. London & New York: Routledge, 2020.

Saunders, Doug. *Arrival City: How the Largest Migration in Human History Is Reshaping Our World*. First US edition. New York: Pantheon Books, 2010.

Scott, James C. *The Art of Not Being Governed: An Anarchist History of Upland Southeast Asia*. Yale Agrarian Studies Series. New Haven, CT & London: Yale University Press, 2009.

Sigona, Nando. "Campzenship: Reimagining the Camp as a Social and Political Space." *Citizenship Studies* 19, no. 1 (2015): 1–15. https://doi.org/10.1080/13621025.2014.937643

Ullah, Akm Ahsan. "Rohingya Refugees to Bangladesh: Historical Exclusions and Contemporary Marginalization." *Journal of Immigrant & Refugee Studies* 9, no. 2 (2011): 139–61. https://doi.org/10.1080/15562948.2011.567149

Vermeersch, Peter. *The Romani Movement: Minority Politics and Ethnic Mobilization in Contemporary Central Europe*. Studies in Ethnopolitics. New York: Berghahn Books, 2006.

Wacquant, Loïc. *Urban Outcasts: A Comparative Sociology of Advanced Marginality*. Cambridge: Polity Press, 2008.

# Part III

# Sea as a Site of Statelessness

Chapter 8

# The Tragic Journey of *Komagata Maru*

## Empire, Immigrants, and Anxiety

Subhas Ranjan Chakraborty

## Introduction

The *Komagata Maru* incident that took place more than a century ago prefigures the experiences of refugees, migrants, and stateless people of our time. The story of the journey of *Komagata Maru* begins like most journeys, but it ends with a tragedy. Gurdit Singh, a Sikh businessman, chartered the ship *Komagata Maru* in Hong Kong to help some Sikhs and other Indians migrate to Canada. The ship reached Vancouver in British Columbia on May 23, 1914, with 376 passengers. Canadian immigration authorities allowed only twenty-two passengers to disembark because others did not fulfill the requirements of a continuous journey under Canadian law. The ship remained anchored in Vancouver Harbor for two months until July 23 without adequate provisions for the large number of passengers. Gurdit, leading the passengers, challenged the existing provisions. He told the reporters, "we are British citizens and we have a right to visit any part of the empire . . . if we are refused entry the matter will not end here." For three months, Gurdit negotiated with the authorities and exhausted all legal appeals. Finally, the Court of Appeals of Canada unanimously decided that it had no jurisdiction in the matter and that the authorities could begin legal deportation.

The passengers were compelled to return literally at gunpoint when a Canadian navy cruiser was brought in. Gurdit was forced to negotiate the return of the ship with all its passengers. The ship left Vancouver on July 23 and while it stopped at Yokohama, Kobe, and Singapore, no one was allowed to disembark. The British authorities ultimately ordered the ship to go to Calcutta. On September 26, the ship was stopped at Kulpi, where Donald, the District Magistrate, Slocock of the Criminal Intelligence Office, and Humphreys, the Deputy Commissioner of a Punjab district, boarded the ship. The ship was searched for arms and seditious literature, but the search yielded nothing, and on September 29 the ship came to the town of Budge Budge, about twenty-seven kilometers from Calcutta. In fact, the decision was taken earlier that the ship would never reach Calcutta.

The Commissioner of Police in Calcutta, Sir Frederick Halliday, personally led a group of British and Indian officers and asked the passengers to disembark and proceed to a special train, waiting at the railway station to take them to Punjab. Gurdit felt suspicious of the move and refused. He informed them that they were carrying the sacred *Guru Granth Sahib*, which they would install at the *Gurdwara* in Howrah. Then they would seek an interview with the governor. The passengers were eventually persuaded to come down, with Gurdit carrying the *Granth Sahib* on his head. The whole group walked in a procession to the railway station and started squatting. The Ingress to India Ordinance (Ordinance V of 1914) was read out to the passengers, and they were asked to board the train. In response, Gurdit argued that it would be sacrilegious to take the sacred book on the train. The situation became increasingly confrontational, and the authorities appealed to Calcutta for more troops. Between 3 and 4 o'clock in the afternoon, the passengers stood up and started marching toward Calcutta with the *Granth Sahib* being carried in front of them. The police followed them, while Halliday and Donald made phone calls to Calcutta for reinforcements. Eastwood, of the Reserve Police, got together thirty European sergeants and constables and started from Calcutta around 4 o'clock in the afternoon. Members of the 150 Royal Fusiliers were also sent from Calcutta. The procession was stopped about six or seven kilometers from Budge Budge by Eastwood and his forces until the Royal Fusiliers arrived. With them came Cummins, the Chief Secretary to the Government of Bengal, and Duke, representing the governor. They asked Gurdit and others to go back to Budge Budge to continue the conversation.

On their return, the passengers were asked to go back to the ship for the night. They refused and sat on the road. The Punjab police was asked to be on the right side of the passengers, and the European forces positioned on the left. The passengers gathered around the Sacred Book, which was placed on a portable platform. As the Police Commissioner walked toward the level crossing, a few shots were heard. Donald asked Gurdit to come up and talk to him, but Gurdit remained where he was. Eastwood plunged into the crowd and was allegedly knocked down. At that moment, the firing had begun. The Commissioner of Police later alleged that he had seen thirty or forty Sikhs firing, but as Johnston wrote, the impression was not shared by some of his own officers. He writes, "some of the shots came from the four police sergeants, now engulfed by the crowd, and discharging their revolvers at such close quarters that one man, Badal Singh, was hit six times" (Johnston 2014, 157). As the passengers now surged forward, the Calcutta and Punjab forces retaliated. The Royal Fusiliers entered the scene late, but the Commanding Officer, Captain Moore, secured Halliday's permission to order firing. Most of the passengers now found shelter in a nearby ditch, or in the fields, and some even jumped into the river (Johnston 2014, 96–104). By 8 p.m., it was quiet again.

The number of passengers dead was officially put at twenty, of whom eighteen died as a result of wounds suffered from service rifles, as recorded by the inquest report submitted to the Commission of Enquiry later ("Proceedings of the *Komagata Maru* Commission of Enquiry" 1914). Varying estimates of the total number of dead was put between twenty-six and forty, but the number was probably higher. Some people probably died later in the hospital. Only about sixty-two passengers were sent back to Punjab under police escort, while 211 were arrested and twenty-eight others, including Gurdit, escaped. After wandering for seven years, Gurdit, reportedly on the advice of Gandhi, voluntarily surrendered in November, 1921.[1]

The unsuccessful immigrants to Canada were forced to spend several months on the sea and found that they did not enjoy freedom of movement even in their land of origin. Did this not foreshadow what would be a familiar global scenario a century later? These people did experience the virtual fate of the stateless. They were not admitted to Canada, and they were not allowed to move freely in India, their home. They were the early boat people, floating in the sea, for more than six months in search of land. When they found land, they also found bullets.

## Migration, Racist Response, and Radicalization

In a way, the journey of *Komagata Maru* represents a moment in history, but a significant moment in Indian, perhaps global, history. It exposed the plight of the Indian migrants, usually poor peasants/laborers/artisans/small traders, and what they experienced in their quest for a better life in a new environment. Michael Fisher spoke of the counter-flow to colonialism, but this migration was different, arising as it did out of subsistence crisis, attributed to the broad economic impacts of the colonial rule (Fisher, 2004). When slavery was abolished in the British colonies in 1834, a new "system of slavery," as it were, was inaugurated with the introduction of "indentured labor" (Tinker 1974). The coercive character of the merchant-controlled coolie trade did produce serious protests, leading to the temporary suspension of the practice in 1839. One estimate is that between 1834 and 1876, 9.8 million people left Indian shores, but about 7.8 million returned (Chakraborty 2011, 12). Between 1871 and 1930, an annual average of between 2,40,000 and 6,00,000 migrated from India (2011, 9–10).

Such migration was predicated on coercion used to recruit labor for projects in the colonies on the one hand, and the denudation of resources by colonial policies in India on the other. A majority of the emigrants were from rural areas where "crop failure could plunge sections of the village community into near-starvation" (Chakraborty 2011). In fact, there was a strong correlation between emigration and harvest conditions. Frequent famines made the situation worse. Most of the emigrants probably left their villages for the first time in their lives and were often victims of disease and even death during the long, arduous journeys. The overall impact of colonialism was indeed negative. There was no increase in per capita income between 1757 and 1947; income probably declined in the second half of the nineteenth century. It is an abiding irony that the cash crop boom accompanied a decline in agrarian productivity. The export boom benefited money lenders, absentee landlords, urban merchants, and a handful of Indian industrialists. During what was, in the imagination of Kipling and Curzon, "the glorious imperial half century," life expectancy of ordinary Indians fell by a staggering 20 percent (M. Davis 2017, 311). Pax Britannica, it would appear, had more victims than decades of war. India was now a part of the capitalist "world system," but ironically, India's increasing integration with world trade produced pauperization (Davis and Huttenback 1986). As Hugh Tinker puts it, the whole indentured labor system and the Indian diaspora were the consequences of British exploitation (Tinker 1974). The majority of Indians who emigrated gained little, exchanging a situation of casual, intermittent, poorly paid labor for a similar situation in the new country (1974). Massive movements of people, then, were more often than not the product of denial of entitlement to livelihood in rural areas.

Migration from the Punjab, writes Raza, dates back to 1867 when about one hundred Sikh emigrants went to Hong Kong to join the new police force. One aspect of the movement of people from Punjab related to the military requirements of the colonial state (Tatla 1999). Thousands of laborers, peasants, small traders, and students ventured to travel to distant lands. The vast majority of these people were moved by the hope of better economic opportunities. "This was the case in Central Punjab where fragmented landholdings and rural indebtedness, combined with the highest population densities . . worked as 'push' factors for many migrants" (Raza 2015, 90). On the other hand, it has been suggested that records indicate close relations among these factors and the migration, settlement, and radicalization of Indians in North America.[2]

North America turned out to be an important destination from the 1890s. The immigration of people from Punjab to Canada and the United States perceptibly increased in the early years of the twentieth century. These migrants to the New World created an anxiety which became more and more acute as the nineteenth century drew to a close in the minds of the imperial authorities about immigrants. The harassment and endless misery to which the Indian immigrants into Canada were subjected was the result of this new feeling of anxiety within the Empire. There was a blatant display of racism as well. Attacks on immigrants in Washington State in 1907 pushed about 400 to enter Canada. A crowd of over 10,000 in Vancouver protested against the arrival of the ship Monteagle, carrying 914 Indian passengers. Canada was trying to follow a policy of exclusion from the opening of the new century. The government of Canada's action was predicated on suspicions about Indians, some of whom were even arrested in the late nineteenth century and "a sudden surge brought 4,700 Indian immigrants in 1906 and 1907 leading to an eruption of 'white nativism,' resulting in the riots of 1907" (Chakraborty 2016, 112). In the decade before the First World War, successive "outbursts of racial animus marked relations between East Indians and whites in British Columbia" (Ward 1990, 179–93). The Federal Immigration Act drastically reduced the number of Indian immigrants. Between 1905 and 1914, only 5,300 Indians were allowed to enter, while the total number of immigrants had been 2.5 million (179–93). Between 1909 and 1913, only twenty-seven Indians were allowed to enter. In 1907, Canada even suggested the introduction of passports. In 1908 came the stipulation of a continuous voyage from Asia, an impossible proposition at the time. It is important to note that in November 1913, when the Ghadar Party was established, Gandhi was leading the striking Indian mine workers across the Natal border into Transvaal to protest discriminatory legislation and to launch his *satyagraha*. Indeed, an Indo-Canadian publication, *Sansar*, had earlier reported the Indian campaign against discriminatory immigration laws in South Africa. The Indian leaders in Vancouver, Seattle, and San Francisco publicized the events in South Africa to argue that Indians in North America as well as other colonies of the British Empire were suffering from "racial discrimination and injustice" (Sohi 2014, 112).[3]

What is perhaps less appreciated is the signal role that the abortive journey of *Komagata Maru* to Vancouver played in closing borders to Indian migrants not just from Canada, but the United States and other parts of the British Empire. Lala Lajpat Rai wrote that the Indians aboard *Komagata Maru* posed a challenge to Canadian immigration laws (Lajpat Rai 1978). They exposed the continuity between forms of imperial expansion in the nineteenth century and the practice of immigrant exclusion at the beginning of the twentieth: "A shipload of Indians is not superficially a matter of much importance, and yet it is not impossible that if we could see events of our time through the eyes of the historian of 2014, we should find that the most significant thing in the world today is the *Komagata Maru* with 376 passengers abroad. It is a challenge thrown down not only to the Empire but to the claim of the white man to possess the earth" (Rai quoted in Munshi 2016, 51–52).

The policy of the Canadian government regarding the immigrants linked Canadian authorities with those in India. The Canadian government became wary of some of the immigrants, especially those perceived as disloyal. Not many Indians (mostly Sikhs) in Canada moved toward the east, but quite a few crossed the southern border into the United States. Peter Ward would believe the number to be around 1,500 (Ward 1990). Some of these immigrants were looking to form their own social and religious associations soon after their arrival in the new country. The first such organization was the *Khalsa Diwan Society* founded at Vancouver in 1907. They realized this to be an urgent need to preserve their collective interests in the face of legislative discrimination. Another such organization was the United India League of Vancouver. These two organizations submitted a petition to the minister of the interior protesting against the deportation of Bhagwan Singh, who came to Canada via San Francisco in 1913. He was deported, but "jumped ship in Yokohama, Japan and made his way back to San Francisco the following year, where he became a prominent leader of the Ghadar Party" (Sohi 2014, 86).[4] Indians in Canada argued, like their counterparts in the United States and South Africa, that in terms of the Queen's Proclamation of 1858, the

Indians, as British subjects, were free to travel to any part of the Empire. They were also beginning to take a keen interest in Indian politics. The Sikh temple became a center of nascent political activities. Other societies were formed in the course of time with two goals emerging as the immediate ones: self-defense in Canada and Indian nationalism.

The Indians had divisions among themselves, but alienation from the whites appeared to give them more cohesion. The Canadian government, on the other hand, divided the Indians into two broad categories: loyal and disloyal. They gradually developed an understandable obsession to control and, if necessary, deport the disloyal. The link between some activists and their counterparts across the border added to their anxiety. The disloyal Indians were suspected of being part of a grand international plan to hatch a conspiracy against the government. The surveillance and the efforts to exclude the Indians, it would appear, were coordinated between the United States and Canada. "Pacific Coast representatives and the immigration authorities used the specter of the 'Hindu' agitator freely crossing the US–Canadian border to advocate for greater border policing, surveillance and enforcement" (Sohi 2014, 2).

## Control by Empire

The need to control the subjects and their movements was urgent for the Imperial government. In the mid–nineteenth century, Lord John Russell had instanced immigration as a matter which of necessity must remain subject to imperial control. By the beginning of the twentieth century, the British Empire had established its right to control access to its territories by officially endorsing that the Dominions had the right to restrict or prohibit the entry of Indian immigrants. In 1911, Lord Crew said, "His Majesty's Government fully accepts that each dominion must be allowed to decide for itself what elements it desires to accept for its population" (Chakraborty 2018). There is little doubt that a dimension of racism was associated with such a policy. Was it just a coincidence that in 1914 the British Nationality and Status of Aliens Act, which stipulated that the aliens had no right in common law or by statute to be admitted into the United Kingdom, was passed? "The policy of free movement that facilitated the growth of the British Empire in the first place became a matter of suspicion and state control" (Banerjee 2003, 84). In India it was a long journey from the Foreigners' Act of 1864 to the Passport Act of 1920. It was in 1914, coincidentally again, that the

Ingress into India Ordinance (V of 1914) was promulgated, authorizing the Government of India to control and regulate the entry of foreigners into India by sea or land. Search for ships became a routine affair after the tragic incident of *Komagata Maru*. On October 24, an order, issued in the name of the Governor-General, laid down: "Whereas by Section 3 of the Foreigners' Ordinance of 1914 read with Section 2 of Ingress into India Ordinance of 1914 the entry of foreigners into British India by sea or by land can be regulated and restricted. The Governor-General in Council is pleased to direct that the persons named in the attached schedule (with the exception of the nine who are in Medical College Hospital) should be interned there temporarily" (Sd/- J. C. Cummins, Chief Secretary, Government of Bengal. "IB File" 1914) This is related to the interns of the *Komagata Maru* and shows how the Ordinance came in handy to control the disaffected immigrants (their failure to emigrate notwithstanding).

Control and surveillance were seen as necessary in view of the suspected link between the immigrants and India. There was a strong protest in India against the continuous journey provision. When the Khalsa Diwan Society decided to send delegations to Ottawa, London, and India, the delegations to Ottawa and London were not accepted by the imperial authorities, but the one in India proceeded to Punjab in 1913. British police officers, Isemonger and Slattery, commented on the activities of the delegates and noted, "it is now apparent that it formed a distinct step in the development of the revolutionary movement and was intended to establish a link of sympathy between Indians at home and emigrants abroad" (quoted in Sohi 2014, 115). The Punjab Governor, Sir Michael O'Dwyer, felt that the delegates initially criticized the immigration laws, but their messages were becoming increasingly "menacing and inflammatory." B. Ketttleswell, OSD, Punjab Civil Secretariat wrote to the Chief Secretary of Bengal on September 17, 1914, from Simla, stating, "Request from Sir Michael O'Dwyer, the Governor of Punjab, to secure all passengers coming by *Komagata Maru* and send them by a special train to Punjab under Ordinance V of 1914 (Ingress into India). Humphreys, the Punjab Commissioner and Petrie of the CID are proceeding to Calcutta to meet the steamer" ("Proceedings of the *Komagata Maru* Commission of Enquiry" 1914).

It seems from such "request" that the perception of both the Canadian and Indian governments was that the passengers of *Komagata Maru* and the Indian revolutionaries were linked. The decision to search the ship repeatedly and to restrain the passengers from traveling freely in the country was apparently taken earlier, perhaps on the basis of intelligence reports. The links were not established, nor were arms found during the searches. That this was shared by the metropolitan government as well is amply borne out by the correspondence between the Criminal Intelligence Office (CIO), Simla, on the one hand, and the Intelligence departments in Bengal, Punjab, and the Central Provinces, on the other. These exchanges were to share information and, on that basis, apprehend those suspected of seditious activities. The department of interior and the emigration branch of British Columbia kept the CIO, Simla, posted about the possible departure of suspects from Victoria, British Columbia, and other places with the names of ships, the dates of their journeys, and the names of the suspects. The authorities in Hong Kong, Shanghai, Penang, Singapore, and Rangoon also shared information and warnings on a regular basis. That Ingress was linked to anticolonial movements is seen from the fact that the Ordinance was applied to the Indians in Chandernagore, a French territory near Calcutta.

A letter, marked secret, from the Secretary of State to the Governor General, dated October 6, 1914, drew the attention of the latter to an earlier secret telegram of August 14 about Indians returning from Canada. The new letter said that two people were arrested in Victoria on September 9 in possession of bombs. It was later found that three bombs were taken by people who had left in August. J. W. Nelson of CIO, wrote from Simla that one Harnam Singh, s/o Labh Singh, was deported from Canada and that he was reported to have left San Francisco on September 25 for Hong Kong. It was likely that he would come to India. The CIO wrote on October 20 about some publications: the Indian Agitators Abroad, 1913; Indians in Germany, 1913; Draft Circular of Indian Agitators in America, April 1914. The investigating officer was advised to consult these publications for possible clues about names. By October 10, three officers—Hutchinson, Tegart, and Colson—were authorized in terms of Ingress into India to search all vessels bound for Calcutta. A note from Hughes-Buller of the CID department suggested that all ships with fifty or more Indian passengers should be searched at Diamond Harbour.

Names of the ships with their expected dates of arrival from Singapore, Rangoon, Vietnam, and Hong Kong were duly collected. Systematic searches were made. The Colonial Office, Hong Kong, wrote to the Secretary, Government of India, about return of emigrants on November 12 by *Foo Song*. It said that there were two "bad men" among the passengers. A search took place, and two men were suspected of carrying bombs. In their luggage, a copy of Savarkar's *Indian War of Independence* and another proscribed book were found. It was suspected that some Sikhs might go to

Chittagong from Rangoon, and the Superintendent of Police in Chittagong was asked to examine all Sikh passengers there. Other ships like *Yet Shing*, *Nam Sang*, *Choy Sang*, *Tosa Maru*, *Hang Sang*, and *Kut Sang* were all searched in October and November.

On October 13, Cleveland, Director, CIO, Simla, wrote to Slattery, DIG, Punjab Police:

> I send you . . . lists . . . of Punjabi passengers who left Victoria by *Shidzukoo Maru* on August 25, *Empress of India* from Vancouver on August 22 and *Kwang Sang* from Hong Kong on October 1. . . . an official of the India Office wrote to me on September 4, "It looks to me as if a number of Sikhs . . . upset over the *Komagata Maru* incident, are leaving British Columbia, and a lot of them may stay in Hong Kong or Chinese ports . . . Hopkinson does not, I think, discriminate between Indians who give trouble to the Canadian authorities over immigration restrictions and Indians who are plotting against the Government of India. And though the Sikhs who went to Canada loyal subjects of the Raj, may, unfortunately, leave there in a rather different mood, I must say that I am inclined to discount the value of the label 'seditionist' when affixed in Canada by subordinate officials." While sympathizing with this kindly view . . . the practical sedition of the Gurdit Singh party has shown that the ravings of the Far Eastern Sikhs, who have been converted to the Ghadar doctrines, are not mere froth. ("D.O. Letter No. 1357" 1914)

Hopkinson had earlier sent a list of thirteen people traveling by *Canada Maru* on September 1, of whom seven were marked as suspicious. Cleveland, in a confidential note on October 28, reported the activities of a group of disloyal Indians in Canada. He gave a number of names and suggested their links with the Ghadar Party. He also noted that Inspector Hopkinson was murdered by a "Hindu" in Vancouver about a week earlier. Mewa Singh was later executed for this in November 1914.

A comprehensive and wide network was established across the Empire to gather intelligence and to act. The outline of the story reveals that the *Komagata Maru* incident was not the cause but rather the result of imperial anxiety about immigrants. The decision to force the passengers to go to Punjab was taken not because they were found to be "seditious," but out of a panic about the suspected link between them and Indian leaders.

## Militant Nationalism in India

Benedict Anderson (2007) suggested that the last two decades of the nineteenth century witnessed the onset of what he calls "early globalization" as seen in nationalists' struggles in the Spanish global empire—Cuba (1895) and the Philippines (1896). Likewise, Indian expatriates were seeking to coordinate their efforts in Europe, America, East and South East Asia, and with the revolutionaries in India. The *Komagata Maru* incident may become more comprehensible in a larger perspective. "The global arena also played host to a variety of political networks that engaged with Indian politics . . . Circles surrounding the clergyman J. T. Sutherland in USA, and the *Gaelic American* . . . supporting the cause of Irish nationalism included space for other movements such as the Indian" (Raza, Roy, and Zachariah 2015, xv). By the beginning of the twentieth century, India had witnessed the consolidation of the nationalist as well as the beginning of a revolutionary movement. The Ghadar Party had already been founded, and many Indians had left for East and South East Asia, Europe, and America to establish networks and coordinate revolutionary activities. The impending war was seen as an opportunity, and they worked with the existing networks of exiled Indians in Europe and America. Clusters of Indian exiles built up in Berlin and Switzerland, as well as in Paris and London (Zachariah 2015). M. N. Roy, Tarak Nath Das (United States, Canada, Germany), Bhupendra Nath Datta (Germany), Virendra Nath Chattopadhyay (Germany, Sweden), Abani Mukherjee (South East Asia, Germany), Champakraman Pillai (Switzerland, Germany), Har Dayal, Barkatullah, Mohendra Pratap, and others were active and traveled across countries. The Indian Independence Committee in Berlin was a very important forum, facilitating the exchange of ideas. Sudhindra Bose of the State University of Iowa wrote in the *Modern Review* in August 1914 that more than three hundred "Hindu" students in American colleges and universities had set up the Hindusthan Association in America. It had fairly strong centers in many cities across the United States, including New York. While they looked after the interests of the students, they were not unmindful of the "patriotic program." They started the magazine *The Hindusthan Student* and *Women's Auxiliary* under Kamala Devi and sought affiliation with the Association (Bose 1914). Seema Sohi has talked of the "organic intellectuals" of the Ghadar party and their collaboration with other Indians in the United States and Canada. She notes that an anticolonial movement for self-determination in India got connected with battles waged by racialized and colonized people across the world fighting for racial equality and political independence. Like Canada, the United States also "tightened restrictions against radicals and immigrants" (Sohi 2014, 3–4). Sohi has effectively explored "how Indian anti-colonial resistance was densely inter-woven with anti-Asian exclusionary campaign and state anti-radical practices that extended from North America to India in the years leading up to and during the First World War" (3–4). It is relevant to note that Jose Rizal, the pioneer of the Philippine nationalism, was angered at being kept for days on board a ship for "quarantine purposes"; in fact, the ship had about 650 Chinese on board, "very useful for racist, anti-immigration campaigns" (Chakraborty 2016). The parallel developments are not without historical significance (Anderson 2007).

Sho Kuwajima cites a book in Japanese entitled *The Komagata Maru Incident*, written by Sadao Yoshida, the captain of the ship. Here, Yokichi Shiosaki, an owner and engineer of *Komagata Maru*, suggested that several passengers of the ship had only recently left their military services. He mentions that Indian policemen and soldiers agitated when the Hong Kong government was delaying the permission for the ship's departure. Kuwajima feels that the problems that Gurdit Singh faced in Hong Kong were probably known to the Indians in Singapore, as Gurdit often stayed in Malay and Singapore. Yoshida mentioned Gurdit as a "leader of an Indian revolutionary group . . . [who] espoused the cause of Ghadar." The *Osaka Ashahi Shimbun* reported the plight of the *Komagata Maru* passengers in Vancouver and mentioned the assertion of the rights of the Indians to enter Canada as British subjects (Kuwajima 2006, 13–24).

It would appear that Japanese missions in Ottawa and Vancouver were watching the situation closely, as the Captain and the crew were Japanese and had a perception of threat from the passengers. During the return journey, the Indian communities in Yokohama and Kobe established contact with the passengers who were not allowed to disembark. English dailies like the *Japan Chronicle* occasionally referred to *Komagata Maru*. They reported what they called the pitiable condition of the passengers at Kobe. The *Osaka Asahi Shimbun* on September 4, 1914, reported that the ship had finally left Kobe and sailed for Calcutta when they were denied permission to land in Hong Kong. The ship arrived in Singapore on September 16 and stayed until September 19. Here also, the passengers were not allowed to come down from the ship, nor was the ship allowed to go either to Shanghai or Bombay. Sohan Singh Josh believes that it was in Singapore that Calcutta was decided as the final destination (Kuwajima 2006; Josh 1975).

The British authority in Singapore sought to keep the Indian community and the passengers isolated from each other, but the Indians developed their own network of communication. They came to know of the fate of the passengers after they had reached Budge Budge. Indeed, the Court of Enquiry set up after the Singapore Mutiny in 1915 did refer to what they called "outside influences" as contributing factors. It noted, "The town and settlements of Singapore together with the neighboring states enjoyed a widespread . . . notoriety as being a focus of Indian seditious passengers to and from Far East and America." The governor of Singapore, Arthur Young noted, "At that time . . . the passage of *Komagata Maru* through Singapore was a recent event, [and] though the ship had no communication with land, yet it had left a bad effect" (Kuwajima 2006, 25).

What placed *Komagata Maru* at the center of the conjuncture we have been trying to understand was the anonymous letter received by Major General Reade, the GOC. It communicated the opinion of the soldiers that they would not fight any other country than the ones mentioned in their engagement sheets, namely, the Malay Peninsula and the Straits Settlements. "As our brethren who have been shot in the *Komagata Maru* case have troubled and grieved us, some of us have lost dear brothers and other blood relations, we can never forget the *kindness* of the British Indian government for shooting and slaughtering the passengers" (Kuwajima 2006, 25–26) (emphasis added). The suspected link between the immigrants in *Komagata Maru* goaded the Canadian government to deny permission to land. Hapless immigrants spent more than six months on the sea in virtual statelessness.

## The Global Context

The refusal of Canada to admit the immigrants, the agonizing wait at the harbor, the forced return journey, and the massacre at Budge Budge transformed the journey of *Komagata Maru* into a historic one. It became a symbol of racist and imperial prejudice, on the one hand, and the resistance to them, on the other. The tangled tales of the frustrated immigrants, diasporic discontents, and political activism of exiled Indians look forward to the world a hundred years later when the immigrants continue to have similar experiences of being obliged to chart a journey to nowhere land. The epic journey of *Komagata Maru* may very well be seen as part of what Anderson calls "the infinitely complex inter-continental networks that characterize the age of Early Globalization" of a different kind (Anderson 2007, 233). This essay has simply tried to connect some of these different aspects in an attempt to understand the conjuncture that the incident represented in its broader world-historical perspective.

## Notes

1. This brief outline is based on Ganesh Ghosh, *An Episode of India's Struggle for Freedom: Komagata Maru* (Budge Budge: Gurdware Sahhedganj, 1998), 1–30; also see, Hugh Johnston, *The Voyage of the Komagata Maru: The Sikh Challenge to Canada's Colour Bar*. Expanded and fully revised edition (Vancouver: UBC Press, 2014); Maria Ramnath, *Haj to Utopia: How the Ghadar Movement Charted Global Radicalism and Attempted to Overthrow the British Empire* (Berkeley: University of California Press, 2011), 47–49.

2. The links had been very elegantly established by Seema Sohi in *Echoes of Mutiny: Race, Surveillance and Indian Anticolonialism in North America* (New Delhi: Oxford University Press, 2014).

3. Sohi (2014) has enumerated several incidents of unjust treatment meted out to immigrants. See especially in chapter 4.

4. Sohi (2014) cites a report by Inspector Hopkinson entitled, "Note on the Hindu revolutionary movement in Canada."

## References

Anderson, Benedict. *Under Three Flags: Anarchism and the Anti-Colonial Imagination*. London & New York: Verso Books, 2007.

Banerjee, Paula. "Aliens in the Colonial World." In *Borders, Histories, Existences: Gender and Beyond*, edited by Ranabir Samaddar, 3–38. New Delhi: SAGE, 2010. https://doi.org/10.4135/9788132107989

Bose, Sudhindra. "World's Hindusthan Students' Federation." *Modern Review* 16, no. 1–2 (1914): 143–44.

Chakraborty, Subhas Ranjan. "Colonialism, Resource Crisis and Forced Migration." Mahanirban Calcutta Research Group. Policies and Practices Series, 2011: www.mcrg.ac.in/PP42.pdf

———. "The Journey of Komagata Maru: Conjuncture, Memory and History." South Asian *Diaspora* 8, no. 2 (2016): 111–24. https://doi.org/10.1080/19438192.2016.1165929

———. "The Journey of Komagata Maru: Conjuncture, Memory and History." In *Diasporas and Transnationalisms: The Journey of the Komagata Maru*, edited by Anjali Gera Roy and Ajaya Kumar Sahoo. Chapter 3. London & New York: Routledge, 2018.

Davis, Lance E., and Robert A. Huttenback. *Mammon and the Pursuit of Empire: The Political Economy of British Imperialism, 1860–1912. Interdisciplinary Perspectives on Modern History*. Cambridge [Cambridgeshire] & New York: Cambridge University Press, 1986.

Davis, Mike. *Late Victorian Holocausts: El Niño Famines and the Making of the Third World*. London & New York: Verso Books, 2017.

"D.O. Letter No. 1357." 1914, October 13, 1914. 1105/14. West Bengal State Archives.

Fisher, Michael Herbert. *Counterflows to Colonialism: Indian Travellers and Settlers in Britain, 1600–1857*. Delhi: Permanent Black, 2004.

Ghosh, Ganesh. *An Episode of India's Struggle for Freedom: Komagata Maru 1914*. Budge Budge: Gurdware Sahhedganj, 1998.

"IB File." 1914. West Bengal State Archives. No. 1105/14. Sl.No.57/1914.

Johnston, Hugh J. M. *The Voyage of the Komagata Maru: The Sikh Challenge to Canada's Colour Bar*. Expanded and Fully revised edition. Vancouver: UBC Press, 2014. www.komagatamarujourney.ca

Josh, Sohan Singh. *Tragedy of Komagata Maru*. New Delhi: People's Publishing House, 1975.

Kuwajima, Sho. *The Mutiny in Singapore: War, Anti War and the War for India's Independence*. New Delhi: Rainbow Publishers, 2006.

Munshi, Sherally. "Immigration, Imperialism, and the Legacies of Indian Exclusion." SSRN Scholarly Paper 2571412. Rochester, NY: Social Science Research Network, 2016. https://papers.ssrn.com/abstract=2571412

"Proceedings of the Komagata Maru Commission of Enquiry." Bengal Secretariat Press, 1914.

Ramnath, Maia. *Haj to Utopia: How the Ghadar Movement Charted Global Radicalism and Attempted to Overthrow the British Empire*. The California World History Library, no. 19. Berkeley: University of California Press, 2011.

Raza, Ali. "Straddling the International and the Regional." In *The Internationalist Moment: South Asia, Worlds, and World Views, 1917–1939*, edited by Ali Raza, Franziska Roy, and Benjamin Zachariah. 86–123. Los Angeles: SAGE, 2015.

Raza, Ali, Franziska Roy, and Benjamin Zachariah, eds. *The Internationalist Moment: South Asia, Worlds, and World Views, 1917–1939*. Los Angeles: SAGE, 2015.

Sohi, Seema. *Echoes of Mutiny: Race, Surveillance, and Indian Anticolonialism in North America*. New York: Oxford University Press, 2014.

Tatla, Darshan Singh. *The Sikh Diaspora: Search for Statehood*. Illustrated edition. Hoboken: University of Washington Press, 1999.

Tinker, Hugh. *A New System of Slavery: The Export of Indian Labour Overseas, 1830–1920*. London & New York: Institute of Race Relations by Oxford University Press, 1974.

Ward, Peter. *White Canada Forever: Popular Attitudes and Public Policy toward Orientals in British Columbia: Popular Attitudes and Public Policy Toward Orientals.* Reprint edition. Montreal: McGill-Queen's University Press, 1990.

Zachariah, Benjamin. "Internationalisms in the Interwar Years: The Traveling of Ideas." In *The Internationalist Moment: South Asia, Worlds, and World Views, 1917–39*, 1–21. New Delhi: SAGE, 2015. https://doi.org/10.4135/9789351507994

Chapter 9

# Subjects at Sea

## *Jahaji* Relationships and Their Discontents

Samata Biswas

Amitav Ghosh might be the best known and most celebrated author currently writing about India in English.[1] Primarily a novelist, his books have received the highest literary honors in India, such as the 54th Jnanpith Award (2018), the Sahitya Akademi Award (for the 1988 novel *Shadow Lines*), and he was also shortlisted for the Man Booker, among other prizes. Since the 1980s, he has written consistently and prolifically about two of the issues that have acquired academic and critical mass in the current world: migration and climate catastrophe. His novels are always rife with historical and anthropological details, sometimes carrying bibliographies of their own, often highlighting and fictionally reconstructing some aspect of the many blind spots of history, and writing history from the margins. Migration has been a recurrent trope that enables Ghosh to write his "histories from below" (Burton 2012), investigating the human cost of empire and colonialism (Gangopadhyay 2017).

His 2008 novel, *Sea of Poppies*, is the first in the *Ibis* trilogy (*River of Smoke* and *Flood of Fire*, being the second and the third, respectively). The title of the novel indicates two important sites and tropes that it engages with—tropes that shape and change countless subcontinental lives; the sea, route for trade and traffic; and opium, that which is traded.

*Sea of Poppies* is set against the backdrop of two important exploitative phenomena in British India: the system of indentured labor export and forced cultivation of opium. The sugar plantations in the Caribbean (Jamaica,

Trinidad), Mauritius, Fiji, British Guyana, Suriname, South Africa (Natal), the French colonies at Réunion, Martinique, Guadeloupe, and plantations in Malaysia, Myanmar, and Sri Lanka were supplied with indentured laborers from the Indian subcontinent (Bates 2017), immediately following the legal termination of slavery in the British empire in 1834 (Tinker 1974). In the colonies, the workers produced sugar, coffee, tea, and rubber (Tinker 1974), and worked in mines and railway tracks. The system of indenture required the laborers to be bound by contract to provide service for a specified period of time (three, four or five years) at a location usually overseas (with the exception of the tea plantation laborers in Assam, popularly and derogatorily known as hill coolies). At the end of their service, laborers would be eligible for a free passage home. The *Ibis* trilogy does not follow the indentured workers to their destination; in *Sea of Poppies*, their recruitment from the Gangetic plains, their journey to Calcutta, and time spent in the immigration depot, and finally their sea voyage, are represented. Deeti (a Brahmin widow of an opium farmer, Hukam Singh, in Ghazipur,[2] under the rule of the East India Company) and Kalua (a "low" caste man of prodigious strength, who rescues Deeti from her immolation pyre) serve as the primary focalizers in this life-world of the indentured workers. Deeti also enables the reader to explore the world of the nineteenth-century opium farmer. Opium had been a stable crop in the Indian subcontinent since the eighth century. By the late eighteenth century, the British East India Company had monopolized the production and sales of Bengal opium, a legal business managed by government officials, which accounted for every little bit of the opium grown (Richards 1981). The farmers were often given advanced loans for cultivation, which trapped them in a web of contractual and legal obligations (Bauer 2019). But the cost of manure, rent, expenditure on hired workers, and irrigation was far higher than what could be recovered from the sale of raw opium (Biswas 2019). Deeti and her husband were victims of this exploitative system, another form of indentureship that resulted in penury, death, threats of sexual violence, and murder. Signing up to become one of the *girmitiyas* (the vernacular for indentured worker) provides for Deeti a temporary safe passage and a shot at a life outside of rigid caste structures. Historians agree that while indentured workers were primarily men, wives (often without contracts) accompanied their husbands on sea voyages, as did many single/unattached women who migrated to avoid unwanted marriages and other hardships. We shall have cause to revisit this later.

Why did the indentured workers migrate at all? Both Crispin Bates (2017) and Hugh Tinker (1974) agree that their movement overseas was part of an already established pattern of labor migration during the Mughal Empire, from what is now Bihar and Uttar Pradesh. Ashutosh Kumar draws on D.H.A. Kolff to show that peasants used to get recruited as soldiers of the Sultanate (the Delhi Sultanate reigned until 1526, and the Mughals came into power immediately afterward) (Kumar 2017). After 1857, many decommissioned soldiers, as well as soldiers whose families had lost land as punishment for participating in the revolt, entered into indentured contracts (Bates 2017). In *Sea of Poppies*, the abject poverty induced by forced opium cultivation and the prospects of sexual violence work together to make Deeti join the laborers, but she had already been aware of people moving for work—her own brother was employed as a soldier.

Historically, the events in *Sea of Poppies* are set immediately before the first Opium War (1839–1842, present in *Flood of Fire*), right after the time the first group of indentured laborers are sent to the sugar plantations in Mauritius in 1834. Central to the novel is *Ibis*, once a vessel that carried slaves, now carrying both opium and indentured laborers. The *Ibis* exists in the novel as both a physical object as well as a metaphor. The narrative comes into existence through the mental image of it: "the vision of a tall-masted ship, at sail on the ocean, came to Deeti on an otherwise ordinary day, but she knew instantly that the apparition was a sign of destiny" (Ghosh 2009, 3). Deeti would then try to draw the ship into existence, trying to explain its contours to her daughter, Kabutri. In her domestic shrine filled with line drawings of her loved ones on "papery poppy-petal discs," Deeti draws the two-masted ship with sails unfurled, and places it in the family pantheon (Ghosh 2009, 8–9). Deeti's role here is akin to that of the author, creating through signs and significations. As a physical object, *Ibis* was a "blackbirder" (Ghosh 2009), a ship used to carry enslaved persons from the West Coast of Africa into the middle passage. It was repurposed into a ship carrying indentured workers and opium, after slavery was formally abolished, making trade in slaves virtually impossible. Hugh Tinker's (1974) book compares indentured labor to slavery, calling it, "a new system of slavery." In its transformation from a slave-carrying ship to one carrying indentured workers, the narrative compares the two systems, just as Deeti learns to get familiar with the "little scratches that had been carved into [the ship's] surface by the nails of others who had lain where she lay" (Ghosh 2009, 394). John Scoble described rampant instances of kidnapping for purposes of indentureship, and said that the recruits had to be pushed onto the ships by the chowkidars (Kumar 2017, 3). Gail Omvedt and Prabhu Mohapatra follow Tinker's arguments. But many historians after Tinker have delineated the considerable differences in the conditions of the enslaved persons vis-à-vis that of the indentured workers, highlighting differences such as the permanent nature of the arrangement of slavery, which was in contrast with the temporary freezing of personal liberty of the indentured worker (8). Others have highlighted the elements of choice and agency that the indentured workers are believed to have displayed. In other instances, the role of the sirdar/maistries, or the intermediary, often a returnee recruiting people from his village/kinship networks, is seen to have worked in favor of the workers, with a larger scope of family reunification and greater mobility across plantations (Bates and Carter 2017).

My entry into the central idea of the present volume, that is, into statelessness, becomes possible through the optics of slavery and the role of intermediaries in the system of indenture. Although the notion of statelessness is integrally linked with modern nation-states—could we, as a sociological phenomenon, consider conditions of slavery to be a precursor of statelessness? Captured, bought, or abducted into slavery, forced to suffer the middle passage across the Atlantic, the enslaved persons literally and figuratively changed hands and authority, before finally being sold to one plantation owner. While the sugar plantations were often marked by absentee owners, the practical authority over the enslaved persons would be that of the manager and the overseer, who would in turn be supervised by an attorney in charge of several estates (Tinker 1974). Would the enslaved person, if she were to reside and work on a plantation owned by a British man, automatically become a British subject, although without inalienable rights? Or would her status be indeterminate, chattel-like, doomed to a continued existence as private property? In *Statelessness and Contemporary Enslavement*, Jane Gordon proposes political membership as a spectrum—with Euromodern nation-states being full members and disenfranchised groups being marked by degrees of statelessness (Gordon 2020). Gordon argues elsewhere that while there may be "crucial differences between enslavement and other fundamentally exploitative labor regimes," those differences depend on institutions that have irrevocably eroded (Gordon 2020, 155). She further traces modern forms of enslavement to the racialized forms inaugurated in the trans-Atlantic world, which have now crossed the boundaries of the trans-Atlantic region to become a global phenomenon where the already vulnerable are likely to be enslaved and made stateless—which may occur within or outside states (156–57).

During the period of indenture, how different were the indentured workers from those they had replaced in the sugar colonies, such as the enslaved persons, in terms of their rights and the authority of the bodies that conferred upon them the same rights? Throughout the nineteenth century, abolitionists in England as well as social reformers in India decried the abysmal treatment of the indentured workers, the harsh conditions of travel, the duplicity that may have made them sign up in the first place, the back-breaking labor, and the likelihood of debt traps. The indentured workers were invoked as subjects of the Government of India, whose well-being was dependent on the government's will. However, records also show that despite multiple negative reports, the plantation owners' lobbies and the government of India were keen to keep the indenture system growing with some checks and balances (Hossain 2017).

The indentured laborers were also subjects of multiple authorities: before boarding the ships they were under the guidance and rule of their recruiters; at the depot, they were dependent on the agent; and at sea, they were under the authority of the ship's captain. There is at least one instance of academic engagement with the authority of the sirdars/recruiters cum leaders operating outside the ambit of the authority of citizenship and state. In his March 2019 lecture at the Silver Jubilee celebrations of Patna's Asia Development Research Institute, Crispin Bates claims, "They [the recruiters—the intermediaries] do not fit with the modern ideas of what a free labor force should be, individuals moving as sovereign subjects within the labor market, relating directly to the employer as to the state. Intermediaries breach national boundaries and defy also territorial ideas of citizenship. They serve both the employers and labourers and they can be the butt of criticism on both sides" (Bates 2017). While I have not managed to locate a direct enunciation of this liminal and subversive position of the intermediaries in Crispin Bates's published work, this helps us in addressing the indentured laborers and those recruiting and guiding them in their employment as occupying a contested terrain in terms of their spheres of influence and subjectification, as well as of subjecthood. While not completely analogous to the modern understanding of citizenship—their position as subjects to and subjects of multiple influences enables us to enter into the discussion on sites of statelessness.

The multiple authorities that the indentured workers are subjected to at sea are summarized succinctly by the Captain of *Ibis*, conveyed to the workers via Baboo Nobo Kissin's translation: "The greatest and most important difference between land and sea is not visible to the eye. In this, and note it well . . . The difference is that the laws of land have no hold on the water. At sea there is another law and you should know that on this vessel I am its sole maker" (Ghosh 2009, 404). This law then rests on the person of the Captain, but also has nonhuman keepers—the lash and the noose. After him, Subedar Bhyro Singh (Deeti's brother-in-law) holds the authority over the *girmitiyas*; he is to be obeyed just as the laborers would "obey" their "own zeminders" (404) The authority the laborers are subjected to can be established only by invoking older forms of authority that they have left behind and by bypassing their subjectivation by the colonial government. The word "subject" carries within it both notions of subjection and subjectification where the indentured workers are both subjected to rapidly changing forms of authority. But as subjects at sea, they also create new subjectivities, as much of the critical literature on the *Sea of Poppies* points out.

Existing critical work on *Sea of Poppies* has commented on its historically accurate juxtaposition of different dialects. "Bhojpuri dialect, the shipman's lingo, commands often distorted beyond recognition when a Desi lascar shouts it, along with others like Paulette's heavily accented English, Babu Nob Kissin's pidgin English that sounds even funnier when juxtaposed with the 'propah' English spoken by characters like Mr. Burnham" (Panwar 2009, 205–8). This blend of languages makes a multiplicity of voices heard within the English that is the language of the novel. Maroua Touil considers *Sea of Poppies* a postmodern novel, characterized by its celebration of difference and blurring of hierarchical oppositions (Touil 2016). For Rudrani Gangopdhyay, the ship, *Ibis*, serves as a microcosm of what would become a full-fledged society in Mauritius, the unusual circumstances of indentureship and punishment bringing together a cross section of Indian society who would have otherwise remained strangers to each other (Gangopdhyay 2017). This creates the ship into a liminal space where a new relationship is forged, a *jahaji nata* "forged by the experience of crossing turbulent seas together" (59–60). I agree with each of these formulations and enquire closely into the construction of the new and multiple identities facilitated by the *Ibis* on the sea. *Sea of Poppies*, unlike later Ghosh novels, does not end with an annotated bibliography. The postscript, however, contains a long list of researchers whose work Ghosh is indebted to, listing all existing research in the different fields this novel traverses. Given the scope of the novel (divided into three parts: Land, River and Sea) a dramatis personae would have enabled the future critic in her job of summarizing the novel, however briefly.

At the same time as Deeti's vision of the *Ibis*, Zachary Reid, a freeman carpenter, takes charge of the vessel through circuitous means and the aid of the leader of the lascars, Serang Ali, delivering it safely to its owner, former slave-trader and current opium magnate, Benjamin Burnham. Paulette, the orphaned daughter of an unconventional French botanist is Burnham's ward and needs to escape. Jodu, the son of her wet nurse also needs to escape his penury. *Ibis* provides these means. The novel brings together merchants, indentured laborers and their guards, convicts undergoing a sentence of *kala-pani*,[3] lascars who ply their trade, one white woman trying to build an independent life in another country, and a Black man passing as white, among other characters. As mentioned above, this coming together and interaction of people from such diverse backgrounds would not have been possible in the highly stratified society of India without the extraordinary circumstances that befall most of the important characters in the novel. The same convergence of disparate and distant identities allows the narrative to underscore the idea that on board the ship, everyone, especially the marginalized, are part of a unified community of forced migrants, irrespective of the reasons behind their migration and their previous situations in life. I will tease out the tensions inherent in the creation of a homogenous migrant identity.

Baboo Nob Kissin, the wily *gomusta* traveling aboard the *Ibis*, slowly realizing his woman self, first through acts of cross dressing and then, a changed physiognomy, views the ship as a powerful force, giving birth to new identities for himself as well as for the convicts, lascars, and the immigrants. In extension, the ship serves as a powerful metaphor for the passage, the experience of forced migration, within the novel, and the craft of fiction itself, both, in several broad sweeps, obliterating difference and engendering new, multiple identities. The narrative posits the transformative potentials of the ship centrally: "the *Ibis* was not a ship like any other; in her inward reality she was a vehicle of transformation, travelling through the mists of illusion towards the elusive, ever-receding landfall that was truth" (Ghosh 2009, 422–23). In *Ibis*, Ghosh brings together multiple, historical marginalities: the widowed Hindu woman; the impoverished opium farmer; the half-caste opium addict, Ah Fatt, son of a Parsi merchant and a Chinese woman; son of a former slave Zachary Reid, now passing off as a white officer; lascars, the most ubiquitous yet most disprivileged of South Asian mariners; the single woman migrant; and the indentured workers. The ship, and the sea on which it sails, becomes a site for creation of new identities, transformation, and consequent forging of new solidarities. At the moment of *Ibis*'s sailing from Calcutta, each of the three sections containing detailed description of its movement, people's feelings, the mechanics of sails, and waves ends with a prayer, with the crucial difference that the three prayers are uttered in three different languages and express three separate religious faiths. The narrative also describes how irrespective of caste and creed all the members of the marginalized population on board join into these prayers. The prayer to the almighty, seeking safe passage across the *kala-pani*, undercuts the religious difference that would have kept the adherents of these religions separate in other circumstances.

There are detailed descriptions of individual transformations: Deeti emerges from being Kaubtri's mother to claiming a name she had forgotten—she is now Aditi; Kalua's caste markers transcend his new name, Maddow Culver; while Paulette sheds her white privilege by turning into Putlishwari, covering her head with a ghunghat and hiding her learning. For some, the transformation is more physical. Baboo Nabo Kissin, the native official performing multiple duties, actually notices his own bodily transformation. His spiritual leader, Taramony, is manifesting herself in his body, through growing hair, developing breasts, and an irritable bowel. In Nabo Kissin's imagination, Zachary's transformation must also be the same: originally designated as Black, but marked by his light skin, Zachary must also be transforming like the Hindu god Krishna, and on the ship, displaying one of his many avatars. Neel, a high-caste landlord extremely mindful of caste-based notions of purity and pollution, is transformed into the caregiver of his fellow convict and cellmate, cleaning and feeding him. He had been brought up "to regard his body and its functions with a fastidiousness that bordered almost on the occult" (Ghosh 2009, 198). As a convict, he is first made to face the ignominy of a strip search, and then, on the ship, in his narrow cell with Ah Fatt, he is faced with a body "so thickly mired in dirt that it was impossible to tell whether the man was naked or clothed" (315). Neel's transformation also involves transcending the disgust that had been his prerogative as a high-caste zamindar, a disgust that when aimed at "low"-caste bodies, ensured the maintenance of the hierarchy whose beneficiary Neel was.

These diverse transformations also serve to unite the ones who are being transformed (with the exception of Zachary, who occupies a tenuous position of power, albeit under the dubious control of Serang Ali, the master lascar who has made his authority possible). It is possible to somewhat neatly divide the population aboard the ship along the lines of the oppressor and the oppressed. The indentured laborers have been brought to the ship under the sometimes brutal authority of the maistries. On board the ship, the Subehdar will be their *mai-baap* (mother and father). The convicts are at the mercy of their guards, and the lascars at the behest of the high-ranking officers. It is possible to map the oppositions set up in the novel in the following manner: the colonized versus the colonizers; the lascars versus the officers; the convicts versus the guards; and finally, the indentured workers versus the laborers. The alignment of different sections of the oppressed against the oppressors (again of diverse identities) is crucial in framing the migrants as a unified whole, whose fortunes are inexorably linked to that of the ship. Oppression is widespread in the novel, as is the systematic exploitation of the farmers by the opium traders and their arm, the colonial government. The intricate web of money lenders, the requirement of opium in the absence of food crops, and the alienation of the producers from their produce are all represented in great detail in the novel. But the attention with which poverty as systemic is represented is not replicated in the representation of the role that landed Indian upper-caste aristocrats played in its production. On one hand, the division between the migrants is elided upon (men and women of different castes seem to be on equal footing), and on the other, the Indian gentry (here represented in the person of Neel) is absolved of its responsibility in the production of marginalization by making its sole representative extraordinarily sensitive, learned, and learning. Within the novel, a certain section of the natives is directly responsible for the miseries of the migrants: some who were instrumental in getting them to sign up and others who are the guards who treat them unkindly. But this conflict of interests does not find an easy expression. In fact, it gets congealed within the person of one or two exceptionally villainous characters, leaving the others free of blame. There is a function that portraying a few characters with all villainies performs: in the narrative's moral universe, most characters continue to be free of blame, and forge solidarities with each other easily. This solidarity is expressed evocatively by Paulette/ Putlishwari/ Pugli: "On a boat of pilgrims, no one can lose caste and everyone is the same: it's like taking a boat to the temple of Jagannath, in Puri. From now on, and forever afterwards, we will all be ship-siblings—*jahaz-bhais* and *jahaz-behns*—to each other. There'll be no differences between us" (Ghosh 2009, 356).

The novel repeatedly celebrates multiple identities: be it that of a Black carpenter who, mistaken as white, becomes the second mate of a ship; that of a simultaneously religious and money-minded native official who embraces his guru's manifestation in his body, both materially and spiritually; an upper-caste landlord who goes through various degradations before learning to care for his fellow convict, and so forth. An upper-caste widow emerges as the leader of her new community with a new caste identity. The ship then, as mentioned in the beginning, is a metaphor for both the physical journey as well as a shared experience of oppression and lack, which, together with physical and mental hardship, engender a new community, that of the ship brotherhood/sisterhood.

The inclusivity of marginalized identities forms another insistent feature of the novel. In Canton (where the next part of the trilogy is set and the destination of the opium trade that informs the novel and its economy), not all foreigners are excluded from the forbidden city, as Neel's fellow convict Ah Fatt informs him. Without fail, the foreigners kept out are the Americans, the Europeans, and the Parsis, owners and employees of Opium trading houses. In short, the Fanquis: the aliens. The outsiders who nevertheless are present within the gates of the city are Javanese, Malayalis, Malays, and Black hat Arabs (Ghosh 2009, 377). Representatives from nations and nationalities all besieged by Western imperialism and capital find space and perhaps a common cause with the Chinese fighting opium. The Lascars are another similar case in point: "they came from spaces that were far apart, and had nothing in common, except the Indian Ocean; among them were the Chinese and east Africans, Arabs and Malays, Bengalis and Goans, Tamils and Arakanese" (13). In their shared occupation and dedication to the Serang, and not least in the pidgin they speak in, the Lascars are, in the novel, the quintessential representatives of this new migrant community, and narratively, its helpers.

At the end of the novel, the reader sees Jodu (an orphaned Bengali Muslim boatman), Neel (erstwhile landowner, avid practitioner of the caste system, and caregiver of his fellow convict), Ah Fatt (the illegitimate son of a Parsi businessman in Canton, a convict, and an opium addict to boot), Kalua (a *chamar* ox cart driver of enormous strength, who rescued Deeti from her *Sati*-pyre), and Serang Ali (the leader of the Lascars, of indeterminate origin and background) escape from the *Ibis*. The group that looks on in farewell is equally motley: Paulette, Baboo Nob Kissin, Deeti, and Zachary (with their origins and occupations as widely different as the one before). But in spite of their differences, both of these groups can come together due to some shared experiences of dispossession, difficulty, and their migration from the familiar and the familial, and their marginality.

In spite of the differences in their identities, some common factors help create a group out of them. Dispossession, threat to personhood and bodies, lack of wellbeing, or simply gullibility is cited as the reason behind the migrants signing up for the trip to Mauritius. In "Refugees, Forced Resettlers and 'Other Forced Migrants,'" David Turton argues for "focusing on forced migrants as 'purposive actors' or 'ordinary people' " (Turton 2003, 10), while cautioning about thinking of them as "identical members of homogeneous categories" (Turton 2003, 11). This is a caution we will do well to follow with respect to the *Sea of Poppies*. Without exception, immigrant women in the novel are on the ship owing to matters sexual, some thwarted, some forced upon, and some in anticipation. Hence, even within their shared marginalization, the agency of the women on the ship is determined by their sexualities, whereas the men's is not. After Deeti's husband Hukam Singh's death, she would have been forced to sleep with her brother-in-law to ensure her survival. She had already been raped on her wedding night, which resulted in Kabutri's birth. Before being rescued by Kalua, she had been set on a funeral pyre, the just reward for "chaste" wives. Heeru had been taken to a fair at Sonepur and abandoned by her husband, who remarried after deserting her. Munia had been courted by a pykari agent of the opium factory at Gazipur, who eventually raped her. The child born out of this violence was burned alive along with Munia's parents, forcing her to leave in search of employment in Mareech, tracing a trajectory her brothers had followed earlier. As Burnham's ward, Paulette was invited to his chambers regularly, where he would read her passages from the Bible and then encourage her to hit him on the buttocks in lieu of chastisement, completely overlooking the acute discomfort this sado-masochistic ritual caused her. The fictional resolution to contested sexualities offered by the novel, that is, migration, nevertheless occurs within the limits of this contestation and never transgresses it. Crucial twists in the plot are brought to a head by questions of desire and operations of power that seek to discipline women's bodies.

The narrative also disciplines marginal and subversive bodies, bodies that do not conform to the heteronorm, like Baboo Nobo Kissin, the cross-dressing *gomusta* slowly becoming a woman. Despite being wily, intelligent, kind, as well as manipulative, Nobo Kissin is an object of ridicule. While Ah Fatt's incontinence with respect to his bowel is treated kindly by the narrative voice and with care by Neel, Nobo Kissin's inability is portrayed in a flippant manner. The first mate, Mr. Crowle, is cruel and responsible for humiliating both the laborers and the convicts. But his death is a result of the transference of his unrequited desire for Zachary into extreme aggression. He tells Zachary, "All ye'd have to do is cross the caddy from time to time. That isn't so long a walk, is it? . . . Comes a day, Mannikin, when every Tar has t'learn t'work ship in headwinds and bad weather" (Ghosh 2009, 508). He tries to pass off his desire as a rite of passage for seamen and a price for keeping his mouth shut about Zachary's race. But faced with Zachary's rejection, his knife falters, and he exclaims, "God damn yer eyes, Reid!" (Ghosh 2009, 510) and has to die. The extreme physical and emotional proximity that the two convicts share is wondered upon by the narrative, but not treated homosocially. Perhaps the slightest hint of homosexual desire within the novel's universe of sexual politics would have precluded their possibility of rescue. On the other hand, heterosexual love moves the plot forward. Deeti is saved by Kalua twice: once from being burned alive and again from a violent rape. Paulette manages to divert Zachary's attention by feigning intimacy, so that the escapees succeed. However, in spite of being crucial to the movement of the plot, and in fact, being the one who conjures the entire novel into being with her line images of the important characters and the ship, Deeti has no place in the final action. The crossdresser, the French woman who wants to roam freely like men, and the pregnant woman look on as the rest of the central characters embark upon a new adventure.

Sexuality bubbles over *Sea of Poppies* in abuses, references, songs, and celebrations. Through its deviations from the norm, as well as its acceptance of the heteronorm, sexuality provides impetus to the plot and carries the action forward. But as Serang Ali instructs Zachary, "What for wanchi flower-girl? He not big pukka sahib now?" (Ghosh 2009, 22), the resolution, at least in this part of the trilogy, has to be brought about through a disavowal of women's sexuality. It has to be built by the actions of marginalized men, even as women or those wanting to be women, look on.

This tension, about women indentured laborers, governed much of Indian reformist and nationalist thought across the nineteenth and twentieth centuries. Brij Lal's "Kunti's Cry: Indentured Women in Fiji Plantations" narrates the incident of Overseer Cobcroft's attack on Kunti while she had been sent to work alone on a patch of isolated land as punishment. Kunti managed to run away and report the attack (Lal 1985). This 1913 incident was widely covered in Indian newspapers, which prompted the Government of India to try to expose the event as a fabrication. Through the inquiry and reportage surrounding Kunti's experience, Brij Lal shows the widespread stereotyping of indentured female workers as mercenaries, "who were responsible for all the major social and moral ills in plantation society" (Lal 1985, 56). While historical evidence showed that women of all castes and religions emigrated under the indentureship system, colonial officials nevertheless designated the migrant women as belonging to the low caste and having a "loose" character, having neither ties of religion nor of family to stop them from falling into the "depths of degradation and vice" (Lal 1985, 58). The kind of women being recruited for indentureship was a cause of concern for the colonial government, located in the tension between the planters' desire for short-term adult male workers versus the need to create self-sustaining, cheap, and stable laboring communities. For this purpose, there was a need to find the "right kind of women"—docile, secluded, controllable (Reddock 2008, 44).

Tejaswini Niranjana, in "Indian Nationalism and Female Sexuality," looks at the changing government-mandated ratio of men and women as a testimony to growing colonial and nationalist anxiety over the status of women indentured workers in the colonies. Between 1857 and 1879, the recommended ratio changed multiple times, from 1:3 to 1:2 to 1:4, in an attempt to ensure that the "right kind of women" (as Reddock has already described above) get recruited and there is an end to polyandry as well as wife murders (Niranjana 2011). A labor recruiter in Suriname wrote about the laughable prospect of a bunch of dancing girls who had come over as indentured workers—Mohammed Orfy considered the women to have "absolutely no knowledge whatever of the value of being in virginhood" (quoted in Reddock 2020, 44). Gandhi in *Indenture or Slavery* writes, "Women, who in India would never touch wine, are sometimes found lying dead-drunk on the roads" (Niranjana 2011). Dwarakanath Ganguly and Ramkumara Bidyaratna raised concerns of sexual violence and immorality regarding the hill coolies, or Adivasi indentured workers, in the tea plantations of Assam. In *Sea of Poppies*, there is also a similar moral and social concern with the bodies of women—with their sexualities and the narrative functions they fulfill.

*Sea of Poppies* celebrates the unity of the migrants and of the dispossessed, locating in the ship and at sea, both solidarity and subjectivity. But in doing so, it continues to harbor an uneasy relationship with women's bodies and sexualities, concerns that had constructed the fulcrum of much of the nationalist engagement with indentured workers. In the novel, each of the women migrants has displayed agential action, they take decisions to migrate, act on their desire, and intervene on behalf of others. Gauitra Bahadur's *Coolie Woman: The Odyssey of Indenture* presents a picture that sheds more light on this situation. In trying to trace the roots of her great grandmother Sujaria, a single Brahmin woman migrant to Guyana, who gave birth to her son on the ship, Bahadur finds that even before Sujaria was recruited on the day that the ship was to set sail, she had left her native village for work (Bahadur 2014). While there were debates about laws preventing married women from abandoning their families and signing up as indentured workers, the reality for women like Sujaria was that they were often married off as children, and continued to live lives of degradation. For some—widows, abandoned woman, and those who escaped unhappy/violent marriages—indentureship provided a way out, something the colonial government was keen to stop (Bahadur 2014).That is the case for the *Sea of Poppies* as well! But narratively, the novel's conclusion leaves the women behind, trapped in their bodies, trapped in narratives more than a hundred years old.

## Postscript

Since the title of my chapter is "Subjects at Sea," I have paid no attention to the characters who do not participate in the sea voyage. Such an outlier is Elokeshi, a name drawn from the young bride murdered by her husband, Nobin, upon accusations of her infidelity by a powerful religious leader (Mohanto) of the Hindu holy place, Tarakeshwar. The criminal case came up for hearing in 1873, in which the husband was acquitted by the local courts. Elokeshi lived on in popular plays, paintings, and artifacts (Sarkar 2001). In *Sea of Poppies*, Elokeshi is the name of Neel's mistress, a professional courtesan, proficient in music, dance, and the erotic arts. Neel loses interest in his business while languishing, literally trapped in Elokeshi's saree and dupatta, in a post-coital haze. He heaps property and jewels on her, only to be betrayed into imprisonment and transport across the dark waters. Tanika Sarkar in *Hindu Wife, Hindu Nation* locates Hindu revivalist anxieties in the enthusiastic support Elokeshi's husband received from the native population, even after her most gruesome murder. The bodies of women were the last remnants of native patriarchal authority, the wife's chastity and fidelity protecting the Hindu man from every other sphere where he had already lost control to colonial authorities. She also comments on the absence of Elokeshi, the dual victim of seduction by a man in a position of authority and spousal violence, from the debates of the time. It is simply not possible that Amitav Ghosh chose the name Elokeshi for Neel's mistress arbitrarily. Elokeshi's sexuality and betrayal go hand in hand in *Sea of Poppies*—awakening Neel to the recognition of his wife's worth and the importance of family. Elokeshi, although not aboard the ship, joins the migrant women in the novel in the way her actions are determined by her sexuality. This prompts me to wonder about the location of women as rights-bearing citizens—subject both to patriarchal and colonial authority at the same time. Despite their differences in status and action, Elokeshi and her indentured counterparts may well have been comrades, stateless in a country for no women.

## Notes

1. A much shorter version of this chapter was presented as part of a workshop titled "Interrogating Forced Migration," organized by Mahanirban Calcutta Research Group in collaboration with MAKAIAS, ICSSR, and Taft Foundation, in March 2015. A portion of the same was published on the forced migration blog, Refugee Watch Online. The present version builds on its earlier self, and has been greatly impacted by the comments of Prof. Lydia Potts.

2. In northern Bihar, 400 miles from the coast of the Bay of Bengal.

3. Punishment by deportation across the dark waters, that is, the seas. Considered one of the most stringent forms of punishment for orthodox Hindus, as crossing the seas entailed a fall from the hierarchical caste structure.

## References


Bahadur, Gaiutra. *Coolie Woman: The Odyssey of Indenture*. Chicago: University of Chicago Press, 2014. https://press.uchicago.edu/ucp/books/book/chicago/C/bo13393932.html

Bates, Crispin. "Migration in the Time of Empire." *Open Democracy*. December 12, 2017. www.opendemocracy.net/en/beyond-trafficking-and-slavery/migration-in-time-of-empire

Bates, Crispin, and Marina Carter. "Sirdars as Intermediaries in Nineteenth-Century Indian Ocean Indentured Labour Migration." *Modern Asian Studies* 51, no. 2 (2017): 462–84. https://doi.org/10.1017/S0026749X16000238

Bates, Crispin. Silver Jubilee Lecture 16. Adri Silver Jubilee Celebrations, 2017. www.youtube.com/watch?v=0eQnELwot58

Bauer, Rolf. *The Peasant Production of Opium in Nineteenth-Century India*. Library of Economic History, volume 12. Leiden & Boston: Brill, 2019.

Biswas, Soutik. "How Britain's Opium Trade Impoverished Indians." *BBC News*, September 5, 2019, sec. India. www.bbc.com/news/world-asia-india-49404024

Burton, Antoinette. "Amitav Ghosh's World Histories from Below." *History of the Present* 2, no. 1 (2012): 71–77. https://doi.org/10.5406/historypresent.2.1.0071

Gangopadhyay, Rudrani. "Finding Oneself on Board the Ibis in Amitav Ghosh's Sea of Poppies." *WSQ: Women's Studies Quarterly* 45, no. 1–2 (2017): 55–64. https://doi.org/10.1353/wsq.2017.0012

Ghosh, Amitav. *Sea of Poppies*. London: John Murray, 2009.

Gordon, Jane Anna. *Statelessness and Contemporary Enslavement*. London & New York: Routledge, 2020.

———. "Critical Allies: On Contemporary Enslavement and Statelessness." *Statelessness & Citizenship Review* 2, no. 1 (2020): 153–58.

Hossain, Purba. "Protests at the Colonial Capital: Calcutta and the Global Debates on Indenture, 1836–42." *South Asian Studies* 33, no. 1 (2017): 37–51. https://doi.org/10.1080/02666030.2017.1297054

Kumar, Ashutosh. *Coolies of the Empire: Indentured Indians in the Sugar Colonies, 1830–1920*. Cambridge: Cambridge University Press, 2017. https://doi.org/10.1017/9781316556627

Lal, Brij V. "Kunti's Cry: Indentured Women on Fiji Plantations." *The Indian Economic & Social History Review* 22, no. 1 (1985): 55–71. https://doi.org/10.1177/001946468502200103

Niranjana, Tejaswini. In *Sex and the Citizen: Interrogating the Caribbean*, edited by Faith Smith. New World Studies. Charlottesville: University of Virginia Press, 2011.

Panwar, Purabi. "Saga of Colonialism." *Indian Literature* 53, no. 3(251) (2009): 205–8. http://www.jstor.org/stable/23340337

Reddock, Rhoda. "Indian Women and Indentureship in Trinidad and Tobago 1845–1917: Freedom Denied." *Caribbean Quarterly* 54, no. 4 (2008): 41–68. https://doi.org/10.1080/00086495.2008.11829735

———. "The Indentureship Experience: Indian Women in Trinidad and Tobago." In *Women Plantation Workers: International Experiences*, edited by Shobita Jain and Rhoda Reddock, 29–48. London & New York: Routledge, 2020.

Richards, J. F. "The Indian Empire and Peasant Production of Opium in the Nineteenth Century." *Modern Asian Studies* 15, no. 1 (1981): 59–82.

Sarkar, Tanika. "Talking about Scandals: Religion, Law and Love in Late Nineteenth Century Bengal." In *Hindu Wife, Hindu Nation: Community, Religion, and Cultural Nationalism*. Bloomington: Indiana University Press, 2001.

Tinker, Hugh. *A New System of Slavery: The Export of Indian Labour Overseas, 1830–1920*. London & New York: published for the Institute of Race Relations by Oxford University Press, 1974.

Touil, Maroua. "The Endless Process of Becoming and the Transformation of Identity in Amitav Ghosh's Sea of Poppies." *International Journal of Humanities and Cultural Studies (IJHCS)* 1, no. 4 (2016): 516–23.

Turton, David. "Refugees, Forced Resettlers and 'Other Forced Migrants': Towards a Unitary Study of Forced Migration." UN High Commissioner for Refugees (UNHCR), 2003. www.refworld.org/docid/4ff2afa93b8.html

Chapter 10

# Governing Migrant Mobilities in the Aegean Sea

## From Moral Rhetoric to Blatant Use of Violence

Sibel Karadağ

On the night of August 2018, we, as the volunteers in rescue operations on the northern shore of the island of Lesbos, received a WhatsApp message from the Hellenic Coast Guard (HCG) that read: "Twenty-two migrants are detected in Efthalou [the northern shore of Lesbos] and stopped while they were walking on the roads. Get prepared and approach to the location." When we arrived at the specified location, we found twenty-two people sitting on the sidewalk with their clothes wet and looking around with scared eyes. As is usually the case, none of them spoke English. A Greek port police officer asked me to learn the details of their journey and how they ended up on the roads of Efthalou. Throughout my fieldwork, I translated between migrants, most of whom understood Turkish due to having spent time in Turkey, and border officials/rescue humanitarians, thanks to my Turkish and English. They were all Afghans. The group had left the Turkish shores ten hours earlier, reached the northern shores of Lesbos, got off the boat by themselves, and started walking on the island. "We were twenty-four at the beginning, but two middle-aged men decided to leave the group and went another direction. I have no idea where they are now," said one of them (2018). When I translated them to the port police and Frontex personnel, a call for an "emergency situation" was given, and all of us (including HCG, Frontex, member of UNHCR, and rescue humanitarians) started to search for and "rescue" the two men who had left the group in the northern part of the island more than three hours earlier. Shortly after, we found them in an open restaurant where they were eating by the time we arrived. The two men were taken to the transit/temporary camp in our village (Sikamineas) where I accompanied their documentation and transfer to the main camp of Moria the next morning. This whole process was called a "rescue operation" by both the armed forces and rescue humanitarians.

On March 21, 2020,[1] a group of thirty-one Syrians (16 men, 3 women, 12 children) left Turkish shores on a rubber boat and arrived at the Greek island of Symi without being intercepted. They climbed the hills and walked alongside roads in search of the authorities to submit their asylum request. After they had walked for six hours, the Greek police spotted them and detained the group on an unofficial site for two days without documenting them or providing first aid or food. Even worse, their personal possessions, including phones, passports, identification documents, money, and medication, were permanently confiscated. On March 23, they boarded a military ship where armed authorities in masks told them they would be taken to Athens to apply for asylum. It did not take long for the migrants to realize this was not the case. The military vessel anchored in the middle of the Aegean waters, and the group was pushed by batons to jump into a three-meter-long, orange, inflatable life raft with no engine. The raft is originally designed to save lives in the rescue operation. After their dangerous jump into this floating tent on the waves, the group was abandoned to the currents of the Aegean. After hours of helpless waiting in the middle of the water, they were found by the Turkish Coast Guard (TCG).[2]

These two representative cases reveal not only the political technologies generated to monitor, police, capture, contain, and expel clandestine migrant mobilities at sea, which, at times, were adorned with humanitarian rhetoric, but also the changes and new technologies deployed as a tactic for border enforcement. Interrogating the web of discourses, border practices, and novel political technologies constituting the political space of the Aegean Sea, this chapter generates insights into the ways of governing and policing human movements at sea, which constantly reproduce certain modes of statelessness. Additionally, the aim is to approach the issue by presenting its historical development since the mass refugee movement of 2015. It is elucidated in the chapter that, until 2020, the main mode of governance in the Aegean, covered by the moral rhetoric of rescue, was the moderated violence of interception, whether to stop, pull, or push back the migrant boat. However, this has transformed into a brutal and fatal use of violence through the introduction of carceral spaces as a new infrastructure of expulsion since the year 2020. By paying particular attention to the specificities of the Aegean Sea, which has received relatively less academic attention compared to the Central Mediterranean in the European context, the extensive empirical analysis elaborates on how spatial and judicial configurations of the sea lead to certain power projections and political technologies in the case of the Aegean.

The chapter is organized into three main parts. First, the distinctive semi-closed geophysicality of the Aegean Sea will be elaborated by mapping out its spatial and juridical configuration, which leads to specific border practices. Second, the changing infrastructures and political technologies seeking to deter, discipline, and police the migrant mobilities in Turkey and Greece will be empirically analyzed, along with the everyday practices of pushback from 2015 onward. Third, a novel infrastructure and technology of expulsion will be addressed in relation to the transformation of the political space both at sea and on land in the Aegean region since Turkey's announcement of opening its borders for migrants to cross into Europe in March 2020. With that, a new technique of using life rafts, which I call *floating carceral spaces*, has been put into practice as a necropolitical intervention in the Aegean Sea. The chapter draws upon ethnographic research carried out for three years (2015–2018) across the two sides of the Aegean, in Turkey and Greece (Lesbos), including participant observation in Search and Rescue operations of a local NGO in northern Lesbos (Skala Sikamineas). Participant observation is accompanied by interviews (84) with the actors in the Aegean Sea, including the Hellenic and Turkish coast guards, the Frontex personnel, and the rescue NGOs. In addition, the recent developments in the Aegean are kept up to date by means of subsequent field visits to the coastal cities of Turkey in 2020.

## Spatial and Judicial Configuration of the Aegean Sea

Manifestations of disciplining human mobility on seas and oceans are neither recent phenomena nor specific to the European context. Ships as an infrastructure incarcerating and transporting African bodies across the Atlantic to the Americas played a key role in shaping the history of colonial expansion, expropriation, and accordingly capitalism from the seventeenth century onward (Bose 2009; Benton 2009; Gilroy 2003; Rediker 2008; Mawani 2018; Samaddar 2020). In the last decade, when the European external seascape started to witness ever-increasing migrant crossings, the Mediterranean Sea has become a contested space in which the European externalized border politics are enacted and expanded while certain configurations of forms of violence are projected mostly onto migrant bodies, consequently turning the sea into a "death world" (Mbembé 2003). In the Mediterranean context, a recent body of work critically examines the forms of statelessness at sea that are crystallized into conflicting state jurisdictions, ambiguous spatialities, and jurisdictional regimes. Thus, the "patchy legal space" has resulted in a systematic violence of irresponsibility, nonaction, and *letting boat people to die* (Heller, Pezzani, and Situ Studio 2012; Heller and Pezzani 2014; Stierl 2016; Casas-Cortés et al. 2017; Cuttitta 2018; Davies, Isakjee, and Dhesi 2017; Cuttitta and Last 2020). More recently, studies on *offshore carcerality* in the Mediterranean investigate how rescue ships turn into confinement spaces for migrants at sea due to the ban on disembarking (Stierl 2021). When we pay particular attention to the Aegean Sea, though the watery and liquid space of the sea has certain modes of governance in common with the Mediterranean, it is still possible to distinguish the Aegean due to its spatial and judicial context.

The scope of the Aegean Sea surface, its insular geography, and the proximity between territorial waters have a decisive impact on the art of governance and the juridical distribution of the space. The Aegean Sea is a unique, semi-closed geography with an extremely complicated insular dispersion. There are numerous insular features scattered throughout the small geography of the Aegean, some of which are islands while others are small islets and rocks. In contrast to the geophysicality of the Central Mediterranean, there is no high sea between the Greek islands targeted by the migrants (Lesbos, Samos, Kos, and Chios) and Turkish coasts, given the short distance (around six miles). Since Turkey is not a party to the 1982 Law of the Sea, the two states adopt the principle of midline *de facto* for territorial partition.

First, due to the lower volume of the sea and the proximity, clandestine migrant boats and patrol vessels are smaller than their counterparts in the Mediterranean. Both the Hellenic and Turkish Coast Guards, as well as Frontex, use small speed boats through which they carry out systematic acts of pullbacks and pushbacks thanks to their high maneuver capacity. Second, the two neighboring territorial waters (Turkey and the Greek islands) are distributed based on the principle of equal division due to the lack of geographical Search and Rescue (SAR) zones. The absence of high seas between Lesbos and Turkish shores is what distinguishes the Aegean case from the highly multitudinous and complex maritime legal space of the Mediterranean. As numerous studies discuss within the context of the

Mediterranean, SAR zones represent "uncertain sovereignties" (Cuttitta 2018) and "patchy" jurisdictional regimes (Heller and Pezzani 2014) where states elude their rescue responsibility and pass it on to others. What is different in the Aegean case is that both the states (Greece and Turkey) pursue an interceptionalist approach rather than a politics of nonaction. In this context, the notion of "distress" becomes an effective source of legitimacy for intercepting the boats on the sea. The moment a dingy leaves the Turkish shores, people on the boat are considered as the ones in danger and the ones who "need to be searched and rescued" (Frontex Personnel interview 2017). The strategy of intercepting in the guise of rescue as a moderated violence is produced and materialized in different manners in Turkey and Greece, as will be discussed in the upcoming sections. This interpretation obviously bears a humanitarian claim; however, in reality, it simultaneously lays the ground for practices of interception and justifies the operations of armed forces under the pretext of rescue. The next section will elaborate on the border and humanitarian actors operating in and constituting the political space of the Aegean. The organizational structure of border governance in Turkey and Greece has differences due to their composition of actors. In addition to that, the section traces the changes on the Greek side, particularly since 2020.

## A Trend toward Further Centralized and Militarized Monitoring

The Turkish and Hellenic Coast Guards are the primary actors in the governance of migration in the Aegean. Since 2015 and until 2020, as opposed to the sole authority of the TCG, multiple actors were involved on the Greek side, namely, the EU border agency—Frontex and the rescue NGOs, ProActiva Open Arms that left in 2017, and Refugee Rescue/Mo Chara whose operations were terminated in 2020. The year 2020 marks a critical juncture in transforming the political space of the Aegean. Until that year, there were different organizational structures on both sides of the Aegean, with Turkey having a highly centralized infrastructure compared to its counterpart.

Until 2020, the Greek side participated in joint operations with the HCG and Frontex, as well as permitting the involvement of rescue humanitarians, albeit with certain restrictions in the field, whereas the TCG has been the one and only authorized body in Turkish territorial waters. As of

July 25, 2016, four months after the EU–Turkey Statement, the Turkish Coast Guard Command was taken under the control of the Ministry of Interior and became a part of the general armed law enforcement. This structural change was followed by the foundation of the Aegean Sea Region Command in 2016. With its Regional Operational Center (ROC) located in İzmir, the Command started to control and govern the whole Aegean coastline of Turkey from Çanakkale to Muğla (Turkish Coast Guard interview 2018). The emergence of the operational center represents Turkey's post-2016 tendency toward an overcentralized governing technology in border management. As TCG explains:

> The operational center can observe the whole map of the Aegean. The data of mobile radars enable to scan the whole horizon along the whole length of the Aegean coastline. The operational coordinator at the center designates the schedule of patrolling and rescue operations. The center directs us when there is a case and says the exact coordination that we shall target. The ROC monitors the whole schedule, location and coordination of coast guard boats in the Aegean. When there is an order from the center, the particular closest unit approaches to the case in 5 minutes. (Turkish Coast Guard interview 2018)

The infrastructure of the entire surveillance system in the Aegean is connected to this main center. To capture a better vision of the Aegean, the coastal districts are additionally reinforced with mobile radars in the form of vans equipped with thermovision cameras (thermovision vans—TVVs) scanning the horizon, sorting out the "bad guys" from the "good" ones in the dense traffic. Considering the information overload coming from all sorts of vessels in the Aegean, automated technological apparatuses were installed (e.g., an algorithm that automatically detects "anomalies" and "threats" from maritime metadata). By scanning the surface of the sea, the algorithm detects "moving things" that are unregistered and without light. The entire surveillance system, consisting of the data from satellite receivers and the imagery generated by the TVVs in various coastal districts, is gathered in the Regional Operation Center (ROC) in İzmir. Meanwhile, the ROC has not only a total vision of the Aegean coastline but also centralized authority in scheduling the patrolling shifts and coordinates of coast guards, which indicates vertical governance in its operations. From the moment a dingy that takes off from the Turkish coast is detected by the radar algorithms visualized and gathered in the operational center, the commander verifies the exact coordination and then orders the responsible unit to engage (or not) with the dingy (Turkish Coast Guard interview 2018).

The affiliation to the Ministry of Interior facilitated the radical structural changes in the organizational body of the TCG. Since 2016, it has gradually become the all-encompassing unit in border management in the Aegean. This centralized role simultaneously excludes all non-state actors, except members of the International Organization for Migration (IOM), from the border zone. As the IOM staff are not allowed to partake in patrolling, rescue, landing (provision of first aid and basic needs), or documentation, they are merely authorized to cover the expenses of provision distributions at the port. In this setting, the involvement of non-state actors in the Turkish border space is foreclosed.

Throughout my ethnography, I visited four coast guard units in Turkey along the Aegean coastline (Küçükkuyu, Dikili, Çeşme, and Bodrum) several times, and did interviews with forty-four members of the TCG, including the commander at ROC. In these interviews, I constantly came across how the TCG displays its "superior operational capacity" vis-à-vis the European "other" (Karadağ 2019). In their projection, the vertical composition of the ROC and its monopoly on the surveillance of the Aegean are indicative of their superiority as opposed to multitudinous and "jumbled," to quote them, environment in Greece.

The multiplicity of actors composed of the rescue NGOs on the Greek side continued to be present until March 2020. Furthermore, unlike the highly centralized structure of Turkey's border control, the Greek/EU side has relied on a more localized and horizontal organizational infrastructure in the islands, which is still the case. Although the local headquarters are in charge of scheduling the patrolling shifts and monitoring the division of labor between the HCG and the Frontex, the data gathered from radar systems is directed to the boat on the ground rather than being concentrated in the hands of a single operational center. In contrast to Turkey, the boat crew has direct communication with TVVs situated on the hills of Lesbos (Frontex Personnel interview 2017). When these TVVs spot an "anomaly," the coordinates are sent to the closest patrolling boat to take the necessary action. "In each Frontex boat, we have a Greek liaison officer, this is the law because they [the Frontex] are not in their countries, and they do not have enforcement power" says the HCG to highlight the hierarchy of authorization, and adds: "So, the Greek officer gives them the enforcement power—we just make patrolling plan and they follow it" (Hellenic Coast Guard interview 2017).

When a boat is spotted, the closest patrolling boat (the HCG or the Frontex) approaches the dingy and stops it by using various techniques. After interception, they transfer migrants to their own patrolling boats and bring them to the shores of Lesbos to disembark. There are two locations of disembarkation on the island: Mytilene (the capital) and Skala Sikamineas in the north. During the approach of the patrolling boat carrying migrants to the port, the land crew of the rescue NGOs stands ready to provide first aid and basic needs (rescue blankets to prevent hypothermia, water, etc.) and accompany the boarding of migrants on the UNHCR buses, which take them to the temporary camp in Skala Sikamineas (see figure 10.1). The whole process, called "landing," is carried out by the NGO workers and with the NGO's own budget. During each landing, I took part as a volunteer in Skala Sikamineas for two years, while the Greek port police, the HCG, and the Frontex members were simply passive observers inspecting the whole process, which was again unlike the case of the TCG. They often intervened in succinct fashion, using a strict voice and top-down manner to discipline migrants (and occasionally volunteers). While the rescue NGOs

Figure 10.1. The boats of Refugee Rescue/Mo Chara and ProActiva leave the port to approach the boat on the sea, Skala Sikamineas. Author photo.

were the only subjects handling the entire process at the port, they also had relatively limited authorization at sea. They were allowed to carry out boat exercises within time periods determined daily by the HCG: they had to inform the HCG as soon as they spotted a dingy, and they could not approach the dingy without permission. Nevertheless, their presence as a civilian actor and a witness on the sea enabled both the archival and revelation of violent acts of the armed forces against migrants despite increasing restrictions and criminalization.

As the anecdote at the beginning indicates, the rescue NGOs were active in daily cases both on land and at sea. In general, volunteers were not notified when a pushback was to take place, but they still had opportunities to record and archive some of the cases while they were at sea. On the other hand, they were in charge of providing aid during the "landing," running the temporary camp, and transferring migrants to the camp of Moria (see figure 10.2).

On February 27, the Turkish President intensified his exploitative bargaining to obtain Western approval of his military operations in northern Syria. In order to do that, he announced that Turkey would no longer prevent migrants from reaching Europe (İşleyen and Karadağ 2023). Right after

Figure 10.2. A night at which I was in the kitchen preparing dinner for more than fifty people in the temporary camp, called Stage 2, Skala Sikamineas. Author photo.

the announcement, thousands of people rushed to Turkey's Pazarkule border gate in Edirne, located at the Greek–Turkish border, and to the Evros River. As a result, an estimated 12,000–25,000 asylum-seekers and migrants from twenty-nine nationalities gathered at the border-crossing points in Edirne (International Organization for Migration 2020; UNHCR 2020). Greek's immediate response was to consolidate and militarize its land border and to suspend all new asylum applications.

The reflections of these events on the Aegean Sea were considerable. The anti-immigrant discourse exacerbated in the islands; the NGOs operating on the island since 2015 were attacked almost on a daily basis;[3] the temporary camp in the village of Sikamineas, which I helped run (see figure 10.2), was burned down by masked individuals in May 2020; the last remaining NGO, Refugee Rescue/Mo Chara,[4] could not stand the pressure and had to terminate its operations; dozens of volunteers were accused of spying and disclosing state secrets;[5] and finally, the main camp of Moria was burned down due to fatal COVID-19 conditions, and the asylum seekers in the camp were transferred to a new camp situated at the edge of the island by the sea, which is surveilled around the clock by an ever-increased military gaze that does not allow visitors (Wallis 2020). In a nutshell, in just one year, the events led to catastrophic consequences both on the Greek islands and in the Aegean Sea.

## Pushbacks Upgraded: Floating Carceral Spaces as a Novel Infrastructure

As mentioned, both on the Greek and Turkish sides, the modus operandi of governing migrant mobilities in the Aegean is based on the interception techniques of border officials under the name of rescue. In Turkish territorial waters, the dominant practice is to pull back the migrant boats in line with the principle of border security. Meanwhile, on the Greek side, interception techniques are practiced in order to prevent the free and independent arrival of migrants to the islands. In cases of detection of migrant boats around the imaginary midline, the techniques of interception are used by the HCG and Frontex to push the boats back to Turkish waters. While this was the modus operandi before 2020, the situation has evolved into a more pervasive and fatal use of systematic pushbacks endowed with novel techniques and technologies of violence, namely, the introduction of life rafts as *floating carceral spaces*.

During one of the landings, we conducted in Skala Sikamineas in 2017, one Afghan migrant who was completely soaked in water said: "They first sunk our boat and then rescued us." This ostensibly paradoxical symbiosis reveals how the practice of rescue has been carried out through interception. During my two years of stay on the island, we witnessed numerous cases in which a dingy safely reached the shores of Lesbos without being detected due to the proximity of the shores, lower volume, and relatively less fatal nature of the sea in the Aegean. Despite the ever-increasing surveillance mechanisms aiming to get a "totalizing panoptic view" (Heller and Pezzani 2014) of the Aegean, the radar sensing capacity was limited in the dark and under the wet ontology (Steinberg and Peters 2015) of the sea with its waves, winds, and currents that disrupt the resolution. As a TCG member once said, "the sea is different you know, you cannot build a stone wall, and a migrant boat usually burst[s] onto the scene." Considering this proximity, migrants can see the lights of the opposite shore in Lesbos as soon as they get on a dingy on the Turkish side. What they need to do is move ahead on the sea until they reach those lights. They stubbornly try to evade military boats to avoid pull- or pushbacks to Turkey.

Whenever a dingy is spotted on the sea, whether by the TCG or Greek border officials, a tug-of-war begins between the dingy of migrants and the speed boat of border officials. The former tries to run away, while the latter chases to intercept. In Turkish territorial waters, the interception techniques are shaped around the objective of border security, which consists of taking people onboard and pulling them back. When a dingy is about to pass the imaginary line and enter the Greek territorial waters, the space of the imaginary midline aptly represents the crystallization of pushbacks. The Frontex patrol boats particularly prefer to stay close to the geographical midline in the Aegean, which enables them to respond swiftly in cases where migrant boats are about to enter Greek waters. Through various maneuvers, such as creating waves or throwing rope to take out the fuel hose by the hook, they aim to push the dingy back to Turkish territorial waters and prevent its entry into European space. The same method is used by the Turkish side, with the aim of pulling the boat back to the Turkish shores. The coast guard teams of the two countries communicate among themselves "sometimes directly boat by boat or sometimes by central level" (Hellenic Coast Guard interview 2017). In some cases, Greek forces detect a dingy that is about to pass the line, and they prefer to inform the TCG to approach and take the boat back. Therefore, the space around the midline designates a space of encounter and a ferocious struggle between the border officials of the two states, as well as migrant boats. However, although rescue NGOs operating in the Aegean Sea witness daily transgressions of the border space by the officials of two states, coast guards never accept that.

The space of the midline additionally becomes a kind of laboratory to observe the contentious cooperation between the two states. Although it is quite apt to argue that borders are "jointly administered" (Longo 2018) by neighboring countries in line with the logic of co-bordering today, such cooperation is always contentious—particularly in the case of Turkey and Greece, who have a long history of frictions and strife. Given the current state of EU–Turkish relations, this "cooperation" plays out in an even more contested fashion. During my interviews, this became crystal clear in the accusations that transpired between the two sides. The TCG sees itself as the "benevolent" and "professional" one as opposed to the "harsh" and "jumbled" operations of the Greek side (Turkish Coast Guard interview 2018). For Greek border officials, the Turkish side presents a great mystery. During our daily encounters in search-and-rescue operations, the Greek officials did not miss a chance to ask me about Turkey's operations. What they generally think is that the Turkish officials intentionally let the boats pass and had close connections with the facilitators. The dispute between the border officials of the two countries reflects itself on the field via *ad hoc* practices of impugning the blame on the other side when it comes to the acts of violence and pull- or pushbacks.

When I revisited the field in 2020, a TCG member stated, "Everything has changed since your last visit [in 2018]." This refers to the catastrophic consequences of the year 2020 after which the space of the Aegean has become incredibly militarized and equipped with the new and more fatal techniques of border enforcement. As events continued throughout March 2020 on the Turkish–Greek land border, specifically around the Evros River, migrants for the first time, started to be found drifting in orange, tent-like inflatable life rafts on the Aegean, as noted at the beginning of the chapter. Since then, more and more images of migrants in tent-like life rafts have begun to circulate online (Kingsley and Shoumali 2020; Keady-Tabbal and Mann 2023. It was the TCG that publicized these images on their official website (see figure 10.3).

According to the annual statistics of the Aegean Boat Report, the total number of arrivals has decreased substantially, by 84.1 percent, compared to the year 2019. There were 33,775 migrants who set out on their journeys in 2020, and 25,158 of them were stopped by the TCG en route to Greece ("Annual Reports" 2019). More strikingly, throughout the year 2020, 324

Figure 10.3. Migrants in a life raft in the Aegean, May 15, 2020. *Source*: Turkish Coast Command Official Website. Public domain.

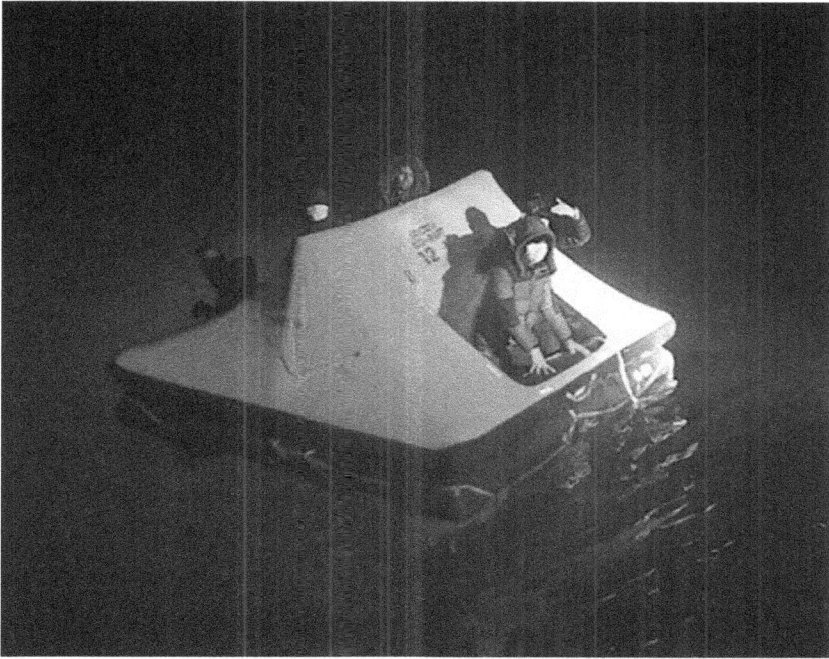

pushback cases were registered by the platform, involving 9,741 individuals who were pushed back by the Greek authorities. As stated, one-third of these pushbacks did not occur at sea, as was the case before. Rather, they were arrested after having arrived on the Greek islands, forcibly put into life rafts, and sent back to Turkey adrift on the sea. In more detail, the annual report notes that 6,116 people were pushed back at sea in 207 rubber boats with the familiar military techniques of maneuvering, creating waves, or deactivation of engines. The new pattern of expulsion, however, is using life rafts, which has amounted to 103 cases (one-third of total pushbacks), with 3,067 people taken from the islands and forced into the life rafts ("Annual Reports" 2019). Life rafts are indeed designed and manufactured for emergency situations in cases of shipwreck and rescue, with the intention of keeping survivors afloat and accordingly alive until help arrives. Rafts have no engine or other propellant and, accordingly, cannot be steered on the water. According to the 1974 Safety of Life at Sea Convention, maritime vessels are obliged to have such protection tools available. Being considerably cheap in price, the rafts are shaped like two-meter-wide square tents, which cannot be steered whatsoever but simply drift on the waves of the Aegean.

This novel technique started to be operationalized once the rescue NGOs terminated their missions on the islands, and thus when the Aegean Sea became definitively a militarized zone with no civilian involvement. Until the year 2020, the rhetoric of border officials was still shaped around moral sentiments, which were palpable in their daily language despite the actual practices (see Karadağ's piece in El Qadim et al. 2021). The strategy of interception through rescue as a proportioned and moderated violence (Weizman 2011) prepared the necessary conditions for the moral economy and its justification in the Aegean. By this way, the spatial control of territorial water was managed; the lethal consequences of interception techniques were moderated; and finally, a constant search for legitimacy and moral superiority was established. As a TCG member once revealed: "we transform the prevention of an illegal action into a lifesaving operation" (Turkish Coast Guard interview 2018). Today, there are almost no attempts to justify interceptions anymore, at least on moral grounds, at the border space of the Aegean.

What is referred to as the "lesser evil" (Weizman 2011; Ignatieff 2005; Ophir 2005) in the previous cases of interception and pushbacks has turned into the fatal incarceration of migrants on the waves of the sea. Although the regular practices of pull- or pushback have always comprised acts of violence, in those cases, migrants had the chance of using their phones to call rescue or, at times, redirect their boats if the engine was still working. Within these floating carceral spaces—life rafts—none of that is possible anymore. In most reported cases, migrants who land on the islands are captured and beaten; their possessions are confiscated; and they are incarcerated within the rafts at sea. This new technique of border enforcement extends the concept of incarceration beyond its conventional notion of confinement and urges us to explore the varied im/mobile sites of its manifestation in today's world.

## Conclusion

The logics of deterrence, incarceration, and refoulment of migrant mobilities that systematically undermine migrants' rights and dignity are not peculiar to the European external borders. Instead, they are accelerating in different geographies with a range of creative strategies, where each geography has its own characteristic of border governance shaped by geographical and sociohistorical context. The specificity of the Aegean Sea involves such authenticity when we consider its geophysicality as well as the social universe of its actors, which have been empirically explored in this chapter. Within the circumstances of the spatial and juridical configuration of the sea—the proximity, the lack of SAR zones, the lower volume of the sea, smaller dinghies, and patrolling speed boats—the politics of control as well as of resistance are shaped and constantly reconfigured.

The chapter lays out the transformation of border enforcement in the Aegean Sea in the post-2015 period, during which new techniques and infrastructure have been introduced, especially from 2020 onward (see also İşleyen 2021). Until 2020, the main mode of governance in the Aegean Sea was based more on the politics of interception under the guise of rescue. Everyday battle occurred with the techniques of interceptions on the waves of the Aegean; evidence was erased with the swallowing of migrant bodies by the sea; and the ones who remained alive were depicted as rescued. Accordingly, the practice of rescue inevitably provided a special opportunity for the justification of interception techniques for spatial control and border security. The same strategy was used for the acts of pushback, which spatially occur around the imaginary midline separating the territorial waters of the two states. Since accountability and evidence are hard to achieve on the waves of the sea, rescue becomes a *thick* field, providing a wide spectrum of maneuver for the armed forces to justify this systematic violence.

However, since March 2020, the Aegean Sea has been witnessing a novel infrastructure, such as life rafts, incarcerating migrants on the waves of the sea, usually with no method to call for rescue. This new fatal practice no longer needs the previously obtained moral sentiments or justification mechanisms for rescue. Rather, it is used as a way of collectively expelling migrants, even those who have already landed. In such a militarized environment, "cleared" of NGOs, migrants are captured on the islands, contained, and tortured in unofficial sites without documentation, and then forced into tent-like carceral spaces. This shows us the transformation of the Aegean Sea from a space of border governance relying on moderated violence shrouded in moral rhetoric to one that operates on a blatant and coarse use of violence.

## Notes

1. For a detailed summary of the case, please visit the report of Legal Centre Lesbos, available at www.infomigrants.net/en/post/26039/legal-ngo-documents-collective-expulsions-by-greek-authorities-in-aegean.

2. Turkish Coast Guard occasionally publicize the photos of life rafts on their official website. The announcement and photos of this event can be found at: https://en.sg.gov.tr/31-irregular-migrants-were-rescued-off-the-coast-of-mugla-23-3-20.

3. For detailed information on attacks in the island, please read the news available at https://tr.euronews.com/2020/03/04/midilli-de-gocmen-karsitlarinin-hedefi-olan-sivil-toplum-orgutleri-faaliyetlerine-son-veri.

4. The Refugee Rescue, the only remaining rescue boat in the Aegean, had to terminate its operations and moved to the Mediterranean recently. For its official website please visit www.refugeerescue.org.

5. For the testimonies of the volunteers who face charges of espionage, see www.reuters.com/world/europe/aid-workers-accused-spying-go-trial-greece-over-refugee-rescues-2021-11-18.

## References

"Annual Reports." Aegean Boat Report, August 25, 2019. https://aegeanboatreport.com/annual-reports

Benton, Lauren A. *A Search for Sovereignty Law and Geography in European Empires, 1400–1900.* Cambridge & New York: Cambridge University Press, 2009.

Bose, Sugata. *A Hundred Horizons: The Indian Ocean in the Age of Global Empire.* Cambridge, MA: Harvard University Press, 2009.

Casas-Cortés, Maribel, Sebastian Cobarrubias, Charles Heller, and Lorenzo Pezzani. "Clashing Cartographies, Migrating Maps: The Politics of Mobility at the External Borders of E.U.Rope." *ACME: An International Journal for Critical Geographies* 16, no. 1 (2017): 1–33.

Cuttitta, Paolo. "Inclusion and Exclusion in the Fragmented Space of the Sea. Actors, Territories and Legal Regimes between Libya and Italy." In *Contemporary Boat Migration: Data, Geopolitics, and Discourses*, edited by Elaine Burroughs and Kira Williams. London & Lanham: Rowman & Littlefield, 2018.

Cuttitta, Paolo, and Tamara Last, eds. *Border Deaths: Causes, Dynamics and Consequences of Migration-Related Mortality.* Amsterdam: Amsterdam University Press, 2020.

Davies, Thom, Arshad Isakjee, and Surindar Dhesi. "Violent Inaction: The Necropolitical Experience of Refugees in Europe: Violent Inaction." *Antipode* 49, no. 5 (2017): 1263–84. https://doi.org/10.1111/anti.12325

El Qadim, Nora, Beste İşleyen, Leonie Ansems de Vries, Signe Sofie Hansen, Sibel Karadağ, Debbie Lisle, and Damien Simonneau. "(Im)Moral Borders in Practice." *Geopolitics* 26, no. 5 (2021): 1608–38. https://doi.org/10.1080/14650045.2020.1747902

Gilroy, Paul. *The Black Atlantic: Modernity and Double Consciousness.* Cambridge, MA: Harvard University Press, 2003.

Heller, Charles, and Lorenzo Pezzani. "Liquid Traces: Investigating the Deaths of Migrants at the EU's Maritime Frontier." In *Forensis: The Architecture of Public Truth*, edited by Forensic Architecture (Project), Anselm Franke, Eyal Weizman, and Haus der Kulturen der Welt. Berlin: Sternberg Press, 2014.

Heller, Charles, Lorenzo Pezzani, and Situ Studio. "Forensic Oceanography: Report on the 'Left-To-Die Boat.'" Forensic Architecture. London: Centre for Research Architecture, University of London, 2012. https://forensic-architecture.org/investigation/the-left-to-die-boat

Ignatieff, Michael. *The Lesser Evil: Political Ethics in an Age of Terror : with a New Preface by the Author*. The Gifford Lectures. Princeton, NJ: Princeton University Press, 2005.

İşleyen, Beste. "Tecnology and Territorial Change in Conflict Settings: Migration Control in the Aegean Sea." *International Studies Quarterly* 65, no. 4 (2021): 1087–96.

İşleyen, Beste, and Sibel Karadağ. "Engineered Migration at the Greek-Turkish Border: A Spectacle of Violence and Humanitarian Space." *Security Dialogue* 54, no.5 (2023): 475–92.

Karadağ, Sibel. "Extraterritoriality of European Borders to Turkey: An Implementation Perspective of Counteractive Strategies." *Comparative Migration Studies* 7, no. 1 (2019): 12. https://doi.org/10.1186/s40878-019-0113-y

Keady-Tabbal, Niamh, and Itamar Mann. "Weaponizing Rescue: Law and the Materiality of Migration Management in the Aegean." *Leiden Journal of International Law* 36, no. 1 (2023): 61–82.

Kingsley, Patrick, and Karam Shoumali. "Taking Hard Line, Greece Turns Back Migrants by Abandoning Them at Sea." *The New York Times*, 2020. www.nytimes.com/2020/08/14/world/europe/greece-migrants-abandoning-sea.html

Longo, Matthew. *The Politics of Borders: Sovereignty, Security, and the Citizen after 9/11*. Cambridge: Cambridge University Press, 2018. https://doi.org/10.1017/9781316761663

Mawani, Renisa. *Across Oceans of Law: The Komagata Maru and Jurisdiction in the Time of Empire*. Durham, NC: Duke University Press, 2018.

Mbembé, J.-A. "Necropolitics." Translated by Libby Meintjes. *Public Culture* 15, no. 1 (2003): 11–40.

"More than 13,000 Migrants Reported Along the Turkish-Greek Border." International Organization for Migration 2020. www.iom.int/news/more-13000-migrants-reported-along-turkish-greek-border

Ophir, Adi. *The Order of Evils: Toward an Ontology of Morals*. New York: Zone Books, 2005.

Rediker, Marcus. *The Slave Ship: A Human History*. New York: Penguin Books, 2008.

Samaddar, Ranabir. *The Postcolonial Age of Migration*. London & New York: Routledge, 2020.

Steinberg, Philip, and Kimberley Peters. "Wet Ontologies, Fluid Spaces: Giving Depth to Volume through Oceanic Thinking." *Environment and Planning D: Society and Space* 33, no. 2 (2015): 247–64. https://doi.org/10.1068/d14148p.

Stierl, Maurice. "The Mediterranean as a Carceral Seascape." *Political Geography* 88 (June, 2021): 102417. https://doi.org/10.1016/j.polgeo.2021.102417

———. "A Sea of Struggle—Activist Border Interventions in the Mediterranean Sea." *Citizenship Studies* 20, no. 5 (2016): 561–78. https://doi.org/10.1080/13621025.2016.1182683

"UNHCR Turkey: March Operational Update." UNHCR, 2020. www.unhcr.org/tr/wp-content/uploads/sites/14/2020/05/UNHCR-Turkey-Operational-Update-March-2020.pdf

Wallis, Emma. "Oxfam: Conditions in 'Moria 2.0' Are Abysmal." InfoMigrants. October 21, 2020. www.infomigrants.net/en/post/28042/oxfam-conditions-in-moria-20-are-abysmal

Weizman, Eyal. *The Least of All Possible Evils: Humanitarian Violence from Arendt to Gaza*. London & New York: Verso, 2011.

Chapter 11

# Sea, Refugees, and Stateless Migrants on the Bay

## The Rohingya

Sucharita Sengupta

> A map is a two-dimensional representation with arbitrary symbols and incised lines that decide who is to be our enemy . . . and friend. Cartography is another name for stories told by winners; for stories told by those who have lost, there isn't one.
>
> —Elif Shafak[1]

## Prelude: A Short Vignette

"Could you guess the identity of this person sitting right next to you is a Rohingya, trying to escape the camps"? The army guard (border police) asked me with a chuckle while pushing the man toward the exit of the bus. "That was a false citizenship document he showed, and this is a regular occurrence here. Every day, we stop illegal trespassers like these pretending to be nationals of Bangladesh. They are not supposed to go outside the camps like this. Most of them go to India via land after crossing the checkposts or cross over by sea to Malaysia from Cox's. These people have completely changed our locality. Criminal activities have increased manifold here."

Heart racing from the sudden incident, I managed a puzzled smile and asked, "How did you realize whom to interrogate on the bus?"

"It's normally the 'look'[2] that first triggers our suspicion, and then after checking documents, it becomes clearer, as you just witnessed."[3]

He then went on to show me the paper (see figure 11.1) and box where the name of the place was written; the color was a tad brighter than the rest the of the document, and spelling was misspelled, along with a few minor errors not easily noticeable. "No official document will have a misspelled word with vital spaces left blank," the officer continued. The man carrying this document was seated next to me in a crowded public bus commuting back from one of the world's largest refugee camp sites in Bangladesh (hosting more than a million refugees) to the main town area. It's nearly a two and half to three-hour ride from the camps to my destination with stopovers/ transport changes. There are three main big checkpoints along with other small gates, that any public transport must cross after exiting the camps through this main bypass route. This was the second checkpoint when four

Figure 11.1. A person (daily laborer working in the camps) carrying his citizenship document while commuting from Camp in Ukhia to Cox's Bazaar. Author photo.

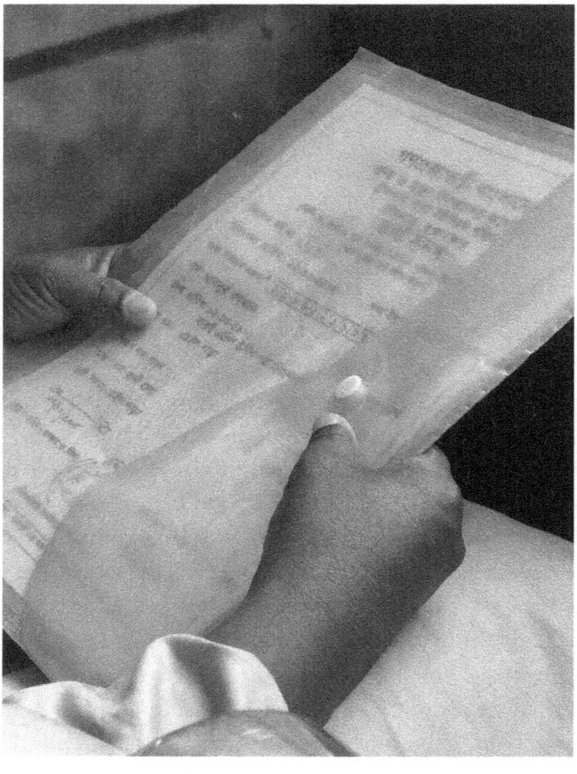

to five officials came inside the bus to check our documents. Incidentally, I was not checked at any of the check posts. In fact, except for two days, I was never checked while commuting to/and from the camps during my stay in Bangladesh. The officer, meanwhile, continued while the bus waited for clearance to restart: "We do not check everyone. Hence, we will not check you, but women who are Burkha-clad and have their faces hidden with the hijab are our usual suspects. You look decent, madam, so we will not bother." Another smile, a sly one this time, replaced the chuckle.

I was nervous, not only because, contrary to what the official had imagined, I was not a citizen of Bangladesh hailing from the capital city Dhaka but a Bengali (my mother tongue) from West Bengal, a state in the east of India that shares the longest border with Bangladesh. I was slightly scared also because, despite having "managed" a formal access/permit to the camp, it ran the risk of getting canceled anytime. This snippet from our long exchange above provides a glimpse into a range of issues that emanated from my stay in Bangladesh as days went by, including how governance functions on the ground, the bureaucracy surrounding identity, the efficacy of papers/documents, and my subjectivity, along with the politics of location—a female ethnographer, a Bengali from West Bengal, and a Bengali Hindu from India whose family had been forced to migrate from Bangladesh (Pre-partition East Bengal) to West Bengal in the 1940s. "The longing" for a forlorn home, or the imagination of a landscape never seen before, but felt through memories that pass down through generations are therefore not unknown or unheard for me. However, the part that complicates this narrative is that refugees who are recognized as citizens have a sense of belonging without having to try and prove it, for instance, partition refugees in the Indian subcontinent. For refugees, the claim to memories of a lost home derives from the claim to territory, which, in the case of stateless persons, become difficult even while reminiscing about the past. There are just so many multifarious issues that stateless people face, from rightlessness to dispossession, which are way more poignant than those faced by the refugees.

Quite like the story above, in the latter part of this chapter, I note another instance when simply for the lack of documentation, either attesting citizenship or refugeehood, a community of nomads suddenly found themselves as "illegal migrants" by crossing over the sea from one territory to the other. Is documentation the answer to dispossession or citizenship? According to human rights laws, there is no general right to documentation. Countries that have signed the 1954 Convention on Statelessness which I enumerate later, should supposedly provide documentation confirming a said people's statelessness. Article 27 of the 1954 statelessness convention denotes identity documents as necessary to prove that a person is stateless and that s/he has the right to reside within the state. On the other hand, documentation on births and marriages are the other forms of identity documents that can resolve statelessness, as per the UNHCR. The next subsections attempt to explore this premise in detail.

## Introduction to the Problematic of Statelessness in the Sea

A recently published news article at the end of January 2022 narrates the tragic event of seven Bangladeshi nationals passing away from hypothermia while trying to reach Italy on a boat full of 280 migrants from Bangladesh and Egypt. The boat was intercepted on Lampedusa, an island in Italy. Three were already dead after the boat passengers were brought to Lampedusa, and four died after reaching the island, unable to withstand the extreme cold. The rest of the boat passengers were taken to a facility in Contrada Ibriacola that already accommodates 365 people. It is suspected that the migrants were trafficked to the boat, and an investigation is still ongoing to trace the traffickers. According to the Italian news agency ANSA, the rest of the migrants were able to be saved from the distressed boat only because the Italian authorities were alerted by an organization called "alarm phone" that monitors migrants crossing the Mediterranean Sea. Despite the call, help was delayed, resulting in casualties. According to the UNHCR, more than 2,000 migrants have already arrived in Italy in 2022 (Jha 2022). In 2021, around 66,770 people had crossed the Mediterranean Sea in difficult conditions to reach Italy, of whom 1,496 were either lost in the sea or were found dead (Jha 2022).

The situation at the Bay of Bengal is no different. It is as unfortunate in terms of the risks involved, resulting in severe loss of lives. For instance, in a news piece published by Al Jazeera, UNHCR notes that in 2020, five years after the 2015 boat crisis in the Bay of Bengal and Andaman Sea, when thousands of migrants in distress at the sea were denied asylum or lifesaving amenities, the situation at the sea has come to the same alarming point once again. Thousands of migrants and refugees were again found to be stranded. They have noted that 2020 was the deadliest year on record for the Rohingya crossing the Bay of Bengal and Andaman Sea (Al Jazeera 2021). The pandemic has made the situation far more complicated. Due to more stringent border restrictions, many were left stranded at sea for days before being rescued.

Between February and June 2020, especially amidst the COVID lockdown in Bangladesh, numbers of refugees trying to cross the Bay in dire precarity had swelled mainly because of two reasons: fear pertaining from disinformation regarding the spread of the virus in camps; and the inaccessibility of help. This disinformation was mainly due to the lack of Internet access in the camps and partly to a need to escape the growing deterioration of living conditions in the camps. Why? Because, even if the initial phase of camp livelihood of a million plus refugees from 2017 in Cox's Bazar of Bangladesh ensured a steady supply of ration (food) and shelter, reports of back-to-back blazing devastating fires engulfing a large part of the camp in March 2021, rendering many homeless, only prove the extreme precarity of such an existence. It comes as no surprise, therefore, that refugees will want to risk their lives in trying to "escape" the dire hopelessness of the camps, even if that means sailing on the sea for more than ten weeks and being prevented from docking (Beech 2020).

A joint statement issued by the UNHCR, IOM, and UNODC on protection at sea in the Bay of Bengal and Andaman Sea notes that there is no quick solution to the irregular maritime movements of refugees and migrants (UNHCR 2020). Deterring movements will be unlawful, so instead, the international agencies have called upon states in the region to uphold the commitments made at the 2016 Bali Declaration to protect the most vulnerable and leave no one behind at sea. Not doing so could jeopardize the lives of many, like the Rohingya refugees in 2015, 2020, and some parts of 2021. The statement further puts emphasis on a "regional solution for a regional problem" and that saving lives is the top priority in the case of stranded migrants on the sea (UNHCR 2020). States should ensure proper disembarkation and rescue operations to ensure the protection of refugees and stateless people from discrimination, persecution, deprivation, and other violations of human rights. Following this, in December 2021, Indonesia allowed a boat packed with Rohingyas from Bangladesh to disembark in its dock after the boat was stranded off its coast and needed immediate refuge. Passengers in the boat were mostly women and children, and it was running the risk of sinking within days owing to leakages in the boat.

Despite this, why do we witness a surge in the numbers of sea migrants instead of the reverse? Is crossing the sea comparatively easier than crossing land, for which so many migrants risk taking to the sea? In addition to all these queries, two more inquiries are worth pondering upon: (1) since sea margins are different from the land, can migrants crossing the sea for days be considered stateless? And alternatively, (2) how does international law address the rights of stateless persons, who are also refugees, crossing the sea in search of asylum to countries they hope to receive help from? This chapter seeks to delve into these questions.

I shall try to understand the complexities of stateless migrants taking to the sea in a bid to migrate for a safe asylum through the context of Rohingya refugees, who are stateless. I shall also quote a few select pieces of literature on the sea to compare with land borders in so far as boundaries and territoriality are concerned. Here, I am particularly intrigued by how Henry Jones writes about the sea and that "international law might take part in the reconceptualization of the space of the sea" (Jones 2016, 1). While land borders are static, the sea with its constant motion, unsettles our understanding of geopolitics, which throws open new avenues for debate and discussion. Jones, by analyzing Carl Schmitt, Deleuze, and Guattari, visualizes the sea as much more than a space, but as a place. Understanding the sea as a place resonates with thinkers like Henry Lefebvre, for whom space is a concrete place produced by economic transactions, planning, and surveillance. The difference that the sea provides from land is its smoothness, which also facilitates the smooth movements of nomads, migrants, and refugees (Jones 2016). Jatin Dua, in *Captured at Sea* (2019), spins a fascinating tale of life at sea—of fishermen, migrants, smugglers, pirates, and labor—that he says is murkier than those on land. This chapter is discussed from three vantage points: (1) the legal and humane implications of statelessness vis-à-vis the state; (2) borders and statelessness at sea; and (3) the case of the Rohingya, known as the "boat people" since 2015, in this respect.

My experiences of interaction with the Rohingya from 2014 in Indian prisons to Bangladesh camps in 2015 and 2019 show that contemporary notions of citizenship are transitional and largely shaped by the inflow of global capital and market. Recognized globally as deracinated victims of genocide, confined to a crammed space like that of a camp, and relegated to a "bare life" existence as framed by Agamben (1998), is how the Rohingya would be generally described. But, in this narrative of dispossession, what we often tend to ignore is that they are living beings who will naturally want to break free from such prison-like existences. Those drives of desperation across the land and sea are termed "illegal" by states, and it is unfortunate that across countries, the Rohingya are considered as risk and not at risk. The 2015 drives of the Rohingya from Bangladesh across the Bay of Bengal[4] that had made headlines worldwide, were marked by mixed and massive flows, with even citizens of Bangladesh in rickety flotillas taking perilous journeys. In another context, Biswas (2016) writes how factors such as dispossession, lack of a good life, or simply gullibility brought a diverse group of people, very different in their identities otherwise, together to sign up for a journey toward uncertainty. The same could be argued in this context.

## Statelessness and the Importance of the State

I shall start this section with the story of Unggun who lives with his family in a traditional Bajau Laut houseboat in Semporna, a coastal town in Sabah, which is completely cut off from the land. He does not know the calendar year or his age because he has no documents. In the 1970s, the Mindanao civil war caused refugees to flood into Sabah, including Bajau Laut like Unggun. The Bajau Laut, also known as Sama Dilaut (meaning sea nomads), is a subgroup of the Sama-Bajau. Once, around the fifteenth century, they used to roam freely in a borderless Sulu Zone as nomads, now they are considered stateless, scattered across the Southeast Asia, for lack of citizenship documents. Unggun lives perched on the sea without "essentials" of a modern life like electricity, clock, a mobile phone, or television, and he has no complaints. However, since Malaysia is not yet a signatory of the International Refugee Conventions of Refugees and Stateless (1951 and 1964), their movement now has been restricted by the then newly elected government. The Immigration Act of the land (1959/1963) makes no distinction between asylum seekers, refugees, irregular migrants, and undocumented stateless people, for which the Bajau Laut, if raided, could be incarcerated as "illegal immigrants" especially for lack of documents (Chiew 2019). The law, albeit necessary, is like a double-edged sword, as, many times, it fails to protect the very people that are the victims of these legal paradoxes.

Statelessness is therefore not just a legal but also a human problem (Batchelor 1998, 156–82). To put it simply, statelessness is the existence of people without a formal citizen status. It means living without having a nationality or the protection of a state that one is entitled to by virtue of citizenship. Concern with stateless people was prevalent during the decade of the 1920s, following the First World War when many people were rendered stateless in the wake of the international passport system in 1920. In the post–World War I period, the "civil wars in Russia and genocide in the Ottoman empire" had rendered millions of people stateless (UNHCR 2009).

The Nansen passport was created then, which did not grant citizenship status to the families but allowed movement across borders. It was after the end of World War II, in 1954, that we see the definitive emergence of the meaning of the term "stateless." It is 2022, yet the world still endures statelessness and dispossession. Until now, and perhaps in an even greater magnitude, stateless people are left with deprivation, social exclusion, rightlessness, hopelessness, and without basic human rights. The year 2022 was the 62nd anniversary of the 1961 Convention on the Reduction of Statelessness. Yet, thus far, seventy-seven countries had signed the convention (UNHCR 2021).

Discrimination based on ethnicity, gender identity, sexual orientation, race, religion, age, sex, and other factors is determined as the root cause of statelessness. Nationality laws are often discriminatory, which in turn result in the creation of stateless people. Currently, more than 75 percent of the world's known stateless population belong to ethnic, religious, or linguistic minority groups (UNHCR 2021). Discrimination in inheriting citizenship rights at birth is generally the most prevalent cause of statelessness, while discrimination in naturalization procedures too can lead to instances of statelessness. Acquisition of citizenship at birth is based on the principles of jus soli, and it is known as jus sanguinis when nationality is attained by descent. Most countries' nationality laws are a combination of both. For some people, discriminatory provisions lead to statelessness at birth and then result in naturalization at a later stage.

Statelessness has been studied primarily through the lens of citizenship rights and legal provisions. However, it is way more complex, not only in terms of legal implementation but also for humanitarian intervention. Fundamentally, it challenges the state-citizenship relationship without which, stateless people are left vulnerable to various forms of exploitation, abuse, poverty, and marginalization (Malischewski 2018, 134). Any discussion on statelessness generally begins with the memoirs of Hannah Arendt, where she recounts her existential experiences as a stateless Jewish refugee going through pathos, despair, anxiety of waiting, and occasional waves of optimism, or hope (Bernstein 2005). The depiction of a stateless figure here is through the lens of refugee narratives, and the conventional understanding of statelessness has been tied to refugeehood.

This lens, however, is not adequate to explain the legal paradoxes that stateless people are faced with in contemporary times because refugeehood or statelessness is not always about border crossings. People can be made stateless and refugees at home by stripping off their citizenship status, as is the case of Unggun.[5] Scholars like Judith Butler, urging one to go beyond

Arendt's legalistic framework of refugee narratives, says how both spatiality and temporality are important indexes in understanding statelessness, where there might not be neatly outlined points of arrival and departure (Butler and Spivak 2007). This theorization is further developed by the likes of Samaddar (Chaudhury and Samaddar 2018; Samaddar 2020) and Chowdhory (2018) who argue that citizenship is an important parameter in understanding contemporary instances of statelessness and that the notions of "home" and "belongingness" attain new meaning in the process. However, there is a need to go beyond both these binary frameworks of refugeehood/citizenship and explore new avenues for gauging the nuances of the increasing global mobility of stateless people. Seaborne migration further complicates this picture. Maritime movements historically have been a regular feature across the Aegean and Bay of Bengal but recent instances of precarious, desperate boat drives of migrants, including the Rohingya, and the subsequent denial of states in disembarking them have once again raised questions on the efficacy of international law and the production of statelessness on high seas. From the crisis in Bay to the Mediterranean emergency in 2015 to recent times, innumerable news clips testifying to shipwrecks, fences, and racism, have necessitated a renewed discussion on borders (Novak 2017), sovereignty, and citizenship.

There are two main angles from which scholars working on citizenship approach the subject. One side is dominated by the "geopolitical and conceptual borders of citizenship's exclusionary lines of demarcation" by scholars working on immigration, globalization, transnational citizenship, and so on (Somers 2008, 21). The other is the "inside/interior" one that dwells on the meaning and legalities of citizenship. There is thus a binary between citizenship rights, which Hannah Arendt contends as the right to have rights, and human rights (Arendt 1968). While citizenship rights are inclusionary in nature and relational, human rights are believed to be possessed by all humans for simply being humans (Somers 2008, 7). Human rights are universal in nature, and my approach to the subject of statelessness stems from a humanitarian lens.

Unngun's story depicts that statelessness can take several forms. The 1954 and 1961 International Conventions[6] coupled with a few regional conventions form the bedrock of the international legal framework to address statelessness. According to the International Law Commission, the definition of stateless persons contained in Article 1 (1) of the 1954 Convention relating to the Status of Stateless Persons now forms part of customary international law. The article defines "stateless persons" as those who are not recognized as nationals by any state under the operation of its law. They therefore have no nationality or citizenship status and are unprotected by national legislation, and are left in the arc of vulnerability. The 1954 International Refugee Convention deals specifically with defining the status of stateless persons, and 1961 Refugee Convention deal with the reduction of statelessness. In legal terms, there are two forms of statelessness: de jure, when a person is not considered as a national by any state under the operation of its law; and de facto, when people have been described broadly as those who are effectively without a nationality because they are unable to avail themselves of the protection of the state. Recent years have seen debates over the validity of de facto statelessness (Parsons and Lawreniuk 2017, 1). One instance of de facto stateless people in the contemporary world are the ethnically Vietnamese communities in Cambodia, many of whom have never crossed a border (Parsons, Lawreniuk). The Rohingyas are de jure, deracinated and scattered through their mobility across international borders in South and Southeast Asia.

UNHCR, rooting to eradicate statelessness by 2024, mentions how the 1954 Convention is of critical importance in current times, as millions of people are still stateless, yet too few people are signatories to these conventions (Mahanirban Calcutta Research Group, n.d.). Article 15 of the Universal Declaration of Human Rights says that "everyone has a nationality. No one shall be arbitrarily deprived of his nationality or the right to change his nationality" (Mahanirban Calcutta Research Group, n.d.). This bears two implications: "one cannot have the option of remaining stateless" and secondly, deprivation of nationality is possible, given that it is not arbitrary.

## Statelessness and Refugeehood

At this juncture, it is pertinent to refer to the distinction between a refugee and a stateless person, not to highlight the importance of one above the other but to not turn a blind eye to the double marginalization that stateless people face. It is noteworthy that historically, it is basically a cycle when statelessness results in refugeehood, as in the case of the Rohingyas, and protracted refugeehood leads to the situation of statelessness. In both instances, the people living such an existence live on the edge. It is thus interesting to see how mechanisms like the Global Compact become useful in fostering both empathy and consciousness on the part of nation-states to deal with such situations and render protection. On the other hand, the resilience and counter resistance by the people for survival is also interesting, as also in this case they are not powerless and receptive to subjugation, but we can see a gradual emergence of a powerful voice on social media platforms, in the digital world, and in using international organizations like the UN and IMO.

The problem with the definition of a refugee, according to the 1951(1) Refugee Convention by the United Nations High Commissioner for Refugees (UNHCR),[7] is that UNHCR has not provided definitive guidelines on how refugee status can be determined. Refugeehood does not mean not having citizenship of a particular state, unlike stateless people who could be termed refugees or asylum seekers, depending on specific situations or particularities. A person might have citizenship status or nationality or not have them when he becomes a refugee. However, "not all stateless people are refugees" (Malkki 1995, 501–2), and neither are all refugees devoid of a nationality.

We thus see a conflation of categories here, provoking questions on the validity of human rights and refugee laws in rendering protection to the stateless or refugees fleeing persecution. Therefore, the massive flow of people crossing international borders questions not only states but also old polarities and binaries—such as who is an economic migrant/migrant labor/refugee/Internally Displaced Person (IDP)/asylum seeker; between citizen/stateless; movement due to fear/movement due to economic imperative; international norms/national responsibility; human rights/humanitarianism—giving rise to new sets of questions. Does a stateless person fleeing persecution qualify to be a refuge, since refugees do not necessarily lack citizenship status as stateless people do? If stateless people also do qualify to be refugees, then are the host countries they are seeking refuge from liable to render them protection? All these questions provoke critical thinking and enquiry/inquiry within the ambit of refugee studies and have been subjected to critical inquiry in contemporary times.

In the international agreement on the Global Compact on Refugees and the Global Compact for Safe, Orderly, and Regular Migration mandated by the New York Declaration for Refugees and Migrants, 2016, both migration and forced migration have been used synonymously, reinforcing the conflation of the categories (Basu Ray Chaudhury and Samaddar 2018, 1). In the same meeting, it was also highlighted how the existing refugee conventions are increasingly becoming inadequate to render protection to refugees and stateless people seeking refuge. It also shows how, in the wake of global migration crises like the Syrian and European migration crises, categories such as who is a refugee, economic migrant, or asylum seeker are getting blurred increasingly. It is worth pondering upon henceforth: can UNHCR-recognized refugees, and in this context, also Stateless people like the Rohingya, be held responsible for crossing borders without sufficient "documents"? This indicates a lacuna in the way the international legal system functions.

## Is the State Important in Civilian Lives? What Is the Rationality of a "Citizenship" Status?

International law empowers the state to decide who stays within its borders and who remains at the periphery or outside. The relevance of statelessness leading to refugeehood and vice versa, that is, protracted refugeehood leading to statelessness, are important issues in this context. Statelessness or lack of citizenship, is an interesting nodal point to think of the ways the state is important or all-pervasive in civilian lives. This debate on the meaning and implications of statelessness is thus crucial to understand the modes of governance of modern states and international relations, raising important questions geared around how social life is organized within and by a state when it is complex. It also empowers the state to select its citizens. This chapter might not be able to offer solutions to several questions flagged here, but it will address them nonetheless.

In contemporary times, there lies the ambiguity as to the role of the state, which is conceived as both central and marginal. Statehood ascribes rights that a citizen is entitled to. With the advent of globalization, the external and internal sovereignty of the state seems to have been reduced (Randeria 2007). However, it remains indispensable through the policies it frames. Statehood, nationality, or citizenship are the basic mechanisms through which the state can exercise its power of inclusion/exclusion and protect its citizens. Scholars like Giorgio Agamben and Michel Foucault, both of whom have written extensively on how "management of life becomes an affair of the state, thus inaugurating the biopolitical state" (Das 2007, 25). The biopolitical form of sovereignty as envisaged by Foucault, the power to "make" live and "let" die, is aimed to produce, and regulate and "make efficient use of life" (Debrix and Barder 2012, 8–26).

Visualizing from the perspective of Agamben, it can be stated that a biopolitical state strips a life to its naked or bare form, producing thereby bodies "that are killable with impunity" (Das 2007, 16). Samaddar (2016), however, moves away from the Agambenian contention to ask whether the refugee can at all be reduced to a bare life simply because the camp for refugees or stateless people, albeit exceptional, becomes the only place of a possible political life that can question democracy, and does the naked person simply die? Rather, do we not see the emergence of political subjectivity from such spaces like that of the camp that is supposedly rightless? In fact, Samaddar contends that it is only after a thorough historical analysis of the postcolonial studies of refugees and stateless, that we would be able to shelve any a priori knowledge based on extreme binaries of life and death (Samaddar 2016).

This articulation of state of a repressive machinery that constrains or kills finds resonance in the writings of James Scott (2009). Sovereign power exercised by the state is, however, not only about territories but bodies as well (Das 2007, 10). In fact, producing the biopolitical body is the result of the sovereign power of the state. Many anthropologists have used this notion of biopower to understand how power is exercised in society. Yet, as the authors write, the interesting question at this juncture is how "politics becomes the domain in which life is put in question" (10). Here, margin, through its exclusion, provides an important locus for studying the state as "strategies of citizenship, technological imaginaries, and new regions of language" through an analysis of the state and its margins (10). Therefore, it could be said that the state machinery is inherently subjugating and exclusionary. Avoiding the state was perhaps still an option a few centuries ago, but not anymore. The way the balance of power between the stateless and the state is maneuvered shows the omnipresence of the state. This power of nation-states as "the standard and nearly exclusive unit of sovereignty" has proven immensely detrimental to nonstate people (Scott 2009, 10–11). Most nation-states have tried to drive out "disloyal" populations outside its territory or to relegate them to the periphery. However, there are several instances of realizations that the once seemingly useless territories inhabited by stateless people at the margins are of great economic value. They might be rich in mineral resources or be apt for logistical expansions and trading with the big power blocks, contributing to the state revenue. Hence, there is "all the more reason to project state power" to these once ungoverned, out-of-reach lands and bring their inhabitants either under firm control or drive them away completely (11). We see an exact replica of this situation in the case of the Rohingya in Myanmar.

The anthropological turn within studies of state started with the "ethnographic gaze" as written by Ferguson and Gupta (2002). The authors argue that this new literature often stresses states not being just "bureaucratic apparatuses but powerful sites of symbolic and cultural production that are themselves always culturally represented and understood in particular ways" (Ferguson and Gupta 2002, 981). It thus offers a scope to not imagine states as imagined nations following Benedict Anderson but as concrete realities with "certain spatial characteristics and properties" (981).

Liisa Helena Malkki, a key pioneer of legal anthropology, argues that displacement or deterritorialization in the present arrangement of nation-states produces two possibilities: (1) whether the "liminal collectivity" tries to fit within the national order, "to become a 'nation' like the others," or (2) a denial to be categorized, "a refusal to be fixed within one and only one national and categorical identity, and one and only one historical trajectory" (Malkki 1995, 6). Through an anthropological study of classifications, she follows, to name a few, the works of Foucault, Balibar, and Wallerstein and argues that modern nation-states are like single linear systems rather than international relations among nations that concur mobility as natural. The modern system of nation-states "has come to be a natural order of things in many dimensions of human lives" (6). By the natural order of things, she explains that a nation is always associated with particularities—a fixed or a particular place and time. It is this understanding that classifies and sorts people into analytical categories, and she asks, what happens if this natural order is challenged or subverted? "Refugees can present precisely such a subversion. They are an "abomination" produced and made meaningful by the categorical order itself even if they are excluded from it" (6). They are a "dangerous" category of people as they blur national (or, in this case, natural) boundaries and challenge the order of the state by challenging the distinction between nationals and foreigners. Theoretically, notions such as citizenship, nationality, origins, nativeness, nationalism, and racism are linked with the concepts of identity, ethnicity, and culture. She explores categories and critics relating to the making of a citizen, of being a refugee and not being one, and traces the journey of the metamorphosis of a "refugee" to an "immigrant" when they move from camps to towns (Malkki 1995). Much of this resonates with the camp lives and drives of the Rohingya.

## Significance of the Bay of Bengal and Statelessness at Sea

The ancient Arakan state (now Rakhine) is situated on the bank of the Bay of Bengal. It extends to some 350 miles along the eastern shores of the Bay. The northern part of Arakan, now known as the "Mayu District" was her point of contact with East Bengal (now Bangladesh). From time immemorial, this region has witnessed traders sailing across different regions and reaching ports of the Arakan. Thus, explaining both mobility and Muslim presence in Rakhine State, before it was conquered by the Burmese kingdom. The sea is thus not unknown to settlers here and is often a desired route for crossing due to its accessibility. Cox's Bazar in Bangladesh is also on the bank of the Bay; hence, the sea is familiar to the settlers in these places and to people on both sides of the borders. It is through the river Naf which separates Cox's Bazar from Rakhine land, that the Rohingya cross over to Bangladesh by foot. Their migration via sea from either Myanmar or Bangladesh is not a new phenomenon, going by the geographical location and easy accessibility of mobility. What is new, however, is the increasing numbers of such drives through risky conditions in order to seek asylum.

The latest 2021 report of the Asia Pacific Refugee Rights Network (APRRN) mentions a timeline of the Rohingya taking to the sea: 2006–2011—the first phase, when more than 400 Rohingyas had died at the sea after Thailand intercepted but set them adrift once again in rickety flotillas; 2011–2015—when the crisis was at its peak with many Rohingyas imprisoned in border detention centers and jungle camps near Thailand (Asia Pacific Refugee Rights Network 2021). For some time after this, with a lot of international attention and clamping down of traffickers, the migration had stopped temporarily. However, things again started picking up from 2018 and reached a peak during the pandemic in 2020 and 2021. Two of the three boats discovered had only women and children. Their families were asked to pay ransoms for their safe disembarkation. Beating, rape, lack of food, and illness on board are common causes of death (ibid.).

Historically, people taking to the sea, looking for a safe asylum, also known as "boat" people have been perceived as a threat—countless incidents of nation-states refusing shelter and pushing back vessels into the high seas testify to this. For instance, Australia, despite being a signatory of the international conventions, flouted maritime rules by ordering the MV Tampa to return to sea in dangerous weather conditions (Pugh 2004, 50). This was a landmark event in the history of the boat people's migration that made Australia review its policy regarding the disembarkation of boats and providing asylum to the people on board (van Selm and Cooper 2006). This policy, known as the "Pacific strategy or solution," parallels with the Fortress Europe.

In the wake of the Rohingya maritime crisis in 2015, we saw a repeat of gross human rights violations. Historically, maritime migrants have always been more vulnerable than their terrestrial counterparts, especially because they can be tracked more easily, identified as pirates, or can simply drown. Rohingyas have been migrating more visibly since 2015, not only as asylum-seekers but also as economic migrants from Bangladesh over the high seas. They are also trafficked to Southeast Asia, West Asia, and even Australia, which has landed them in border-detention camps, often on the road to death, or turned them into bonded labor, or trapped them in a trafficking nexus that involves many actors. The scenario in Bangladesh vis-à-vis the Rohingya taking to the sea in precarious conditions has traces of this historical maritime context, with trafficking and slavery as epicenters. I will come to this part in a later section. Before that, the next section deals with the possibilities of rescuing sea-stuck migrants from the sea. How safe is the process?

## SAR: Search and Rescue

In situations of boat capsizing, interception is the first step, even for search and rescue operations for the migrants. Interception can also be used by a state to prevent the arrival of a ship within its jurisdiction. Daniele Esibini, the captain of one of the coastguard ships, revealed the dangers of such rescue operations. The first problem is overloaded boats, which "leads to them capsizing—frequently exactly at the point of rescue. He has never come across a boat that was not overloaded" (Baster and Merminod 2015). He further states, "The most dangerous part of a search-and-rescue operation is the moment of rescue. As rescuers approach, the very human reaction is to stand up and wave to guide your rescuers. If the [passengers] stand up, the boat capsizes" (Baster and Merminod 2015). The operation was abandoned after criticism from the European Union.

Normally, interception is followed by Search and Rescue Operations (SAR). Most often, SARs have paradoxically increased fatalities. Often migrants jump into the sea in desperation, failing to comprehend the reasons for interception. Scholars like Charles Heller, in their articles, talk about how the governmentality at sea is shaped by complex legal infrastructure, for which the responsibility of states to protect is often difficult to detect or prove, resulting into/ in the loss of lives (Heller and Pezzani 2017).

In such contexts of protracted "migration crisis" akin to the Rohingya situation, when all states including Myanmar, where they belong, deny citizenship rights, individuals can be compared to empty vessels sailing in the sea without any state flag or state protection. Experts in international law have thus been aiming at reducing migrant casualties at sea while simultaneously trying to uphold the legal right to asylum (Mann 2018).

Even if the initial phase of camp livelihood for a million plus Rohingya in Bangladesh in 2017 ensured a steady supply of ration (food) and shelter, reports of a blazing, devastating fire engulfing a large part of the camp in March 2021, rendering many homeless, only prove the extreme precarity of such an existence. Therefore, it is not surprising that the option of an escape will be alluring even if risky, resulting in sailing on the sea for more than ten weeks and being prevented from docking in Malaysia, their preferred destination, and Bangladesh, their country of origin (Beech 2020).

## Rohingyas from the Camps in Bangladesh

> My Son has crossed the sea over to Malaysia and is working in the fishing market there. He did not inform us at the time of leaving to save us from worrying. We would not have let him risk his life in undergoing such a risky journey but now, I am glad that he has fled the camps. Neither me or my wife have any hope left for us to go back (to Myanmar) but it gives us some hope to see the son is at least able to work and live as a free worker. I have not spoken to my daughter for years since she left home for India. If I give you her number, can you please dial and see whether it's working and connect us? (Mafatlal, personal interview 2015)

I promised I would. It was a warm afternoon in June 2015, and I was chatting with Abdul Mafatlal inside a tea shop located in Leda, the scattered shanty of Rohingyas living as undocumented, "unregistered" migrants in Bangladesh. Although recognized as refugees by UNHCR, they are still not considered so, at least by the terminology, in Bangladesh. The year 2015 was a crucial year on a few accounts, to which I shall come back in a moment. Mafatlal (65) is from Mongdaw, a village in Myanmar, and had been living in the camps of Cox's Bazar for thirteen years at the time of the interview. His daughter was in India then, and they had not met in years. Mafatlal just knows she was in Jammu, India, at the time of the interview. He is the informal head or representative of their makeshift settlement area. There are stages of violence against the Rohingyas in Myanmar, which have led them to flee in huge numbers. While the biggest in dimension and latest was in 2017, before that, it was 2012, when a mass exodus had taken place in Myanmar, following which many had crossed over the river Naf to reach Bangladesh. Mafatlal and most of the residents of this settlement that I visited, came after the violence of 2012. In between the two periods, it was 2015 when the extent of marginalization and haplessness of the people came to the limelight.

Incidentally, Malaysia was a desired location for the Rohingya also because of the interaction that the Rohingya living in Bangladesh had with the locals, because labor migration between Bangladesh and Malaysia was formally agreed upon in 2008. Religion was also a key factor in choosing the destinations. The informal labor migration in this case too was going on for a while but when more and more people started going there, the government of Malaysia in May 2016 refused to accept them, and the then home minister in no uncertain terms remarked, "we have to send the right message that they are not welcome here" (Mafatlal, personal interview 2015). I say this here to project that it is not clear whether the status of refugeehood for the Rohingya at all mattered to these countries because, for them and India, they were no different from the illegal Bangladeshi economic migrants.

While Myanmar harps on the point that the Rohingyas never originally belonged to Myanmar and hence they lose their claim to live there, the argument of the Rohingyas contradicts this claim. The official statement maintained by Rohingya activists and the people is that according to the 1948 Citizenship Law of Myanmar, they were considered as "citizens of Myanmar."[8] It was much later, that a new law was framed under which they lost their citizenship status and became stateless. It is important to understand these dynamics, the war of words, and various interpretations of history to gauge the flight of the Rohingyas from Myanmar in precarious conditions. The most crucial aspect of their existence or precarity is the aspect of their statelessness (Staples 2012, 140). It is here that one is reminded of the postcolonial particularities of the borders that South Asian nationhood is constituted of.

During my second longer stint of PhD fieldwork in Bangladesh in 2019, every other youth that I have interacted with, from Farukh to Zubair and Pormin—my key interlocuters from the camps—vouched that they are not stateless: "Why will we accept us being called stateless when our forefathers have cards that prove their citizenship status in Myanmar? Furthermore, we were born in Myanmar through generations. We are citizens of Myanmar and want our rights back as citizens before going back there" (Faruk, Zubair, and Pormin, personal interview 2019). All three of them are new settlers in the camps after the biggest exodus of Rohingya from Myanmar in 2017.

Over the last few years, the Bangladesh government has decided to resettle registered Rohingyas in a different region since Cox's Bazaar is primarily a tourist area and the smuggling-trafficking nexus in the region has led to a lot of anti-social activities, including drug smuggling. The place where the registered camps might shift is a barren island in the Bay of Bengal called Thengar Bhashan Char—a remote, cyclone and flood prone island. It is being said that the concept of sending the refugees to this island is like the idea of "refugee warehousing" where mobility will be further restricted, bearing similarities to the colonial legacy of penal colonies (Nguyen and Lewis 2022). Even after saving several camp residents from a vessel that was adrift in the sea for months in 2020, they were sent to Bhasan Char instead of the camps. The explanation was that they were to be quarantined on the island, but unofficially, the idea is to keep them there till they can be pushed back to Myanmar from Bangladesh. Much as the fate of the Rohingya as the new boat people reminds one of the dark histories of that of the Vietnamese boat crisis, likewise, the strategy of relocating them to Bhasan Char bears resemblance to the Andaman Islands that served as "penal colonies" during the British rule in the Indian subcontinent. It is estimated that 19,000 Rohingyas have already been shifted from the camps to the islands without adequate infrastructure (ibid.). While the idea of shifting the refugees to Bhasan Char has been around for some time, it was only in 2020 that the first relocation was initiated, following the rescue of a stranded boat that was attempting to reach Malaysia from Cox's Bazar. This only indicates the complexity of the entire scenario when, for the refugees, the questions of life and choice hang on the edge. The sea becomes the dangerous dream that allures them toward a journey of freedom, albeit uncertain, on the other side, failing which their confinement either in the refugee camps or a flood prone island is certain. For the refugee, the hope of attaining citizenship in the destination country or the status of a refugee as per the UNHCR 1951 refugee convention becomes paramount to break free from the condition of statelessness, even if the journeys are fraught with danger.

To conclude, in Bangladesh, as follows from above, the condition of the Rohingya refugees has deteriorated significantly of late, after a million of them were resettled from Myanmar in 2017. Dissatisfaction, dissent, and internal friction have led to the murder of popular Rohingya leader Mohibullah in 2021, triggering panic in the camps, and leading to more people wanting to escape their lives at the camps. Thus, because of its accessibility and familiarity, the sea has emerged as the most preferable medium for bailing out. All these in combination, propelled by the lack of rights that the conditions of statelessness manifest, are causes why the Rohingya take to the sea, albeit at risk, to seek out a better life, employment, and asylum in the Southeast Asian countries, and what remains unsolved to date is the helplessness and lack of protection measures for the floating stateless, seeking refuge in the border states.

## Notes

1. Elif Shafak, *The Island of Missing Trees: A Novel* (Cyprus: Viking, 2021), 1.

2. By which he meant appearance, attire, and attitude or body language of the people, a certain level of nervousness that is easily discernible by trained officers.

3. The official asked him the exact location in the district that was mentioned in the paper, which the person sitting next to me could not answer. When pushed harder to disclose his citizenship status, he admitted to be a Rohingya, from the new influx, 2017, in Bangladesh. This fieldwork done in 2019 was part of my PhD program. My fieldwork in 2015 was supported by the Calcutta Research Group (CRG), for which I remain indebted.

4. An UNHCR report on illegal maritime migration between April and June 2015 mentioned 6,000 refugees had been abandoned by smugglers in the Bay of Bengal and Andaman Sea in May 2015. Since 2014, approximately 94,000 migrants had attempted to cross the seas. In the first three months of 2015, the figure was 25,000, which between April and August 2015 increased to 31,000, with 370 deaths in 2015 alone. This UNHCR report gave a day-to-day account of what unfolded between May and July 2015 after the migrants had been abandoned at sea. See "South-East Asia: Mixed Maritime Movements," UNHCR, April–June 2015.

5. *De Facto* Statelessness. This part is borrowed from the publication proposal of statelessness developed by the Calcutta Research Group, 2021.

6. Article 1.1 of the 1954 UN Convention relating to the Status of Stateless Persons, defines a stateless person as "a person who is not considered as a national by any State under the operation of its law." The 1954 Convention establishes minimum guarantees in areas such as education, health care, employment, and identity as well as travel documents.

7. "[S]omeone who is unable or unwilling to return to their country of origin owing to a well-founded fear of being persecuted for reasons of race, religion, nationality, membership of a particular social group, or political opinion." www.unhcr.org/3b66c2aa10.pdf

8. Taken from the personal website of a Rohingya activist who is also a medical practitioner based in Ireland. He holds several offices in organizations that work for Rohingya rights in the UK and Ireland. www.haikalmansor.com

## References

"2020 Was 'Deadliest' Year Ever for Rohingya Sea Journeys: UNHCR." *Al Jazeera*, August 20, 2021. www.aljazeera.com/news/2021/8/20/rohingya-sea-journeys-un

Agamben, Giorgio. *Sovereign Power and Bare Life. Homo Sacer*. Stanford, CA: Stanford University Press, 1998.

Arendt, Hannah. *The Origins of Totalitarianism*. London: George Allen & Unwin, 1968.

Baster, Tim, and Isabelle Merminod. "Death in the Mediterranean." New Internationalist. May 27, 2015. https://newint.org/features/web-exclusive/2015/05/27/mediterranean-refugee-crisis

Basu Ray Chaudhury, Sabyasachi, and Ranabir Samaddar, eds. *The Rohingya in South Asia: People without a State*. London & New York: Routledge, 2018.

Batchelor, C. A. "Statelessness and the Problem of Resolving Nationality Status." *International Journal of Refugee Law* 10, no. 1–2 (1998): 156–82. https://doi.org/10.1093/ijrl/10.1-2.156

Beech, Hannah. "Hundreds of Rohingya Refugees Stuck at Sea With 'Zero Hope.'" *The New York Times*, May 1, 2020. www.nytimes.com/2020/05/01/world/asia/rohingya-muslim-refugee-crisis.html

Bernstein, Richard J. "Hannah Arendt on the Stateless." *Parallax* 11, no. 1 (2005): 46–60. https://doi.org/10.1080/1353464052000321092

Biswas, Samata. "Migrations and Identities: A Study of Sea of Poppies." *Refugee Watch Online*. July 22, 2016. http://refugeewatchonline.blogspot.com/2016/07/migrations-and-identities-study-of-sea.html

Butler, Judith, and Gayatri Chakravorty Spivak. *Who Sings the Nation-State?: Language, Politics, Belonging*. Kolkata: Seagull Books, 2007.

Chiew, Huiyee. "Bajau Laut: Once Sea Nomads, Now Stateless." Malaysiakini. May 17, 2019. www.malaysiakini.com/news/476595

Chowdhory, Nasreen. "State Formation, Marginality and Belonging: Contextualising Rights of Refugees in India, Bangladesh and Sri Lanka." *In Refugees, Citizenship and Belonging in South Asia: Contested Terrains*, 43–69. Singapore: Springer, 2018.

"Convention and Protocol Relating to the Status of Refugees." United Nations, 2020.

Das, Veena. *Life and Words: Violence and the Descent into the Ordinary.* Berkeley: University of California Press, 2007.

Debrix, François, and Alexander D. Barder. *Beyond Biopolitics: Theory, Violence, and Horror in World Politics*. Interventions. Abingdon: Routledge, 2012.

Dua, Jatin. *Captured at Sea: Piracy and Protection in the Indian Ocean*. Atelier: Ethnographic Inquiry in the Twenty First Century 3. Oakland: University of California Press, 2019.

Ferguson, James, and Akhil Gupta. "Spatializing States: Toward an Ethnography of Neoliberal Governmentality." *American Ethnologist* 29, no. 4 (2002): 981–1002. https://doi.org/10.1525/ae.2002.29.4.981

Heller, Charles, and Lorenzo Pezzani. "Liquid Traces: Investigating the Deaths of Migrants at the EU's Maritime Frontier." In *The Borders of "Europe": Autonomy of Migration, Tactics of Bordering*, edited by Nicholas De Genova, 657–84. Durham, NC: Duke University Press, 2017. https://doi.org/10.1215/9780822372660

Jha, Rajesh. "Seven Bangladeshi Die on Migrant Boat near Italy." *DD News*. January 25, 2022. https://ddnews.gov.in/international/seven-bangladeshi-die-migrant-boat-near-italy

Jones, Henry. "Lines in the Ocean: Thinking with the Sea about Territory and International Law." *London Review of International Law* 4, no. 2 (2016): 307–43. https://doi.org/10.1093/lril/lrw012

Mahanirban Calcutta Research Group. n.d. "Module D: Statelessness in South Asia: (Concept Note, Suggested Readings, and Assignments)." www.mcrg.ac.in/Statelessness/ModuleD.pdf

Malischewski, Charlotte-Anne. "Legal Brief on Statelessness: Law in the Indian Context." In *The Rohingya in South Asia: People without a State*, edited by Sabyasachi Basu Ray Chaudhury and Ranabir Samaddar. London & New York: Routledge, 2018.

Malkki, Liisa H. *Purity and Exile: Violence, Memory, and National Cosmology Among Hutu Refugees in Tanzania*. Chicago & London: University of Chicago Press, 1995.

Mann, Itamar. "Maritime Legal Black Holes: Migration and Rightlessness in International Law." *European Journal of International Law* 29, no. 2 (2018): 347–72. https://doi.org/10.1093/ejil/chy029

"Nansen—a Man of Action and Vision." UNHCR. 2009. www.unhcr.org/events/nansen/4aae50086/nansen-man-action-vision.html

Nguyen, Hanh, and Themba Lewis. "Bhasan Char and Refugee 'Warehousing.'" *The Diplomat*. February 8, 2022. https://thediplomat.com/2022/02/bhasan-char-and-refugee-warehousing

Novak, Paolo. "Back to Borders." *Critical Sociology* 43, no. 6 (2017): 847–64. https://doi.org/10.1177/0896920516644034

Parsons, Laurie, and Sabina Lawreniuk. "Seeing Like the Stateless: Documentation and the Mobilities of Liminal Statelessness in Cambodia." *Political Geography* 62 (October, 2017): 1–11. https://doi.org/10.1016/j.polgeo.2017.09.016

"Promoting Safety of Life at Sea in Selected Coastal Areas in South-East Asia through Local Actors," Asia Pacific Refugee Rights Network, 2021. https://aprrn.org/media/Publications/files/ASRN-Report_ENG_s_W6jgHBX.pdf

Pugh, M. "Drowning Not Waving: Boat People and Humanitarianism at Sea." *Journal of Refugee Studies* 17, no. 1 (2004): 50–69. https://doi.org/10.1093/jrs/17.1.50

Randeria, Shalini. "The State of Globalization: Legal Plurality, Overlapping Sovereignties and Ambiguous Alliances between Civil Society and the Cunning State in India." *Theory, Culture & Society* 24, no. 1 (2007): 1–33. https://doi.org/10.1177/0263276407071559

Samaddar, Ranabir. "Forced Migration Situations as Exceptions in History?" *International Journal of Migration and Border Studies* 2, no. 2 (2016): 99–118. https://doi.org/10.1504/IJMBS.2016.075579

———. *The Postcolonial Age of Migration*. London & New York: Routledge, 2020.

Scott, James C. *The Art of Not Being Governed: An Anarchist History of Upland Southeast Asia*. Yale Agrarian Studies Series. New Haven, CT & London: Yale University Press, 2009.

Selm, Joanne van, and Betsy Cooper. "The New 'Boat People': Ensuring Safety and Determining Status." Migration Policy Institute, 2006. www.migrationpolicy.org/research/new-boat-people-ensuring-safety-and-determining-status

Somers, Margaret R. *Genealogies of Citizenship: Markets, Statelessness, and the Right to Have Rights*. Cambridge Cultural Social Studies. Cambridge & New York: Cambridge University Press, 2008.

Staples, Kell. "Statelessness and the Politics of Misrecognition." *Res Publica* 18, no. 1 (2012): 93–106. https://doi.org/10.1007/s11158-012-9188-0

"UNHCR Fact Sheet: The 1961 Convention on the Reduction of Statelessness." Refworld. 2021. www.refworld.org/docid/612608084.html

UNHCR. "Joint Statement by UNHCR, IOM and UNODC on Protection at Sea in the Bay of Bengal and Andaman Sea." UNHCR. May 6, 2020. www.unhcr.org/news/press/2020/5/5eb15b804/joint-statement-unhcr-iom-unodc-protection-sea-bay-bengal-andaman-sea.html

Chapter 12

# Logistics of Maritime Capitalism

## Flags of Convenience and the Statelessness at Sea

Joyce C. H. Liu, Yu-Fan Chiu, and Jonathan S. Parhusip

The trilogy of the investigation reports conducted by the independent media outlet *The Reporter* in five years, from 2016 to 2021, has allowed us to witness the horrendous crimes of forced labor on Taiwan fishing vessels in the high seas.[1] The fishers on Taiwan vessels are from different countries, mainly the low-waged, third-world countries such as Indonesia, the Philippines, Cambodia, and North Korea, among others. They are forced to work long hours, often up to twenty hours per day when the situation requires. Due to fishing seasons, they must stay on board for eight months to two years. Their salary is low, supposedly 458 USD per month, but it is deductible variably according to the agreement with their brokers. In the worst cases, many of them receive no wages after their service. The working conditions are miserable and unsafe, and they often endure brutal physical abuse from their captain or other crew members close to the captain. If injured during fishing, they cannot receive proper medical treatment and cannot ask for help or appeal for compensation.

Why do the fishers become stateless once they are on the FOC ships sailing on the high seas? In the following sections, we shall first discuss the origin of FOC (Free of Charge) and its role within a composite structure in the logistics of global capitalism. We shall then take the case of Taiwan as one of the major receiving countries of foreign fishers and discuss the formation of "Lawlessness" of fisherman's labor rights concerning the FOC Fishing Vessel Control Policy under the legislation process. We further investigate the recruitment policies in Indonesia, one of the most significant labor-sending countries in the third world, to demonstrate the collaboration of the complex logistics through forgery and fraud in the global supply chain. We will conclude with our theoretical intervention of the New Nomos of the Earth in the age of the neoliberal maritime capitalism of the twenty-first century and the complex apparatus that produces the slavery system at sea today.

## The Logistics of FOC and Global Capitalism

Scholars have pointed out that the genealogy of logistics and racial capitalism originated with the Atlantic slave trade in the sixteenth century. It is the first moment of a large-scale trans-continental and trans-oceanic transportation of commodities by shipping cargo. The shipping of human labor forces is connected with a complete and sophisticated network, involving multi-national laws, institutions, information, infrastructures, military equipment, etc. (Ferrell 2005; Ince 2014; Chua et al. 2018). FOC, in its roots, is also closely linked with the logistics of global capitalism and functions through free trade liberalization in the neoliberal age, playing with the game of law. As we know, the flag in history represents a military legion, a religious clan, or a commercial group. Using a flag as a national emblem began only at the end of the eighteenth century. The flag of convenience is a legal invention to implement the changing phase of global capitalism since the 1960s. Historians traced FOC use to English merchants sailing under the Spanish flag in the sixteenth century to evade trade regulations with the West Indies. Slave ships carried FOCs under Spanish-Cuban registration to escape capture by the British navy until the transatlantic slave trade was ended in the 1860s. US shipping companies have used Panamanian flags since the 1920s (Ferrell 2005, 336).

The transition from the national flag cargo shipping system to the FOC global shipping system has developed rapidly since the late 1960s and early 1970s (van Fossen 2016; Ademun-Odeke 2005). Alongside the rise of neoliberalism and the enormous growth of transnational corporations, international trade, foreign direct investment, and other determining factors, the invention of FOC indicated the emergence of a new stage of global capitalism. With the legal identity a flag of convenience represents, it also gives the applicable laws governing taxation, labor practices, safety regulations, licensing, inspections, and all the offshore management of financial centers (van Fossen 2016; Ademun-Odeke 2005). Countries such as Panama, Liberia, the Marshall Islands, and Vanuatu are the most popular flag states. These governments sought rents from vessel registration powers as a form of state property. FOC states also outsource flag registration, and private companies administer these private flags (Campling and Colás 2021). In this way, FOCs play a game of pseudo-nationhood, with the flags of the flag states but no genuine links between the flag state's law, port states, ship owners, or crews. FOC becomes the epitome of the laissez-faire global logistics system.

Moreover, the legal "denationalization" of shipping capital with the generalized shift to flags of convenience, as Campling and Colás (2021) pointed out, opened maritime labor markets to international crew from the third world. In East Asia, for example, the fast promotion of maritime industries as state-managed industrialization strategies explains the rise of giant shipyards and internationally competitive shipping companies with low-waged fishers from regional developing countries, such as South and Southeast Asia. The opaque operation of ownership and the outsourcing of registries in this global maritime trade contribute to the phenomenon of the sea as a locus for the deep interconnection between "big business and organized crime, open registries, and secret jurisdiction" (Campling and Colás 2021, 267–68).

In the pursuit of maximizing profits limited by their home registries, fishing vessels flag out, purchasing foreign flags that allow them to fish in different maritime zones. They often buy Bareboat Charter (BBC) offered by the flag states with FOC registries. With the sovereignty of the flag states, no other countries or international laws can interfere with the FOC and BBC practices (Ademun-Odeke 2005, 355–56). The legal "offshore" practices allow capital to choose the laws that serve it. The emergence of the new terraqueous space of Special Economic Zones (SEZ), Export Processing Zones (EPZs), and their newly established ports onshore also mimicked "offshore" practices (Campling and Colás 2021, 2550–52). These new ports are often corporatized and privatized, with fast and automated cargo handling, and enjoy exemption from several national laws, including low or no tax, freedom from customs duties, avoidance of labor control, and inspections. As Campling and Colás rightly pointed out, the term "offshore" does not only refer to the geographical location of economic activities but to "the juridical status of a vast and expanding array of the specialized realm" (Campling and Colás 2021, 268–69).

With the belief that the world ocean with the global flows of goods belongs to whoever can join the competition, the sea is liberalized and dominated by a few enormous fishing/shipping companies. The competition among large shipping companies globally is intense. The merger of small shipping groups leads to the emergence of large multinational shipping corporations.[2]

Asian governments also rapidly gain revenues from the number of vessels flying FOCs. In 2014, Japan, China, South Korea, Singapore, Hong Kong, and Taiwan were among the top ten ship-owning nations with foreign and national flags. In a UK Department of Transport study in 2015, 74.8 percent of the world's fleet was under flags of convenience in 2014 (van Fossen 2016, 367). The UNCTAD (United Nations Conference on Trade and Development) statistics show that, in 2019, half of the world fleet was owned by Asian companies, 93 percent of global shipbuilding occurred in China, the Republic of Korea, and Japan, and 16 percent of the global fleet carrying capacity was registered in Panama. The Institute of Shipping Economics and Logistics claimed that, in 2019, China topped Japan for the first time (UNCTADstat 2020).[3]

FOC has been regarded as a "floating piece of the territory" of the nation whose flag it flies, in which no law can intervene (Warner-Kramer 2004, 503, as quoted in van Fossen 2016, 368). The flag states do not care to bother with the ships flying their flags or regulate their working conditions or IUU (Illegal, Unreported and Unregulated) fishing. The fishing companies outsource their recruitment of international fishers to private brokerage. The ship owners' states also do not have jurisdiction over the vessels flying foreign flags or recruiting overseas. Moreover, there is no implementation of domestic law to carry out the international conventions. The international conventions, such as the 1958 Geneva High Seas Convention, the IMCO (Intergovernmental Maritime Consultative Organization) Advisory Opinion in 1960, the negotiations of UNCLOS (United Nations Convention on the Law of the Sea) in the 1970s, or the 188 Convention, all fail to find implementation by the local government, either of the flag states or the ship owners' state, not to mention the transnational corporations. Various loopholes between the laws and policies of different departments and bureaus also expose the gaps between labor law and actual practice on the high seas. Given the laissez-faire attitude among countries towards FOC vessels without direct control mechanisms, fishing activities that violate international fisheries management norms are frequent. To clarify the formation of "lawlessness" of fisherman's labor rights on FOC vessels of the receiving countries, we move on to the case of Taiwan's FOC Fishing Vessel Control Policy and the legislation process.

## Legislation and the Formation of "Lawlessness": The Case of Taiwan's FOC Fishing Vessel and Fishermen's Labor Rights

Taiwan's FOC fishing vessel control policy and legislation Article 92 of the United Nations Convention on the Law of the Sea clearly stipulates that ships shall sail under the flag of one state only and shall be subject to its exclusive jurisdiction on the high seas. All countries have the obligation to formulate the conditions for ship nationality grants, but they also have the discretion to determine the contents of the conditions for ship nationality grants. FOC ship states may formulate more relaxed conditions for the granting of nationality based on the consideration of their national economic interests. At present, there are no restrictions on such discretion in international practice. Therefore, when a country grants nationality to a ship according to its own conditions, other countries should simply recognize the ship's nationality (Hwang 2000; Wang 2008). There were already 251 FOC ships approved by the Taiwanese government by 2021, mainly from Panama (73), Vanuatu (71), Seychelles (40), Nauru (16), and Micronesia (16).[4]

In 2004 and 2005, the International Commission for the Conservation of Atlantic Tunas (ICCAT) imposed sanctions on Taiwan's longline tuna fishery for two consecutive years. Instances in which Taiwan's fishing vessels were reported and protested against by Greenpeace organizations on the high seas also prompted the Taiwanese government to face the issue of the control of distant-water fishing ships (Greenpeace Southeast Asia 2020). In the face of international pressure, Taiwan finally enacted the Act to Govern the Investment in and Operation of Foreign Flag Fishing Vessels in 2008 (hereinafter the Foreign Flagged Fishing Vessel Act). Article 4 of the Act stipulates that no person of Taiwanese nationality is permitted to invest in or operate a non-Taiwan-flagged vessel to conduct fishing business overseas without the permission of the competent authority. Moreover, those who fish in violation of international fisheries management regulations are subject to criminal or administrative penalties, depending on the severity of the situation.

However, Taiwan was still included by the EU in the IUU yellow card list on October 1, 2015. This occurred mainly because the Taiwanese fisheries industry's legal framework was not sound, and the overly lenient penalties were disproportionate to the illegal gains, resulting in problems such as the failure to deter IUU fishing practices, a lack of effective management of ocean-going fleets, and the failure to fulfill the relevant obligations to international fishery organizations. Pressed by the world again, the Taiwanese government passed the new Act for Distant Water Fishing and amended the Foreign Flagged Fishing Vessel Act and the Fisheries Act on July 20, 2016. These regulations were implemented on January 20, 2017 (Chen 2019, 153–54). The most important amendments to the Foreign Flagged Fishing Vessel Act were new provisions on the circumstances of the investment in and operation of foreign-flagged fishing vessels (Article 4, par. 2). The following are examples of circumstances for not granting or revoking permission:

> (1) The flag state of the fishing vessels lacks control mechanisms over its fishing vessels. (2) The fishing vessel's flag state has been listed by other countries, international fisheries organizations, or economic integration organizations as a non-cooperative country in combating IUU fishing operations or a country on the warning list of non-cooperation in combating IUU fishing operations for more than two years. (3) The fishing vessel has been included in the list of fishing vessels engaged in IUU fishing operations by any international fisheries organisation. (Government of Taiwan, 2016)

Operating a foreign-flagged fishing vessel without a permit (including a cancelled permit) is subject to an administrative penalty.

## The Formation of "Lawlessness" of Fishermen's Labor Rights

As for the FOC fishing vessel control policies and legislations, despite those new legislations, Taiwan always attended to them in a passive way only when there was international pressure to prevent Taiwanese nationals' products from being banned from entering the EU market because of their catches being from illegal fishing vessels or products of non-cooperative ship flag countries. The Taiwanese government took these measures not to eliminate illegal acts on fishing vessels, even though it recognized their frequent occurrence. Therefore, despite the implementation of the above regulations, there are no effective regulatory measures. FOC institutions offer strong incentives and measures to expand the open registry of ship flags as much as possible and provide advantages such as shipowners' taxes, confidentiality, financing, labor costs, and anti-environmental protection. Complementing the increase in FOC ships is cost reduction, insecurity, low wages, and poor working conditions (Hwang 2000, 293–96).

Under the structure of transnational capitalism, libertarians are of the view that FOC ships help to improve efficiency, reduce costs, and improve innovation. At the same time, when each country is constantly improving and looking for new ways to attract capital, FOC ships surely provide a benign alternative in the midst of "unfair blackmail" by the government and trade unions. This also further creates opportunities for the globalization of free enterprises. Structuralists, on the other hand, believe that although the FOC open registry has disadvantages, if all FOC registration institutions formulate laws and establish institutional structures to meet the minimum standards, they can facilitate competition and play an important role in the global economy by providing low standards with consistency through "structural isomorphism." As for the regulationists who engage in comprehensive criticism of the FOC, they believe that the FOC should be strictly restricted or even that the whole FOC system should be abolished because its operation violates global public interest and only serves a handful of capitalists with the lowest productivity and the strongest parasitism. They further believe that cross-border cooperation should therefore be strengthened to establish a fairer and more coordinated global maritime system and that the principle of national sovereign equality should be downplayed by requiring adherence to universal high standards (van Fossen 2016, 11–13).

The Taiwanese government's position is between that of the libertarians and the structuralists. It believes that this is only a matter of Taiwanese people investing abroad and should not be prohibited. Since FOC ships are fishing vessels with foreign nationality, restrictions imposed on Taiwanese nationals in the operation of foreign fishing vessels may raise questions about the extraterritorial effect of domestic laws as they regulate events outside one's own territory. However, FOC ships' flag states (such as Panama and Vanuatu) have long been passive in the management of ships granted their nationality, resulting in the problems of IUU and forced labor at sea. Consequently, internationally, there has been demand to switch the administration of FOC ships from the ship's flag state to the state of the shipowner's nationality (Hwang 2000, 296–308). In addition, legally, the legislation on FOC vessels in Taiwan does not violate the principle of territorial jurisdiction because administering the investment in and operation of foreign fishing vessels by nationals of Taiwan is still in line with the nationality principle.

Nevertheless, this has put distant-water fishermen in a dilemma of "lawlessness" in both legislation and practice. First, of the Panama and

Vanuatu FOC ships, which are the most invested in by the Taiwanese, Panama has been warned by the EU for three consecutive years (2019, 2020, and 2021), while Vanuatu has been listed as a key inspection object by the International Transport Workers' Federation (ITF) for many years. These circumstances exactly fit the following stipulation in the Foreign Flagged Fishing Vessel Act: "The fishing vessel's flag state has been listed by other countries, international fisheries organizations, or other economic integration organizations as a non-cooperative country in combating IUU fishing operations or a country on the warning list of non-cooperation in combating IUU fishing operations for more than two years" (Government of Taiwan, 2016). As such, the license to continue to operate foreign-flagged fishing vessels should be revoked. However, such fishing vessels continue to recruit fishermen and operate FOC vessels, reaping many benefits. It renders the Act useless and provides no function for preventing and blocking illegal distant-water fishing from the source. Secondly, on the issue of forced labor and unreasonable labor conditions, the Act does not provide clear labor conditions for operators to implement. In contrast, there are the Regulations on the Authorisation and Management of Overseas Employment of Foreign Crew Members for Taiwan-flagged distant-water fishing vessels with provisions on working conditions such as "the items, amount, and payment method for payment to crew members; the monthly salary of crew members shall not be less than US $450" and "the daily rest time of foreign crew members shall not be less than 10 hours; the monthly rest should not be less than four days" (Government of Taiwan, 2019). The fishermen on the FOC ships, however, are likely in a working environment in which their working conditions are unprotected. The FOC ships usually have no crew members from the flag state; thus, the relationship between the FOC ships and the flag state is quite poor. Hence, the flag state usually has no incentive to regulate the working conditions in a fishery, and even if it does, it lacks supervision and implementation capacity.

Countries around the world use the legislation on basic labor rights to protect their own workers, but they do not provide protections for foreign migrant workers or, instead, they adopt laissez-faire differential treatment for economic reasons. Passive reaction is the current policy with the excuse of "non-interference in flag state sovereignty." If FOC fishing boats are incorporated into Taiwan's migrant policy, migrant workers would be excluded from legal protection to the maximum extent. For distant-water fishermen employed abroad, the government provided a straightforward announcement that the Labor Standard Act (LSA) did not apply and replaced the LSA with the Regulations on the Authorisation and Management of Overseas Employment of Foreign Crew Members. The working conditions of the fishermen on the FOC ships are not protected, thus allowing the formation of a lawless state without labor rights for distant-water fishermen, which allows capitalism to further globalize without hindrance and FOC shipping to become more powerful. We need to further investigate the recruitment policies in Indonesia, as one of the significant labor-sending countries in the third world, to demonstrate the collaboration of the complex logistics in the global supply chain.

## Recruitment Practices in Indonesia: A Complex Web Full of Fraud and Deceit

Private recruitment agencies (PRAs) in Indonesia are various elements of "migration infrastructure" (Xiang and Lindquist 2014, 122–48) with a business license (*Surat Izin Usaha*) in recruiting, selecting, training, sending, and placing Indonesian migrant workers overseas. The Ministry of Labor holds sole authority to issue licenses for PRAs recruiting land-based workers. On the contrary, three ministries have the right to issue licenses for PRAs recruiting seafarers and fishers, namely, the National Board for the Placement and Protection of Indonesian Overseas Workers (BP2MI) under the authority of the Ministry of Labor, the Ministry of Transportation, and the Department of Commerce at the regency level under the supervision of the Ministry of Trade (Rhamdani 2020). In late 2020, BP2MI reported that from 2018 to 2020, the Ministry of Labor had issued licenses (SIU-PJTKI) to 322 companies, and these PRAs had sent 6,169 fishers abroad. About 94 percent of them were employed in Taiwan, but the report does not specify whether those fishers were employed in offshore or distant water fishing (Indonesian Ministry of Labor, n.d.). Dephub (2021) reported that the Ministry of Transportation had issued business licenses to recruit and place crew ships (SIUPPAK) for 178 PRAs, and the Ministry of Trade does not provide how many licenses (SIUP) have been issued. On the other hand, neither the Ministry of Transportation nor the Ministry of Trade provides statistics on the placement of Indonesian crews abroad.

Decentered licensing of manning agencies and overlapping regulations generate lawless gaps in recruitment practices, protection overseas, and supervision from the authorities. Multiple interpretations of different ministerial regulations create loose ends in the recruitment process. These gaps provide an opportunity for PRAs to send as many prospective crews as possible without considering the credibility of their clients overseas. Consequently, the Indonesian government does not have an accurate database of PRAs in the country or how many Indonesians are employed as fishers overseas.

The multiplicity of actors involved in the recruitment process, the overlapping authorities issuing PRAs licenses in Indonesia, and the passive reaction of the Taiwan government put migrant fishers in a vulnerable position. Transnational employment of fishers is exacerbated by the fact that PRAs in the sending countries and employers abroad have no clear division of responsibilities. The 2017 Act for Distant Water Fisheries and the Regulations on the Authorization and Management of Overseas Employment of Foreign Crew Members are arguably inadequate to protect migrant fishers on board, particularly those employed on FOC vessels. Although the vessel is in the territory of a country, for example, a port in Taiwan, the Taiwanese government cannot intervene in a labor dispute that occurs on the vessels flying FOCs. FOC adoption allows flag states to deflect and eschew responsibility for labor disputes, criminal wrongdoing, and labor abuses that arise in their territorial jurisdictions (Yea 2022).

In March 2021, our researcher assisted a group of twenty-nine Indonesian and Filipino fishers who had newly arrived in Kaohsiung's Cijin port to claim their unpaid salary.[5] The salary was due but remained unpaid, so they contacted an NGO. Although the vessel is docked in Kaohsiung port, such a complaint cannot be addressed to the Fishery Agency as they do not intervene in the affairs of FOC fishing vessels (in this case, it was a Vanuatu flagged vessel). After publishing the case on social media, a Fishery Agency officer reached out, offering to find the vessel owner and ask about the situation, making no promises. The officer said, "I can make sure the vessel is FOC, but due to my limited rights, I cannot violate the owner." He offered help and said, "I will try to find the owner and try to know more detail with private communication." So, despite the vessels being owned by Taiwanese investors and the crewing being managed by a manning agency located in Taiwan, relevant authorities cannot intervene in the case of a FOC vessel.

The name of Taiwan and the Taiwan flag become appetizing merchandise in the recruitment process in many Southeast Asian countries. The fishers in the case discussed above were not aware that they were being employed on a FOC vessel because the signed contract clearly stated Taiwan flag (see figure 12.1), and the vessel does not fly its flag until the vessel leaves the port. Such false advertisements and fraudulent contracts are common in sending countries, such as Indonesia, during the recruitment process. In

Figure 12.1. Vanuatu flagged vessel. *Source*: wcpfc.int. Public domain.

Western & Central Pacific
Fisheries Commission

**ESSIEN** [redacted]

**Owner Name** [redacted]FISHERY CO LTD
**Owner Address:**
[redacted] Vanuatu
**Master Name:** CHENG,[redacted]
**Master Nationality:** Chinese Taipei
**Reg Port:** Port Vila
**Built in Country:** Japan
**Built in Year:** 1990
**Crew:** 35
**Length:** 55.45
**Length Units:** Meters
**Length Type:** Overall
**Moulded Depth:** 3.85
**Moulded Depth Units:** Meters
**Beam:** 8.70
**Beam Units:** Meters
**Tonnage:** 598.00
**Tonnage Type:** GRT
**Engine Power:** 1600
**Power Units:** PS
**Freezer Types:** Other (Air (Coils) RC)
**Freezing Capacity:** 6
**Freezing Capacity Units:** MT/DAY
**Number of Freezers:** 4

**Flag:** Vanuatu
**Registration Number:** [redacted]
**IRCS:** [redacted]3
**Vessel Type:** Tuna longliner
**WIN:** Y[redacted]
**IMO-LR:** [redacted]1
**VID:** [redacted]
**Submitted by CCM:** Vanuatu
**Attachments:**

many cases, the recruitment agency sent the fishers to the receiving countries and assigned them to the far sea fishing vessels with FOCs without being noticed. During the two-year contract period, many fishers only stepped their feet off the vessels only twice, once at arrival and once at departure. In some other cases, fishers were trafficked directly to the port-states and ended up working onboard FOC fishing vessels.

Many PRAs advertised the job on FOC vessels as "Taiwan fishing job" or "Taiwan flagged vessels" because fishers do know that Taiwan has stricter regulations than other countries' flags. However, many fishers do not know that about 251 Taiwanese-owned fishing vessels are flying FOCs, and many manning agencies based in Taiwan supply crews to FOC vessels and foreign-owned and flagged vessels.[6] On the other hand, Taiwan does not have adequate laws regulating the operations of crewing companies in Taiwan, which creates space for practices that are detrimental to foreign crews applying to work on Taiwan-flagged vessels.

The PRAs in Indonesia would send anyone who is willing to work abroad, including those who are not qualified as fisher, or without any proper selection and training in the recruitment process. Practically, the PRAs would facilitate all the needs of the prospective crews, including providing loans, managing documents, and licensing. These involved administrative frauds, and forged documents, such as Basic Safety Training (BST), medical check-ups, passports, and permits from the district level. Tempo's investigation reported that a forger they interviewed can make at least a total of 4,000 blank Seamen Books and BST certificates in a year (*Tempo* 2017). The forger would sell a blank Seamen Book for NTD 70 and a BST for NTD 16 to local brokers. Then, the brokers will sell forged documents to prospective fishers who are unqualified or inexperienced and to those who don't want the burden of the recruitment process. Consequently, inexperienced fishers are vulnerable to being victims of bullying and abuse on the vessels due to their incompetence to perform fishing jobs and stress due to the long sailing period on the high seas. This is what was experienced by Supryanto on the *Fu Tzu Chun* vessel before he died in 2015, as well as many other fishers onboard fishing vessels.

During the recruitment process, prospective crews would sign an agreement of loan to cover recruitment, documents, and departure fees. The loans, ranging from USD 400 to USD 1,200, will be deducted from the crews' monthly salaries.[7] Many recruitment companies withhold crews' wages as guarantee-fees to ensure that the fishers fulfill their contract, pay back the loans, and do not run away after they arrive in Taiwan (Parhusip 2021). Therefore, even though the Regulations on the Authorization and Management of Overseas Employment of Foreign Crew Members do not permit recruitment agencies to deduct and withhold the salaries of the crew, such practices still continue today. Hence, since the crews signed the contract with the manning agencies based in the sending countries, Taiwan authorities have no power to intervene in the violation of the crews' rights regarding the terms written in the contract. Certainly, this issue pertained to both FOC and Taiwan-flagged vessels.

As shown above, the political and economic transnationalism of privatized recruitment industries from Indonesia to Taiwan presents a complex web full of deceit with false advertisement, fraud, debt bondage, forging documents, and recruitment of inexperienced fishers. Loose laws to regulate privatized recruitment agencies in both countries and the absence of diplomatic relations fragmented the efforts of each party to protect migrant crews working onboard in distant water fishing vessels.

## New *Nomos* of the Earth and the Neoliberal Void of Slavery Production

We face a new and neoliberalized world order practiced with maritime logistics starting from the sixteenth century, which intensified in the second half of the twentieth century and peaked in the twenty-first century. Back in the seventeenth century, Walter Raleigh claimed: "Whoever rules the sea rules world trade, and whoever rules world trade owns all the treasures of the world and, indeed, the world itself." Carl Schmitt quoted him and stressed in his *Land and Sea: A World-Historical Meditation* (1950) the emergence of a new *nomos* of the earth: "The order of the firm land consists in its division into state dominions; the high sea is free, i.e., state-free and subject to the authority of no state dominion. This *was* the basic law, the *nomos* of the earth in this epoch" (Preface). Schmitt further elaborated: "Liberalism is a doctrine of freedom, freedom of economic production, freedom of the market, and, above all, the queen of all economic freedoms, freedom of consumption. Liberalism also solves the social question with reference to increases in production and consumption, both of which should follow from economic freedom and economic laws" (331)

What Schmitt diagnosed in the mid–twentieth century has become more accurate. As a "fence-word," *Nomos* indicates the political act of enclosure, the management, and the ordering of the space immediately. Any establishment of the new world order involves a long process of spatial revolution and re-distribution of land and power structures. Land appropriation is always the ultimate legal title for further division and distribution, thus additional production (Schmitt 2006, 328). The enclosure of territory, division, and distribution of land discussed by Schmitt are the constitutional moments of primitive accumulation analyzed by Karl Marx, the appropriation of land, and the extraction of pure labor. New rules are established at this moment (Walker 2011; Ince 2014; Onuki 2016).

The liberalized competition on the high seas has created a web of complex logistics. It contributes to a space that allows the flag state to escape from the regulation of any sovereign state. These complex logistics involved a chain of FOC, BBC, SEZ, EPZ, tax havens, offshore financial centers, and outsourcing of private brokerage. The juridical process of the ship owner's state and the labor-sender countries cannot intervene in the lawless practices involved in producing the slavery system in distant water fishing in various maritime zones. Therefore, the practice of FOC is only a symptom of neoliberal capitalism on the surface. Underneath, it is the entire complex logistics that support the topological system of neoliberal slavery production. The link between the surface and the system is the legal exception space that triggers the complex system's production and reproduction.

This zone of legal exception is a dynamic void. This void, we must emphasize, is not a vacuum, but a void with many flying liberalized atoms of interests that serve as a motor or an engine that pushes the traffic of maritime capitalism. Sovereignty is transferred to the multinational actors of maritime capitalism. This zone of legal exception is ensured by the multidirectional enclosures of territories, not of the state, but the multinational corporates' interests. The corporates purchase whatever laws are available to make the most profits, from the flag states, the service of bareboat charters, ports of a tax haven, offshore financial centers, and private brokerage to recruit the cheapest fishing laborers worldwide.

In this chapter, we have argued that the practice of FOC is symptomatic of the complex global logistics of neoliberal maritime capitalism in the twenty-first century. This complex structure is configured by multiple sectors. This composite logistic involves the ship owner's state, the flag state, the countries that recruit the foreign fishers, the countries that send the fishers abroad, the outsourcing of manpower recruitment, and the loopholes of the jurisdictional practices among multiple sectors. At the center of this composite logistic network is a zone of legal exception, participated by liberalized competitive agents from around the world, and constitute a free zone of exemption of jurisdiction for all states. This zone of exemption offers a free space that can be taken by any agent. It serves as the motor that triggers the compound logistics and the movement of maritime capitalism while reproducing the neoliberal slavery of today. On the fishing vessel, the one who dominates the space can enslave the fishers as he wills. In this neoliberal void, along with the slavery system, we see the crudest tortures and deprivations of fundamental human rights on these fishing vessels.

## Notes

1. This work was part of the project of the CHCI-GHI (2019–2021): "Migration, Logistics and Unequal Citizens in the Global Context" awarded by the CHCI-Mellon Foundation. It has also been supported by the Ministry of Education

through the SPROUT Project—International Center for Cultural Studies (ICCS), National Chiao Tung University, Taiwan.

The trilogy referred to is the following: Part I "Falsification, Exploitation, Blood-Tear Fishery: Far Sea Fishing Trans-National Investigative Report" (completed in 2017), Part II, "The Storm of the Human Trafficking at Sea: How Taiwan Became an Accessory to Slavery on the High Seas" (completed in 2018), and Part III, "Insufficient Governance of the Distant Water Fishery: The Illegal Shark Finning, Forced Labor, and the Death of the Observer" (completed in 2021) (Zhe 2017, 2018, 2021).

2. The FOC ship can, for example, register in Panama, be owned by a Japanese company, get the manager registration in Singapore, operate in Thailand, be classified in Japan, be insured in England, and have crew members from different countries of the third world.

3. According to the UNCTAD statistics record, the top five registries in 2020 are Panama, Liberia, Marshall Islands, Hong Kong SAR, and Singapore (UNCTAD 2020).

4. According to a recent report by the Control Yuan of Taiwan, there are 251 FOC ships owned by the Taiwanese, with flags of sixteen countries, but the exact figure might be triple the official record. Taiwan has 1,041 overseas employment fishing vessels, with 19,642 overseas-employed fishers, fishing across more than thirty countries' economic zones, being ranked no. 2 in fishing capacities in the high seas in the world. Fisheries Agency of Taiwan webpage. Authorized vessels list of non-Taiwanese fishing vessels. www.fa.gov.tw/cht/FOC

5. Our researcher Jonathan S. Parhusip assisted this event at the port. Before their departure in late February 2021, the twenty-nine crews signed the contract in their home country and were quarantined for two weeks upon arrival in Taiwan. After being moved to the fishing vessel (and new workplace) for a one-week observation period, they began working and preparing fishing gear before leaving for working at the sea. In late March, the salary was due but remained unpaid. So the group reached out to a local Kaohsiung-based NGO, which visited them three times in their fishing vessels to bring clothes, foods, and medicines.

6. Our researcher Jonathan S. Parhusip has also assisted in several cases where the crews were recruited by Taiwan agencies and employed on foreign owned and flagged vessels.

7. These prices will be determined by the number of documents that need to be handled by brokers. The company also offers loans to cover family expenses before they receive their salary. These practices trapped fishers in debt-bondage practices.

## References


Ademun-Odeke. "An Examination of Bareboat Charter Registries and Flag of Convenience Registries in International Law." *Ocean Development & International Law* 36, no. 4 (2005): 339–62. https://doi.org/10.1080/00908320500308726

Campling, Liam, and Alejandro Colás. *Capitalism and the Sea: The Maritime Factor in the Making of the Modern World.* London & New York: Verso, 2021.

Chen, Po-Chuan. "A Research on Decent Work for Fishing Vessel Workers: Based on Work in Fishing Convention." *Chinese (Taiwan) Review of International and Transnational Law*, no. 15 (2019): 131–59.

Chua, Charmaine, Martin Danyluk, Deborah Cowen, and Laleh Khalili. "Introduction: Turbulent Circulation: Building a Critical Engagement with Logistics." Environment and Planning D: Society and Space 36, no. 4 (2018): 617–29. https://doi.org/10.1177/0263775818783101

Dephub. "Surat Izin Usaha Perekrutan Dan Penempatan Awak Kapal (SIUPPAK) (Business License for Recruitment and Placement of Vessel Crews)." Ministry of Transportation, Indonesia, 2021. https://dokumenpelaut.dephub.go.id/listsiuppak

Ferrell, Jessica K. "Controlling Flags of Convenience: One Measure to Stop Overfishing of Collapsing Fish Stocks." Environmental Law 35, no. 2 (2005): 323–90.

Government of Taiwan. Act to Govern Investment in the Operation of Foreign Flag Fishing Vessels, 2016.

Government of Taiwan. Regulations on the Authorization and Management of Overseas Employment of Foreign Crew Members, 2019. https://law.moj.gov.tw/ENG/LawClass/LawAll.aspx?pcode=M0050061

GreenpeaceSoutheastAsia. "Choppy Waters: Forced Labour and Illegal Fishing in Taiwan's Distant Water Fisheries." 2020. www.greenpeace.org/southeastasia/publication/3690/choppy-waters-forced-labour-and-illegal-fishing-in-taiwans-distant-water-fisheries

Hwang, I. *The Order of the Seas and International Law*. Sharing Press, 2020.

Ince, Onur Ulas. "Primitive Accumulation, New Enclosures, and Global Land Grabs: A Theoretical Intervention." *Rural Sociology* 79, no. 1 (2014): 104–31. https://doi.org/10.1111/ruso.12025

Indonesian Ministry of Labor. n.d. "Data Perusahaan Penempatan Pekerja Migran Indonesia Yang Mendapat Izin Dari Kemnaker RI." BP2MI.

Marschke, Melissa, and Peter Vandergeest. "Slavery Scandals: Unpacking Labor Challenges and Policy Responses Within the Off-Shore Fisheries Sector." *Marine Policy*, no. 68 (2016): 39–46.

Nakamura, Katrina, Lori Bishop, Trevor Ward, Ganapathiraju Pramod, Dominic Chakra Thomson, Patima Tungpuchayakul, and Sompong Srakaew. "Seeing Slavery in Seafood Supply Chains." *Science Advances* 4, no. 7 (2018): e1701833. https://doi.org/10.1126/sciadv.1701833

Onuki, Hironori. "The Neoliberal Governance of Global Labor Mobility: Migrant Workers and the New Constitutional Moments of Primitive Accumulation." *Alternatives: Global, Local, Political* 41, no. 1 (2016): 3–28.

Parhusip, Jonathan S. "The Making of Freedom and Common Forms of Struggle of Runaways in Taiwan." *South Atlantic Quarterly* 120, no. 3 (2021): 663–69. https://doi.org/10.1215/00382876-9155366

Rhamdani, Benny. "Peran Pemerintah Dalam Penempatan Dan Perlindungan Pekerja Migran Indonesia Di Kapal Ikan Asing" (The Roles of the Government in Placement and Protection of Indonesian Migrant in Foreign Fishing Vessels). BP2MI, 2020. https://is.gd/3b9wia.

Schmitt, Carl. *Land and Sea: A World-Historical Meditation*. Candor: Telos Press Publishing, 1950.

———. *The Nomos of the Earth in the International Law of the Jus Publicum Europaeum*. First paperback edition. New York: Telos Press, 2006.

*Tempo*. "Investigation: Slavery at Sea: Undocumented Indonesian Seamen Are Victim of Abuse Aboard Foreign Fishing Boat," January 8, 2017. https://en.tempo.co/read/833777/investigation-slavery-at-sea

Tickler, David, Jessica J. Meeuwig, Katharine Bryant, Fiona David, John A. H. Forrest, Elise Gordon, Jacqueline Joudo Larsen, et al. "Modern Slavery and the Race to Fish." *Nature Communications* 9, no. 4643 (2018). https://doi.org/10.1038/s41467-018-07118-9

UNCTADstat. "Building, Ownership, Registration and Recycling of Ships, 2019," 2020. https://unctad.org/system/files/official-document/tdstat45_en.pdf

van Fossen, Anthony. "Flags of Convenience and Global Capitalism." International Critical Thought 6, no. 3 (2016): 359–77. https://doi.org/10.1080/21598282.2016.1198001

Walker, Gavin. "Primitive Accumulation and the Formation of Difference: On Marx and Schmitt." *Rethinking Marxism* 23, no. 3 (2011): 384–404. https://doi.org/10.1080/08935696.2011.583016

Wang, Mu-Han. "Review on Shipping Registration System." Institute of Transportation, Ministry of Transportation and Communications, Taiwan, 2008.

Xiang, Biao, and Johan Lindquist. "Migration Infrastructure." *International Migration Review* 48, no. 1 suppl (2014): 122–48. https://doi.org/10.1111/imre.12141

Yea, Sallie. "Human Trafficking and Jurisdictional Exceptionalism in the Global Fishing Industry: A Case Study of Singapore." *Geopolitics* 27, no. 1 (2022): 238–59. https://doi.org/10.1080/14650045.2020.1741548

Zhe, Bao Dao. "Part I. Falsification, Exploitation, Blood-Tear Fishery: Far Sea Fishing Trans-National Investigative Report." *The Reporter*, 2017.

———. "Part II. The Storm of the Human Trafficking at Sea: How Taiwan Became an Accessory to Slavery on the High Seas." *The Reporter*, 2018.

———. "Part III. Insufficient Governance of the Distant Water Fishery: The Illegal Shark Finning, Forced Labor, and the Death of the Observer." *The Reporter*, 2021.

# Bibliography

"2020 Was 'Deadliest' Year Ever for Rohingya Sea Journeys: UNHCR." *Al Jazeera* (August 20, 2021). www.aljazeera.com/news/2021/8/20/rohingya-sea-journeys-un

Abourahme, Nasser. "The Camp." *Comparative Studies of South Asia, Africa and the Middle East* 40, no. 1 (2020): 35–42.

Abourahme, Nasser, and Sandi Hilal. "Political Subjectification, the Production of Space and the Folding of Polarity: The Case of De-Heishe Camp, Palestine," in *Peripheries: Decentering Urban Theory*, edited by James Holston and Teresa Caldeira. Berkeley: University of California Press, 2012, 142–66.

Ademun-Odeke. "An Examination of Bareboat Charter Registries and Flag of Convenience Registries in International Law." *Ocean Development & International Law* 36, no. 4 (2005): 339–62.

Agamben, Giorgio. *Homo Sacer: Sovereign Power and Bare Life*. Stanford, CA: Stanford University Press, 1998.

Agier, Michel. "Between War and City: Towards an Urban Anthropology of Refugee Camps." *Ethnography* 3, no. 3 (2002): 317–41.

Agier, Michel. *Anthropologie de la Ville*. Paris: PUF, 2015.

Agier, Michel. *Managing the Undesirables: Refugee Camps and Humanitarian Government*. Cambridge: Polity Press, 2011.

Ahmed, I. "The Rohingyas : From Stateless to Refugee" (2009). www.semanticscholar.org/paper/The-Rohingyas-%3A-From-Stateless-to-Refugee-Ahmed/078b2fc5ec5dc8bae1e03cb699ae7387a704943b

Alice Edwards, and Laura Van Waas (eds.). *Nationality and Stateless under International Law*. Cambridge: Cambridge University Press, 2014.

Anderson, Benedict. *Under Three Flags: Anarchism and the Anti-Colonial Imagination*. London & New York: Verso Books, 2007.

Anghie, Antony. *Imperialism, Sovereignty and the Making of International Law*. Cambridge: Cambridge University Press, 2005.

Arendt, Hannah. *The Origins of Totalitarianism*. London: George Allen & Unwin, 1968.

Arendt, Hannah. *Responsibility and Judgment*. New York: Schocken Books, 2003.

Arendt, Hannah. *The Human Condition*. Chicago: University of Chicago Press, 1958.

Assunção, Thiago. "Apatridia No Brasil: Da Invisibilidade Ao Convite Para Se Tornar Cidadão." *Revista de Estudos e Pesquisas Sobre as Américas* 13, no. 1 (2019): 279–307.

Atkinson, Carolyn, and Lauren Turner. "Covid Pandemic May Increase People Trafficking Says Charity," *BBC News*, October 18, 2021. www.bbc.com/news/uk-58920152

Bagchi, Jasodhara, and Subhoranjan Dasgupta. *The Trauma and the Triumph: Gender and Partition in Eastern India*. Kolkata: Stree, 2003.

Bahadur, Gaiutra. *Coolie Woman: The Odyssey of Indenture*. Chicago: University of Chicago Press, 2014.

Balibar, Étienne. *We, the People of Europe? Reflections on Transnational Citizenship*, trans. James Swenson. Princeton, NJ: Princeton University Press, 2004.

Bandyopadhyay, Anwesha. "Char laksha kore kshatipuran pabe pacharer par uddhar dui kanya." *Ei Samay*, February 28, 2021. https://eisamay.com/west-bengal-news/24pargana-news/trafficked-girls-will-get-4-lakhs-each-as-a-victim-compensation/articleshow/81256837.cms

Banerjee, Paula. "Aliens in the Colonial World," in *Borders, Histories, Existences: Gender and Beyond*, edited by Ranabir Samaddar. New Delhi: Sage, 2010, 3–38.

Bangladesh Bureau of Statistics, Ministry of Planning. "Census of Slum Areas and Floating Population 2014," 2015.

Barrett, Jenny, and Nando Sigona. "The Citizen and the Other: New Directions in Research on the Migration and Citizenship Nexus." *Migration Studies* 2, no. 2 (July 2014): 286–94.

Barth, Gunther. *Instant Cities: Urbanization and the Rise of San Francisco and Denver*. Oxford: Oxford University Press, 1975.

Baster, Tim, and Isabelle Merminod. "Death in the Mediterranean." *New Internationalist* (May 27, 2015). https://newint.org/features/web-exclusive/2015/05/27/mediterranean-refugee-crisis

Basu Ray Chaudhury, Sabyasachi. "Dispossession, Un-Freedom, Precarity: Negotiating Citizenship Laws in Postcolonial South Asia." *South Atlantic Quarterly* 120, no. 1 (2021): 209–19.

Basu Ray Chaudhury, Sabyasachi, and Ranabir Samaddar (eds.). *The Rohingya in South Asia: People without a State*. London: Routledge, 2018.

Basu Ray Chaudhury, Sabyasachi. "Governance of Migration in South Asia: The Need for a Decolonial Approach," in *Displacement, Belonging, and Migrant Agency in the Face of Power*, edited by Tamar Mayer and Trinh Tran. London: Routledge, 2022.

Batchelor, C. A. "Statelessness and the Problem of Resolving Nationality Status." *International Journal of Refugee Law* 10, no. 1–2 (1998): 156–82.

Bates, Crispin. "Migration in the Time of Empire." *Open Democracy*, December 12, 2017.

Bates, Crispin, and Marina Carter. "Sirdars as Intermediaries in Nineteenth-Century Indian Ocean Indentured Labour Migration." *Modern Asian Studies* 51, no. 2 (2017): 462–84.

Bates, Crispin. Silver Jubilee Lecture 16. ADRI Silver Jubilee Celebrations, 2017. www.youtube.com/watch?v=0eQnELwot58

Baud, Michiel, and Willem Van Schendel. "Toward a Comparative History of Borderlands." *Journal of World History* 8, no. 2 (1997): 211–42.

Bauer, Rolf. *The Peasant Production of Opium in Nineteenth-Century India*. Leiden: Brill, 2019.

Bauman, Zygmunt. "Sociological Responses to Postmodernity." *Thesis Eleven* 23, no. 1 (1989): 35–63.

Bauman, Zygmunt. *Life in Fragments: Essays in Postmodern Morality*. Oxford: Blackwell, 1998.

Bauman, Zygmunt. *Wasted Lives: Modernity and Its Outcasts*. Reprint. Cambridge: Polity, 2004.

BBC. "Shamima Begum Will Not Be Allowed Here, Bangladesh Says," *BBC News*, February 21, 2019. www.bbc.com/news/uk-47312207

Beech, Hannah. "Hundreds of Rohingya Refugees Stuck at Sea With 'Zero Hope.' " *The New York Times* (May 1, 2020). www.nytimes.com/2020/05/01/world/asia/rohingya-muslim-refugee-crisis.html

Benhabib, Seyla. *The Rights of Others: Aliens, Residents, and Citizens*. Cambridge: Cambridge University Press, 2004.

Benslama-Dabdoub, Malak. "Colonial Legacies in Syrian Nationality Law and the Risk of Statelessness." *The Statelessness & Citizenship Review* 3, no. 1 (2021): 6–32.

Benton, Lauren A. *A Search for Sovereignty Law and Geography in European Empires, 1400–1900*. Cambridge: Cambridge University Press, 2009.

Benton, Meghan. "The Problem of Denizenship: A Non-Domination Framework." *Critical Review of International Social and Political Philosophy* 17, no. 1 (2014): 49–69.

Bernstein, Richard J. "Hannah Arendt on the Stateless." *Parallax* 11, no. 1 (2005): 46–60.

Billig, Michael. *Banal Nationalism*. London: Sage, 1995.

Biswas, Samata. "Migrations and Identities: A Study of Sea of Poppies." *Refugee Watch Online* (July 22, 2016). http://refugeewatchonline.blogspot.com/2016/07/migrations-and-identities-study-of-sea.html

Biswas, Soutik. "How Britain's Opium Trade Impoverished Indians." *BBC News*, September 5, 2019. www.bbc.com/news/world-asia-india-49404024

Blitz, Brad K. "Statelessness and the Social (De)Construction of Citizenship: Political Restructuring and Ethnic Discrimination in Slovenia." *Journal of Human Rights* 5, no. 4 (2006): 453–79.

Bornman, Jan. "Migrants Excluded from Government Food Aid." *New Frame*, May 13, 2020. www.newframe.com/migrants-excluded-from-government-food-aid

Bose, Sudhindra. "World's Hindusthan Students' Federation." *Modern Review* 16, no. 1–2 (1914): 143–44.

Bose, Sugata. *A Hundred Horizons: The Indian Ocean in the Age of Global Empire.* Cambridge, MA: Harvard University Press, 2009.

Bosniak, Linda. *The Citizen and the Alien: Dilemmas of Contemporary Membership.* Princeton, NJ: Princeton University Press, 2006.

Bouchain, Patrick. *Construire Autrement: Comment Faire?* Arles: Actes sud, 2006.

Branch, Adam. "Gulu in War . . . and Peace? The Town as Camp in Northern Uganda." *Urban Studies* 50, no. 15 (2013): 3152–67.

Brankamp, Hanno. "Camp Abolition: Ending Carceral Humanitarianism in Kenya (and Beyond)." *Antipode* 54, no. 1 (2022): 106–29.

Bulley, Dan. "Inside the Tent: Community and Government in Refugee Camps." *Security Dialogue* 45, no. 1 (2014): 63–80.

Burton, Antoinette. "Amitav Ghosh's World Histories from Below." *History of the Present* 2, no. 1 (2012): 71–77.

Butler, Judith, and Gayatri Chakravorty Spivak. *Who Sings the Nation-State? Language, Politics, Belonging.* Kolkata: Seagull Books, 2007.

Çaglar, Ayse, and Nina Glick Schiller. *Migrants and City-Making: Dispossession, Displacement, and Urban Regeneration.* Durham, NC: Duke University Press, 2018.

Çağlar, Ayşe. "The Multiple Tenses of a Postcolonial Age of Migration: A Commentary on Samaddar, R. 'The Postcolonial Age of Migration.'" *Dialectical Anthropology* 45, no. 3 (2021): 317–20.

Calcutta Research Group. "Kolkata Declaration 2018." www.mcrg.ac.in/RLS_Migration/Kolkata_Declaration_2018.pdf

Campling, Liam, and Alejandro Colás. *Capitalism and the Sea: The Maritime Factor in the Making of the Modern World.* London: Verso, 2021.

Candilis, Georges. *Bâtir la vie: un architecte témoin de son temps.* Paris: Infolio, 1977.

Canefe, Nergis. "Afghanistan and Its Futures." *International Migration* 60, no. 1 (2022): 262–67.

Canefe, Nergis. "Citizens versus Permanent Guests: Cultural Memory and Citizenship Laws in a Reunified Germany." *Citizenship Studies* 2, no. 3 (1998): 519–44.

Canefe, Nergis. "New Faces of Statelessness: The Rohingya Exodus and Remapping of Rights," in *Citizenship, Nationalism and Refugeehood of Rohingyas in Southern Asia,* Nasreen Chowdhory and Biswajit Mohanty. Singapore: Springer, 2020, 197–215.

Canefe, Nergis, Paula Banerjee, and Nasreen Chowdhory. "Gender, Identity and Displacement: Nexus Requirements for a Critical Epistemology," in *Gender, Identity and Migration in India,* edited by Nasreen Chowdhory and Paula Banerjee. Singapore: Palgrave Macmillan, 2022, 1–14.

Carens, Joseph. *The Ethics of Immigration.* Oxford: Oxford University Press, 2013.

Casas-Cortés, Maribel, Sebastian Cobarrubias, Charles Heller, and Lorenzo Pezzani. "Clashing Cartographies, Migrating Maps: The Politics of Mobility at the

External Borders of E.U.Rope." *ACME: An International Journal for Critical Geographies* 16, no. 1 (2017): 1–33.

Chakraborty, Subhas Ranjan. "Colonialism, Resource Crisis and Forced Migration." *Policies and Practices*. Kolkata: Mahanirban Calcutta Research Group, 2011.

Chakraborty, Subhas Ranjan. "The Journey of *Komagata Maru*: Conjuncture, Memory and History," in *Diasporas and Transnationalisms: The Journey of the Komagata Maru*, edited by Anjali Gera Roy and Ajaya Kumar Saho. London: Routledge, 2018.

Chamoiseau, Patrick. *Texaco*. New York: Vintage International, 1998.

Chatterjee, Partha. *The Nation and Its Fragments: Colonial and Postcolonial Histories*. Princeton, NJ: Princeton University Press, 1993.

Chatterjee, Partha. *The Politics of the Governed: Reflections on Popular Politics in Most of the World*. New York: Columbia University Press, 2004.

Chen, Po-Chuan. "A Research on Decent Work for Fishing Vessel Workers: Based on Work in Fishing Convention." *Chinese (Taiwan) Review of International and Transnational Law*, no. 15 (2019): 131–59.

Chiew, Huiyee. "Bajau Laut: Once Sea Nomads, Now Stateless." *Malaysiakini* (May 17, 2019). www.malaysiakini.com/news/476595

Chimni, B. S. "From Resettlement to Involuntary Repatriation: Towards a Critical History of Durable Solutions to Refugee Problems." *Refugee Survey Quarterly* 23, no. 3 (2004): 55–73.

Chimni, B. S. "Globalization, Humanitarianism and the Erosion of Refugee Protection." *Journal of Refugee Studies* 13, no. 3 (2000): 243–63.

Choi, Young Rae. "The Blue Economy as Governmentality and the Making of New Spatial Rationalities." *Dialogues in Human Geography* 7, no. 1 (2017): 37–41.

Chowdhory, Nasreen, and Shamna Thacham Poyil. "Biometrics, Notion of Governmentality and Gender Relations in Rohingya Refugee Camps, Policies and Practices." *Policies and Practices 114*. Kolkata: Mahanirban Calcutta Research Group, 2020.

Chowdhory, Nasreen. "Marginality and the 'State of Exception' in Camps in Tamil Nadu." *International Journal of Migration and Border Studies* 2, no. 2 (2016): 132.

Chowdhory, Nasreen. "State Formation, Marginality and Belonging: Contextualising Rights of Refugees in India, Bangladesh and Sri Lanka," in *Refugees, Citizenship and Belonging in South Asia: Contested* Terrains, 2018. Singapore: Springer, 43–71.

Chowdhory, Nasreen, and Shamna Thacham Poyil. "Interrogating Camps in Forced Migration Studies: The Exceptionality of South Asia," in *Gender, Identity and Migration in India*, edited by Nasreen Chowdhory and Paula Banerjee. Singapore: Springer Nature 2022, 153–79.

Chowdhory, Nasreen, and Shamna Thacham Poyil. "Speaking the Language of the 'Other': Negotiating Cultural Boundaries through Language in Chitmahals in Indo-Bangladesh Borders." *Citizenship Studies* 25, no. 6 (2021): 791–807.

Chowdhory, Nasreen. *Refugees, Citizenship and Belonging in South Asia: Contested Terrains.* Singapore: Springer, 2018.

Chowdhory, Nasreen, Shamna Thacham Poyil, and Kajla Meghna. "The Idea of Protection; Norms and Practice of Refugee Management in India." *Refugee Watch* 53, no. 1 (2019): 36–54.

Chua, Charmaine, Martin Danyluk, Deborah Cowen, and Laleh Khalili. "Introduction: Turbulent Circulation: Building a Critical Engagement with Logistics." *Environment and Planning D: Society and Space* 36, no. 4 (2018): 617–29.

Cole, Philip. "At the Borders of Political Theory: Carens and the Ethics of Immigration." *European Journal of Political Theory* 14, no. 4 (2015): 501–10.

Cole, Philip. "Towards a Symmetrical World: Migration and International Law." *Ethics and Economics* 4, no. 1 (2006): 1–7.

Cole, Philip. *Philosophies of Exclusion: Liberal Political Theory and Immigration.* Edinburgh: Edinburgh University Press, 2000.

Cornwall, Andrea. "Locating Citizen Participation." *IDS Bulletin* 33, no. 2 (2002): i–x.

Cuttitta, Paolo. "Inclusion and Exclusion in the Fragmented Space of the Sea: Actors, Territories and Legal Regimes between Libya and Italy," in *Contemporary Boat Migration: Data, Geopolitics, and Discourses*, edited by Elaine Burroughs and Kira Williams. London: Rowman & Littlefield, 2018.

Cuttitta, Paolo, and Tamara Last (eds.). *Border Deaths: Causes, Dynamics and Consequences of Migration-Related Mortality.* Amsterdam: Amsterdam University Press, 2020.

Dalrymple, William. "The Mutual Genocide of Indian Partition," *The New Yorker* (June 22, 2015). www.newyorker.com/magazine/2015/06/29/the-great-divide-books-dalrymple

Das, Veena. *Life and Words: Violence and the Descent into the Ordinary.* Berkeley: University of California Press, 2007.

Datta, Antara. *Refugees and Borders in South Asia: The Great Exodus of 1971.* Routledge Studies in South Asian Politics. New York: Routledge, 2013.

Davies, Thom, Arshad Isakjee, and Surindar Dhesi. "Violent Inaction: The Necropolitical Experience of Refugees in Europe: Violent Inaction." *Antipode* 49, no. 5 (2017): 1263–84.

Davis, Lance E., and Robert A. Huttenback. *Mammon and the Pursuit of Empire: The Political Economy of British Imperialism, 1860–1912.* Cambridge: Cambridge University Press, 1986.

Davis, Mike. *Late Victorian Holocausts: El Niño Famines and the Making of the Third World.* London: Verso, 2017.

De Genova, Nicholas. "Introduction. The Borders of 'Europe' and the European Question," in *The Borders of "Europe": Autonomy of Migration, Tactics of Bordering.* Durham, NC: Duke University Press, 2017, 1–36.

Debrix, François, and Alexander D. Barder. *Beyond Biopolitics: Theory, Violence, and Horror in World Politics.* London: Routledge, 2012.

Dua, Jatin. *Captured at Sea: Piracy and Protection in the Indian Ocean.* Oakland: University of California Press, 2019.

Edwards, Alice, and Laura Van Waas (eds.). *Nationality and Stateless under International Law.* Cambridge: Cambridge University Press, 2014.

El Qadim, Nora, Beste İşleyen, Leonie Ansems de Vries, Signe Sofie Hansen, Sibel Karadağ, Debbie Lisle, and Damien Simonneau. "(Im)Moral Borders in Practice." *Geopolitics* 26, no. 5 (2021): 1608–38.

Eliassi, Barzoo. *Narratives of Statelessness and Political Otherness : Kurdish and Palestinian Experiences.* Cham: Palgrave Macmillan, 2021.

Ersbøll, Eva. "The Right to a Nationality and the European Convention on Human Rights," in *Human Rights in Turmoil: Facing Threats, Consolidating Achievements,* edited by Stéphanie Lagoutte, Hans-Otto Sano, and Peter Scharff Smith. Leiden: Brill | Nijhoff, 2007, 249–70.

Fassin, Didier. *Humanitarian Reason: A Moral History of the Present Times.* Berkeley: University of California Press, 2011.

Ferguson, James, and Akhil Gupta. "Spatializing States: Toward an Ethnography of Neoliberal Governmentality." *American Ethnologist* 29, no. 4 (2002): 981–1002.

Ferrell, Jessica K. "Controlling Flags of Convenience: One Measure to Stop Overfishing of Collapsing Fish Stocks." *Environmental Law* 35, no. 2 (2005): 323–90.

Fisher, Michael Herbert. *Counterflows to Colonialism: Indian Travellers and Settlers in Britain, 1600–1857.* Delhi: Permanent Black, 2004.

Forth, Aidan. "Britain's Archipelago of Camps: Labor and Detention in a Liberal Empire, 1871–1903." *Kritika: Explorations in Russian and Eurasian History* 16, no. 3 (2015): 651–80.

Fossen, Anthony van. "Flags of Convenience and Global Capitalism." *International Critical Thought* 6, no. 3 (2016): 359–77.

Foster, Michelle, and Timnah Rachel Baker. "Racial Discrimination in Nationality Laws: A Doctrinal Blind Spot of International Law." *Columbia Journal of Race and* Law 11, no. 1 (2021): 83–146.

Foucault, Michel. *Power/Knowledge: Selected Interviews and Other Writings, 1972–1977.* New York: Pantheon Books, 1980.

Foucault, Michel. *The Archaeology of Knowledge,* trans. A. M. Sheridan. New York: Pantheon Books, 1972.

Fromonot, François. "Manières de Classer l'urbanisme.' " *Criticat,* no. 8 (2011): 40–61.

Gangopadhyay, Rudrani. "Finding Oneself On Board the Ibis in Amitav Ghosh's Sea of Poppies." *WSQ: Women's Studies Quarterly* 45, no. 1–2 (2017): 55–64.

Ghosh, Amitav. *Sea of Poppies.* London: John Murray, 2009.

Ghosh, Ganesh. *An Episode of India's Struggle for Freedom: Komagata Maru 1914.* Budge Budge: Gurdware Sahhedganj, 1998.

Ghosh, Sushmita. "Covid-19 Made Poor More Vulnerable to Child Trafficking, Say NGOs—Coronavirus Outbreak News." *India Today* (June 8, 2021).

Gilroy, Paul. *The Black Atlantic: Modernity and Double Consciousness*. Cambridge, MA: Harvard University Press, 2003.

Godin, Marie, and Giorgia Donà. "Rethinking Transit Zones: Migrant Trajectories and Transnational Networks in *Techno-Borderscapes*." *Journal of Ethnic and Migration Studies* 47, no. 14 (2021): 3276–92.

Gordon, Jane Anna. "Critical Allies: On Contemporary Enslavement and Statelessness." *Statelessness & Citizenship Review* 2, no. 1 (2020): 153–58.

Gordon, Jane Anna. "Degrees of Statelessness: Vulnerability and Political Capital." *Journal of Contemporary Thought*, no. 32 (2010): 17–39.

Gordon, Jane Anna. *Statelessness and Contemporary Enslavement*. London: Routledge, 2010.

Grbac, Peter. "Civitas, Polis, and Urbs: Reimagining the Refugee Camp as the City." *Working Paper Series* 96, Refugee Studies Centre, University of Oxford, 2013.

Greenpeace SoutheastAsia. "Choppy Waters: Forced Labour and Illegal Fishing in Taiwan's Distant Water Fisheries," 2020. www.greenpeace.org/southeastasia/publication/3690/choppy-waters-forced-labour-and-illegal-fishing-in-taiwans-distant-water-fisheries

Grosfoguel, Ramón. "The Epistemic Decolonial Turn: Beyond Political-Economy Paradigms." *Cultural Studies* 21, no. 2–3 (2017): 211–23.

Guild, Elspeth, Kees Groenendijk, and Sergio Carrera (eds.). *Illiberal Liberal States: Immigration, Citizenship and Integration in the EU*. London: Routledge, 2016.

Gündoğdu, Ayten. "Arendt on Culture and Imperialism: Response to Klausen." *Political Theory*, 39, no. 5 (2011): 661–67.

Gündogdu, Ayten. *Rightlessness in an Age of Rights : Hannah Arendt and the Contemporary Struggles of Migrants*. Oxford: Oxford University Press, 2015, 90–116.

Hailey, Charlie. *Camps: A Guide to 21st-Century Space*. Cambridge, MA: MIT Press, 2009.

Hanappe, Cyrille, et al. *La Ville Accueillante: Accueillir à Grande-Synthe, Questions Théoriques et Pratiques Sur Les Exilés, l'architecture et La Ville*. La Défense: Plan urbanisme construction architecture PUCA, 2018.

Hanley, Will. "Statelessness: An Invisible Theme in the History of International Law." *European Journal of International Law* 25, no. 1 (2014): 321–27.

Hansler, Jennifer. "Covid-19 Pandemic Increased Number of People at Risk of Human Trafficking, State Department Report Says." *CNN* (2019). www.cnn.com/2021/07/01/politics/2021-trafficking-in-persons-report-covid/index.html

Hart, Gillian. "Denaturalizing Dispossession: Critical Ethnography in the Age of Resurgent Imperialism." *Antipode* 38, no. 5 (2006): 977–1004.

Heller, Charles, and Lorenzo Pezzani. "Liquid Traces: Investigating the Deaths of Migrants at the EU's Maritime Frontier" in *The Borders of "Europe": Autonomy of Migration, Tactics of Bordering*, edited by Nicholas De Genova. Durham, NC: Duke University Press, 2017, 657–84.

Heller, Charles, and Lorenzo Pezzani. "Liquid Traces: Investigating the Deaths of Migrants at the EU's Maritime Frontier," in *Forensis: The Architecture of Public Truth*, edited by Anselm Franke, Eyal Weizman and Haus der Kulturen der Welt. Berlin: Sternberg Press, 2014.

Heller, Charles, Lorenzo Pezzani and Situ Studio. "Forensic Oceanography: Report on the 'Left-To-Die Boat.'" London: Centre for Research Architecture, University of London, 2012.

Herz, Manuel, ed. *From Camp to City: Refugee Camps of the Western Sahara*. Baden: Lars Müller, 2012.

Hossain, Purba. "Protests at the Colonial Capital: Calcutta and the Global Debates on Indenture, 1836–42." *South Asian Studies* 33, no. 1 (2017): 37–51.

Huq, Efadul, and Faranak Miraftab. "'We Are All Refugees': Camps and Informal Settlements as Converging Spaces of Global Displacements." *Planning Theory & Practice* 21, no. 3 (2020): 351–70.

Huq, Efadul. "Seeing the *Insurgent* in Transformative Planning Practices." *Planning Theory* 19, no. 4 (2020): 371–91.

"Human Trafficking at Tea Gardens: Coronay bandha kaj, pachar rukhte tatpar prashasan." *Zee 24 Ghanta* (January 30, 2022). https://zeenews.india.com/bengali/state/government-of-west-bengal-has-taken-a-new-initiative-to-stop-human-trafficking-from-the-closed-tea-gardens_420210.htm

Hutchings, Kimberly. "Decolonizing Global Ethics: Thinking with the Pluriverse." *Ethics and International Affairs* 33, no. 2 (January 2019): 1–11.

Ignatieff, Michael. *The Lesser Evil: Political Ethics in an Age of Terror*. Princeton, NJ: Princeton University Press, 2005.

Ince, Onur Ulas. "Primitive Accumulation, New Enclosures, and Global Land Grabs: A Theoretical Intervention." *Rural Sociology* 79, no. 1 (2014): 104–31.

International Organization for Migration. "More than 13,000 Migrants Reported along the Turkish–Greek Border" (2020). www.iom.int/news/more-13000-migrants-reported-along-turkish-greek-border

International Organization for Migration. "ILO and IOM Sign Agreement to Strengthen Collaboration on Migration Governance," 2020. www.iom.int/news/ilo-and-iom-sign-agreement-strengthen-collaboration-migration-governance

Isin, Engin F. *Being Political: Genealogies of Citizenship*. Minneapolis: University of Minnesota Press, 2002.

Isin, Engin F., and Greg Marc Nielsen (eds). *Acts of Citizenship*. London: Zed Books, 2008.

Isin, Engin F., and Kim Rygiel. "Abject Spaces: Frontiers, Zones, Camps," in *The Logics of Biopower and The War on Terror: Living Dying, Surviving*, edited by Elizabeth Dauphinee and Masters Cristina. New York: Palgrave Macmillan, 2007, 181–203.

Jalal, Ayesha. *The Pity of Partition*. Princeton, NJ: Princeton University Press, 2013.

Jamal, Amal, and Anna Kensicki. "Theorizing Half-Statelessness: A Case Study of the Nation-State Law in Israel." *Citizenship Studies* 24, no. 6 (2020): 769–85.

Jansen, Bram. "The Protracted Refugee Camp and the Consolidation of a 'Humanitarian Urbanism,'" *IJURR* (blog), 2016. www.ijurr.org/spotlight-on/the-urban-refugee-crisis-reflections-on-cities-citizenship-and-the-displaced/the-protracted-refugee-camp-and-the-consolidation-of-a-humanitarian-urbanism

Jha, Rajesh. "Seven Bangladeshi Die on Migrant Boat near Italy," *DD News* (January 25, 2022). https://ddnews.gov.in/international/seven-bangladeshi-die-migrant-boat-near-italy

Johnston, Hugh J. M. *The Voyage of the Komagata Maru: The Sikh Challenge to Canada's Colour Bar*, expanded and fully revised edition. Vancouver: UBC Press, 2014.

Jones, Henry. "Lines in the Ocean: Thinking with the Sea about Territory and International Law." *London Review of International Law* 4, no. 2 (2016): 307–43.

Josh, Sohan Singh. *Tragedy of Komagata Maru.* New Delhi: People's Publishing House, 1975.

Karadağ, Sibel, and Ayşen Üstübici. "Protection during Pre-Pandemic and COVID-19 Periods in Turkey," ADMIGOV, 2021. https://admigov.eu/upload/Deliverable_42_Protection_COVID19_Turkey_Karadag_Ustubici.pdf

Karadağ, Sibel. "Extraterritoriality of European Borders to Turkey: An Implementation Perspective of Counteractive Strategies." *Comparative Migration Studies* 7, no. 1 (2019): 12.

Kazi, Anis Ahmed. "10 Injured in Clash between Two Rohingya Groups." *Dhaka Tribune* (June 19, 2018). https://archive.dhakatribune.com/reeceesh/nation/2018/06/19/10-injured-in-clash-between-two-rohingya-groups

Kazi, Anis Ahmed. "UN Launches Environmental Project for Rohingyas and Bangladeshis," *Dhaka Tribune* (September 23, 2018). https://archive.dhakatribune.com/reeceesh/nation/2018/09/23/un-launches-environmental-project-for-rohingyas-and-bangladeshis

Kerber, Linda K. "The Stateless as the Citizen's Other: A View from the United States." *The American Historical Review* 112, no. 1 (2007): 1–34.

Kesby, Alison. *The Right to Have Rights: Citizenship, Humanity, and International Law*. Oxford: Oxford University Press, 2012.

Khan, Yasmin. *The Great Partition: The Making of India and Pakistan*. New Haven, CT: Yale University Press, 2017.

Kingsley, Patrick, and Karam Shoumali. "Taking Hard Line, Greece Turns Back Migrants by Abandoning Them at Sea." *The New York Times* (2020). www.nytimes.com/2020/08/14/world/reece/reece-migrants-abandoning-sea.htm

Kingston, Lindsey. "Worthy of Rights: Statelessness as a Cause and Symptom of Marginalisation," in *Understanding Statelessness*, edited by Tendayi Bloom, Phillip Cole, and Katherine Tonkiss. London: Routledge, 2018, 17–34.

Kipgen, Nehginpao. "Conflict in Rakhine State in Myanmar: Rohingya Muslims' Conundrum." *Journal of Muslim Minority Affairs* 33, no. 2 (2013): 298–310.

Krause, Monika. "Undocumented Migrants: An Arendtian Perspective." *European Journal of Political Theory* 7, no. 3 (2008): 331–48.

Kreichauf, René. "From Forced Migration to Forced Arrival: The Campization of Refugee Accommodation in European Cities." *Comparative Migration Studies* 6, no. 1 (2018): 7.

Kumar, Ashutosh. *Coolies of the Empire: Indentured Indians in the Sugar Colonies, 1830–1920.* Cambridge: Cambridge University Press, 2017.

Kuwajima, Sho. *The Mutiny in Singapore: War, Anti War and the War for India's Independence.* New Delhi: Rainbow Publishers, 2006.

Labenski, Sheri. "Women's Violence and the Law: In Consideration of Shamima Begum." *LSE Women, Peace and Security Blog*, November 20, 2019. http://eprints.lse.ac.uk/103903/1/WPS_2019_11_20_women_s_violence_and_the_law.pdf

Lal, Brij V. "Kunti's Cry: Indentured Women on Fiji Plantations." *The Indian Economic & Social History Review* 22, no. 1 (1985): 55–71.

Leake, Elisabeth, and Daniel Haines. "Lines of (In)Convenience: Sovereignty and Border-Making in Postcolonial South Asia, 1947–1965." *The Journal of Asian Studies* 76, no. 4 (2017): 963–85.

*Liechtenstein v. Guatemala* (Nottebohm Case), Second Phase (International Court of Justice Reports 1955).

Longo, Matthew. *The Politics of Borders: Sovereignty, Security, and the Citizen after 9/11.* Cambridge: Cambridge University Press, 2018.

Macklin, Audrey. "Citizenship Revocation and the Privilege to Have Rights." *Queen's Law Journal*, 40, no. 1 (2014): 1–54.

Malischewski, Charlotte-Anne. "Legal Brief on Statelessness: Law in the Indian Context," in *The Rohingya in South Asia: People without a State*, edited by Sabyasachi Basu Ray Chaudhury and Ranabir Samaddar. London: Routledge, 2018.

Malkki, Liisa H. *Purity and Exile: Violence, Memory, and National Cosmology among Hutu Refugees in Tanzania.* Chicago: University of Chicago Press, 1995.

Malkki, Liisa. "National Geographic: The Rooting of Peoples and the Territorialization of National Identity among Scholars and Refugees." *Cultural Anthropology* 7, no. 1 (1992): 24–44.

Malkki, Liisa. "News From Nowhere: Mass Displacement and Globalized 'Problems of Organization.'" *Ethnography* 3, no. 3 (2002): 351–60.

Manby, Bronwen. "Statelessness and Citizenship in the East African Community" (UNHCR, 2018). https://data2.unhcr.org/en/documents/download/66807

Manly, Mark, and Santhosh Persaud. "UNHCR and Responses to Statelessness." *Forced Migration Review*, no. 32 (2009).

Mann, Itamar. "Maritime Legal Black Holes: Migration and Rightlessness in International Law." *European Journal of International Law* 29, no. 2 (2018): 347–72.

Mantu, Sandra. " 'Terrorist' Citizens and the Human Right to Nationality." *Journal of Contemporary European Studies* 26, no. 1 (2018): 28–41.

Mantu, Sandra. *Contingent Citizenship: The Law and Practice of Citizenship Deprivation in International, European and National Perspectives*. Leiden: Brill | Nijhoff, 2015.

Marschke, Melissa, and Peter Vandergeest. "Slavery Scandals: Unpacking Labor Challenges and Policy Responses Within the Off-Shore Fisheries Sector." *Marine Policy*, no. 68 (2016): 39–46.

Marushiakova, Elena, and Vesselin Popov. *Gypsies (Roma) in Bulgaria*. Frankfurt: P. Lang, 1997.

Masters, Mercedes, and Salvador Santino F Regilme. "Human Rights and British Citizenship: The Case of Shamima Begum as Citizen to *Homo Sacer*." *Journal of Human Rights Practice* 12, no. 2 (2020): 341–63.

Mawani, Renisa. *Across Oceans of Law: The Komagata Maru and Jurisdiction in the Time of Empire*. Durham, NC: Duke University Press, 2018.

Mbembé, J. A. "Necropolitics." Trans. Libby Meintjes, *Public Culture*, 15, no. 1 (2003): 11–40.

McGarry, Aidan. "The Roma Voice in the European Union: Between National Belonging and Transnational Identity." *Social Movement Studies* 10, no. 3 (2011): 283–97.

McKernan, Bethan. "ISIS Women Languish in Dire Conditions with Nowhere Else to Go," *The Guardian*, February 26, 2021. www.theguardian.com/world/2021/feb/26/isis-women-languish-in-dire-conditions-al-hawl-shamima-begum

Meadows, Fiona. *Habiter le campement*. Paris/Arles: Cité de l'architecture et du patrimoine/Actes Sud, 2016.

Meijers Committee. "Policy Brief on 'Differential Treatment of Citizens with Dual or Multiple Nationality and the Prohibition of Discrimination.' " CM 2016. 2020. www.commissie-meijers.nl/comment/cm2016-policy-brief-on-differential-treatment-of-citizens-with-dual-or-multiple-nationality-and-the-prohibition-of-discrimination/

Meth, Paula "Unsettling Insurgency: Reflections on Women's Insurgent Practices in South Africa." *Planning Theory & Practice* 11, no. 2 (2010): 241–63.

Michel Agier. "Humanity as an Identity and Its Political Effects (A Note on Camps and Humanitarian Government)." *Humanity: An International Journal of Human Rights, Humanitarianism, and Development* 1, no. 1 (2010): 29–45.

Mignolo, Walter D. "Delinking: The Rhetoric of Modernity, the Logic of Coloniality and the Grammar of de-Coloniality." *Cultural Studies* 21, no. 2–3 (2007): 449–514.

Mignolo, Walter D. *The Darker Side of Western Modernity: Global Futures, Decolonial Options*. Durham, NC: Duke University Press, 2011.

Miraftab, Faranak. "Insurgent Practices and Decolonization of Future(s)," in *The Routledge Handbook of Planning Theory*, edited by Michael Gunder, Ali Madanipour, and Vanessa Watson. New York: Routledge, 2018.

Miraftab, Faranak. "Invited and Invented Spaces of Participation: Neoliberal Citizenship and Feminists Expanded Notion of Politics." *Wagadu: Journal of Transnational Women's and Gender Studies* 1, no. 1 (2004): 1–7.

Miraftab, Faranak. "Planning and Citizenship," in *The Oxford Handbook of Urban Planning*, edited by Randall Crane and Rachel Weber. New York: Oxford University Press, 2012, 786–802.

Misselwitz, P., and S. Hanafi. "Testing a New Paradigm: UNRWA's Camp Improvement Programme." *Refugee Survey Quarterly* 28, no. 2–3 (2009): 360–88.

Misselwitz, Philipp. "Rehabilitating Camp Cities : Community Driven Planning for Urbanised Refugee Camps." University of Stuttgart, 2009.

Molavi, Shourideh C. *Stateless Citizenship: The Palestinian-Arab Citizens of Israel*. Leiden: Brill, 2013.

Möller, Frank, and Susan Sontag. "Rwanda Revisualized: Genocide, Photography, and the Era of the Witness." *Alternatives: Global, Local, Political* 35, no. 2 (2010): 113–36.

Mondelli, Juan Ignacio. "Eradicating Statelessness in the Americas." *Forced Migration Review*, 56 (2017): 44–46.

Mondelli, Juan Ignacio. "From the Brasilia Declaration to the Brazil Plan of Action," in *Latin America and Refugee Protection: Regimes, Logics and Challenges*, edited by Liliana Lyra Jubilut, Marcia Vera Espinoza, and Gabriela Mezzanotti. New York: Berghahn, 2021.

Mongia, Radhika V. "Historicizing State Sovereignty: Inequality and the Form of Equivalence." *Comparative Studies in Society and History* 49, no. 2 (2007): 384–411.

Montclos, M.A.P.D., and P.M. Kagwanja. "Refugee Camps or Cities? The Socio-Economic Dynamics of the Dadaab and Kakuma Camps in Northern Kenya." *Journal of Refugee Studies* 13, no. 2 (2000): 205–22.

Morris, Lydia. "Rights and Controls in the Management of Migration: The Case of Germany." *The Sociological Review* 48, no. 2 (2000): 224–40.

Muhammad, Anu. "Rise of the Corporate NGO in Bangladesh." *Economic and Political Weekly* 53, no. 39 (2018): 45–52.

Munshi, Sherally. "Immigration, Imperialism, and the Legacies of Indian Exclusion." *SSRN Scholarly Paper 2571412*. Rochester, NY: Social Science Research Network, 2016.

Murphy, Alexander. "Political Rhetoric and Hate Speech in the Case of Shamima Begum." *Religions* 12, no. 10 (2021): 834.

Nagaraj, Anurandha. "Rescued Child Sex Workers in India Reveal Hidden Cells in Brothels," *Reuters* (December 13, 2017). www.reuters.com/article/us-india-trafficking-brothels-idUSKBN1E71R1

Nagaraj, Anurandha. "Indian Brothel Owners Get First Life Sentence for Trafficking Children," *Reuters* (March 28, 2018). www.reuters.com/article/us-india-trafficking-women-idUSKBN1H419U

Nakamura, Katrina, Lori Bishop, Trevor Ward, Ganapathiraju Pramod, Dominic Chakra Thomson, Patima Tungpuchayakul, and Sompong Srakaew. "Seeing Slavery in Seafood Supply Chains." *Science Advances* 4, no. 7 (2018). https://doi.org/10.1126/sciadv.1701833

National Crime and Records Bureau, Ministry of Home Affairs. "Crime in India 2016: Statistics" (2016).

National Crime and Records Bureau, Ministry of Home Affairs. "Crime in India 2018: Statistics" (2018).

National Crime and Records Bureau, Ministry of Home Affairs. "Crime in India 2019: Statistics" (2019).

National Crime and Records Bureau, Ministry of Home Affairs. "Crime in India 2020: Statistics" (2020).

National Investigative Report. "Part II. The Storm of the Human Trafficking at Sea: How Taiwan Became an Accessory to Slavery on the High Seas," *The Reporter* (2018).

National Investigative Report. "Part III. Insufficient Governance of the Distant Water Fishery: The Illegal Shark Finning, Forced Labor, and the Death of the Observer," *The Reporter* (2021).

Ng'weno, Bettina. "Beyond Citizenship as We Know It: Race and Ethnicity in Afro-Colombian Struggles for Citizenship Equality," in *Comparative Perspectives on Afro-Latin America*, edited by Kwame Dixon, John Burdick, and Howard Winant. Gainesville: University Press of Florida, 2013.

Nguyen, Hanh, and Themba Lewis. "Bhasan Char and Refugee 'Warehousing.'" *The Diplomat.* February 8, 2022. https://thediplomat.com/2022/02/bhasan-char-and-refugee-warehousing

Niranjana, Tejaswini, *Sex and the Citizen: Interrogating the Caribbean*, edited by Faith Smith. Charlottesville: University of Virginia Press, 2011.

Novak, Paolo. "Back to Borders." *Critical Sociology* 43, no. 6 (2017): 847–64.

Office to Monitor and Combat Trafficking in Persons, U.S. State Department. "2021 Trafficking in Persons Report: India" (2021).

Ogilvie, Bertrand. *L'Homme Jetable: Essai Sur l'exterminisme et La Violence Extrême*. Paris: Éditions Amsterdam, 2012.

O'Neill, Onora. "Agents of Justice." *Metaphilosophy* 32, no. 1–2 (2001): 180–95.

Ong, Aihwa. "(Re)Articulations of Citizenship." *PS: Political Science and Politics* 38, no. 4 (2005): 697–99.

Onuki, Hironori. "The Neoliberal Governance of Global Labor Mobility: Migrant Workers and the New Constitutional Moments of Primitive Accumulation." *Alternatives: Global, Local, Political* 41, no. 1 (2016): 3–28.

Ophir, Adi. *The Order of Evils: Toward an Ontology of Morals*. New York: Zone Books, 2005.

Owens, Patricia. "Reclaiming 'Bare Life'?: Against Agamben on Refugees." *International Relations* 23, no. 4 (2009): 567–82.

Panwar, Purabi. "Saga of Colonialism." *Indian Literature* 53, no. 3 (2009): 205–8.

Parhusip, Jonathan S. "The Making of Freedom and Common Forms of Struggle of Runaways in Taiwan" *South Atlantic Quarterly* 120, no. 3 (2021): 663–69.

Parsons, Laurie, and Sabina Lawreniuk. "Seeing Like the Stateless: Documentation and the Mobilities of Liminal Statelessness in Cambodia." *Political Geography* 62 (October, 2017): 1–11.

Patnaik, Amar. "Why a Strong Law against Human Trafficking Is Necessary in Post-Covid Times." *The Indian Express* (September 8, 2021). https://indianexpress.com/article/opinion/web-edits/strong-law-human-trafficking-post-covid-times-7497207

Peteet, Julie. *Landscape of Hope and Despair: Palestinian Refugee Camps*. Philadelphia: University of Pennsylvania Press, 2005.

Petti, Alessandro. "Spatial Ordering of Exile. The Architecture of Palestinian Refugee Camps." *Crios* 1 (2013): 62–70.

Pfister-Ammende, Maria. "Mental Hygiene in Refugee Camps," in *Uprooting and After . . .* , edited by Charles Zwingmann and Maria Pfister-Ammende. Berlin, Heidelberg: Springer, 1973, 241–51.

Pithouse, Richard. "The Shack Settlement as a Site of Politics: Reflections from South Africa." *Agrarian South: Journal of Political Economy: A Triannual Journal of Agrarian South Network and CARES* 3, no. 2 (2014): 179–201.

Pittaway, Eileen. "The Rohingya Refugees in Bangladesh: A Failure of the International Protectin System," in *Protracted Displacement in Asia: No Place to Call Home*, edited by Howard Adelman, 2016. London: Routledge, 83–106.

Potvin, Marianne. "Humanitarian Urbanism: Cities, Technology, and the Hybrid Practices of Humanitarian Planners." Dissertation, Harvard University, Cambridge, Massachusetts, 2019. https://dash.harvard.edu/handle/1/42013101

Pugh, M. "Drowning Not Waving: Boat People and Humanitarianism at Sea." *Journal of Refugee Studies* 17, no. 1 (2004): 50–69.

Quijano, Aníbal. "Coloniality and Modernity/Rationality." *Cultural Studies* 21, no. 2–3 (2007): 168–78.

Ramnath, Maria. *Haj to Utopia: How the Ghadar Movement Charted Global Radicalism and Attempted to Overthrow the British Empire*. Berkeley: University of California Press, 2011.

Rancière, Jacques. "Who Is the Subject of the Rights of Man?" *South Atlantic Quarterly* 103, no. 2–3 (2004): 297–310.

Ranciere, Jacques. "Politics, Identification, and Subjectivization," October, Vol. 61. The Identity in Question (Summer 1992): 58–64.

Randeria, Shalini. "The State of Globalization: Legal Plurality, Overlapping Sovereignties and Ambiguous Alliances between Civil Society and the Cunning State in India." *Theory, Culture & Society* 24, no. 1 (2007): 1–33.

Raza, Ali. "Straddling the International and the Regional," in *The Internationalist Moment: South Asia, Worlds, and World Views, 1917–1939*, edited by Ali Raza, Franziska Roy, and Benjamin Zachariah, 2015. London: Sage, 86–123.

Raza, Ali, Franziska Roy, and Benjamin Zachariah (eds.). *The Internationalist Moment: South Asia, Worlds, and World Views, 1917–1939*. London: Sage, 2015.

Redclift, Victoria. "Abjects or Agents? Camps, Contests and the Creation of 'Political Space,'" *Citizenship Studies* 17, no. 3–4 (2013): 308–21.

Redclift, Victoria, *Statelessness and Citizenship: Camps and the Creation of Political Space*. London: Routledge, 2013.

Reddock, Rhoda. "Indian Women and Indentureship in Trinidad and Tobago 1845–1917: Freedom Denied." *Caribbean Quarterly* 54, no. 4 (2008): 41–68.

Reddock, Rhoda. "The Indentureship Experience: Indian Women in Trinidad and Tobago," in *Women Plantation Workers: International Experiences*, edited by Shobita Jain and Rhoda Reddock. London: Routledge, 2020, 29–48.

Rediker, Marcus. *The Slave Ship: A Human History*. New York: Penguin Books, 2008.

Richards, J. F. "The Indian Empire and Peasant Production of Opium in the Nineteenth Century." *Modern Asian Studies* 15, no. 1 (1981): 59–82.

Rürup, Miriam. "Lives in Limbo: Statelessness after Two World Wars." *Bulletin of the GHI Washington* 49 (Fall 2011): 113–34.

Rygiel, Kim. "Politicizing Camps: Forging Transgressive Citizenships in and through Transit." *Citizenship Studies* 16, no. 5–6 (2012): 807–25.

Sadiq, Kamal. "Limits of Legal Citizenship: Narratives from South and Southeast Asia" in *Citizenship in Question*, edited by Benjamin N. Lawrance and Jacqueline Stevens. Durham, NC: Duke University Press, 2016, 165–76.

Samaddar, Ranabir. "Forced Migration Situations as Exceptions in History?" *International Journal of Migration and Border Studies* 2, no. 2 (2016): 99–118.

Samaddar, Ranabir (ed.), *Refugees and the State: Practices of Asylum and Care in India, 1947–2000*. New Delhi: Sage, 2003.

Samaddar, Ranabir. *Emergence of the Political Subject*. New Delhi: Sage, 2010.

Samaddar, Ranabir. *Karl Marx and the Postcolonial Age*. New York: Springer, 2017.

Samaddar, Ranabir. *The Postcolonial Age of Migration*. London: Routledge, 2020.

Sanders, Doug. *Arrival City: How the Largest Migration in History is Reshaping our World*, New York: Vintage Books, 2012.

Santos, Boaventura de Sousa. *Epistemologies of the South: Justice against Epistemicide*. London: Routledge, 2014.

Sanyal, Romola. "From Camps to Urban Refugees: Reflections on Research Agenda." *IJURR* (blog). 2016. www.ijurr.org/spotlight-on/the-urban-refugee-crisis-reflections-on-cities-citizenship-and-the-displaced/the-protracted-refugee-camp-and-the-consolidation-of-a-humanitarian-urbanism

Sarkar, Tanika. *Hindu Wife, Hindu Nation: Community, Religion, and Cultural Nationalism*. Bloomington: Indiana University Press, 2001.

Saunders, Doug. *Arrival City: How the Largest Migration in Human History Is Reshaping Our World*. New York: Pantheon Books, 2010.

Schmitt, Carl. *Land and Sea: A World-Historical Meditation*, trans. Samuel Garrett Zeitlin. Candor, NY: Telos, 1950.

Schmitt, Carl. *The Nomos of the Earth in the International Law of the Jus Publicum Europaeum*. Candor, NY: Telos, 2006.

Schopenhauer, Arthur. *The Essential Schopenhauer: Key Selections from The World as Will and Representation and Other Writings*. New York: Harper Collins, 2010.

Scott, David. *Conscripts of Modernity: The Tragedy of Colonial Enlightenment*. Durham, NC: Duke University Press, 2004.

Scott, James C. *The Art of Not Being Governed: An Anarchist History of Upland Southeast Asia*. New Haven, CT: Yale University Press, 2009.

Selm, Joanne van, and Betsy Cooper. "The New 'Boat People': Ensuring Safety and Determining Status" (Migration Policy Institute, 2006). www.migrationpolicy.org/research/new-boat-people-ensuring-safety-and-determining-status

Sennett, Richard. *Building and Dwelling: Ethics for the City*. London: Allen Lane, 2018.

Shafique, Tanzil. "300,000 People in a Tenth-of-a-Square-Mile: Analysing the Morphological Evolution of the Largest Self-Organized Settlement in Dhaka." Presented at the International Seminar on Urban Form, Salt Lake City, Utah (September 1, 2020).

Sigona, Nando. "Campzenship: Reimagining the Camp as a Social and Political Space." *Citizenship Studies* 19, no. 1 (2015): 1–15.

Singh, Shiv Sahay. "Lockdown, Amphan Render Girls Vulnerable in West Bengal," *The Hindu* (July 30, 2020). www.thehindu.com/news/national/other-states/lockdown-amphan-render-girls-vulnerable-in-bengal/article32233610.ece

Sohi, Seema. *Echoes of Mutiny: Race, Surveillance, and Indian Anticolonialism in North America*. New York: Oxford University Press, 2014.

Somers, Margaret R. *Genealogies of Citizenship: Markets, Statelessness, and the Right to Have Rights*. Cambridge: Cambridge University Press, 2008.

Sontag, Susan. "Regarding the Pain of Others." *Diogene* 201, no. 1 (2003): 127–39.

Sontag, Susan. *On Photography*. New York: Rosetta 1973.

Spiro, Peter J. "A New International Law of Citizenship." *American Journal of International Law* 105, no. 4 (2011): 694–746.

Spivak, Gayatri Chakravorty. "Can the Subalterns Speak?" in *Colonial Discourse and Post-Colonial Theory*, edited by Patrick Williams and Laura Chrisman. London: Routledge, 1994, 66–111.

Staples, Kell. "Statelessness and the Politics of Misrecognition." *Res Publica* 18, no. 1 (2012): 93–106.

Steinberg, Philip, and Kimberley Peters. "Wet Ontologies, Fluid Spaces: Giving Depth to Volume through Oceanic Thinking." *Environment and Planning D: Society and Space* 33, no. 2 (2015): 247–64.

Stierl, Maurice. "A Sea of Struggle—Activist Border Interventions in the Mediterranean Sea." *Citizenship Studies* 20, no. 5 (2016): 561–78.

Stierl, Maurice. "The Mediterranean as a Carceral Seascape." *Political Geography* (June 2021). https://doi.org/10.1016/j.polgeo.2021.102417

Tatla, Darshan Singh. *The Sikh Diaspora: Search for Statehood.* London: Routledge, 1998.

*Tempo.* "Investigation: Slavery at Sea: Undocumented Indonesian Seamen Are Victim of Abuse Aboard Foreign Fishing Boat" (January 8, 2017). https://en.tempo.co/read/833777/investigation-slavery-at-sea

Tickler, David, Jessica J. Meeuwig, Katharine Bryant, Fiona David, John A. H. Forrest, Elise Gordon, Jacqueline Joudo Larsen, et al. "Modern Slavery and the Race to Fish." *Nature Communications* 9, no. 4643 (2018).

Tinker, Hugh. *A New System of Slavery: The Export of Indian Labour Overseas, 1830–1920.* New York: Oxford University Press, 1974.

Touil, Maroua. "The Endless Process of Becoming and the Transformation of Identity in Amitav Ghosh's Sea of Poppies." *International Journal of Humanities and Cultural Studies* 1, no. 4 (2016): 516–23

Trouillot, Michel-Rolph. *Silencing the Past: Power and the Production of History.* Boston: Beacon Press, 1995.

Tuitt, Patricia. "Rethinking the Refugee Concept," in *Refugee Rights and Realities Evolving International Concepts and Regimes*, edited by Frances Nicholson and Patrick Twomey. Cambridge: Cambridge University Press, 1999, 106–18.

Turton, David. "Refugees, Forced Resettlers and 'Other Forced Migrants': Towards a Unitary Study of Forced Migration," UN High Commissioner for Refugees (UNHCR), 2003.

Tyler, Imogen. "Revolting Subjects: Social Abjection and Resistance in Neoliberal Political Equality." *San Diego Law Review* 45 (2013): 981–88.

Ullah, Akm Ahsan. "Rohingya Refugees to Bangladesh: Historical Exclusions and Contemporary Marginalization." *Journal of Immigrant & Refugee Studies* 9, no. 2 (2011): 139–61.

UNCTADstat. "Building, Ownership, Registration and Recycling of Ships, 2019" (2020). https://unctad.org/system/files/official-document/tdstat45_en.pdf

UNHCR. "UNHCR Fact Sheet: The 1961 Convention on the Reduction of Statelessness." *Refworld*, 1961. www.refworld.org/docid/612608084.html

UNHCR. "UNHCR Turkey: March Operational Update" (2020). www.unhcr.org/tr/wp-content/uploads/sites/14/2020/05/UNHCR-Turkey-Operational-Update-March-2020.pdf

UNHCR. "Convention Relating to the Status of Stateless Persons." United Nations, 1954. www.unhcr.org/ibelong/wp-content/uploads/1954-Convention-relating-to-the-Status-of-Stateless-Persons_ENG.pdf

United Nations. "Global Compact for Safe, Orderly and Regular Migration," 2018. www.un.org/en/ga/search/view_doc.asp?symbol=A/RES/73/195

Van Eert. "Stitching Institute on Statelessness and Inclusion: Annual Accounts for the Year 2020." Stitching Institute on Statelessness and Inclusion (2021). https://files.institutesi.org/year_report_2020.pdf

Vermeersch, Peter. *The Romani Movement: Minority Politics and Ethnic Mobilization in Contemporary Central Europe.* New York: Berghahn Books, 2006.

Vlieks, Caia, and Laura Van Waas. "Stateless Persons," in *Elgar Encyclopedia of Human Rights.* Cheltenham: Edward Elgar, 2022.

Wacquant, Loïc. *Urban Outcasts: A Comparative Sociology of Advanced Marginality.* Cambridge: Polity Press, 2008.

Walker, Gavin. "Primitive Accumulation and the Formation of Difference: On Marx and Schmitt." *Rethinking Marxism,* 23, no. 3 (2011): 384–404.

Wallis, Emma. "Oxfam: Conditions in 'Moria 2.0' Are Abysmal." *InfoMigrants* (October 21, 2020). www.infomigrants.net/en/post/28042/oxfam-conditions-in-moria-20-are-abysmal

Wang, Mu-Han. "Review on Shipping Registration System" (Institute of Transportation, Ministry of Transportation and Communications, Taiwan, 2008).

Ward, Peter. *White Canada Forever: Popular Attitudes and Public Policy Toward Orientals in British Columbia: Popular Attitudes and Pubilc Policy Toward Orientals.* Montreal: McGill-Queen's University Press, 1990.

Weizman, Eyal. *The Least of All Possible Evils: Humanitarian Violence from Arendt to Gaza.* London: Verso, 2011.

Werbner, Pnina, and Nira Yuval-Davis. "Women and the New Discourse of Citizenship," in *Women, Citizenship and Difference,* eds. Pnina Werbner and Nira Yuval-Davis. London: Zed Press, 1999.

"Who Are Chakmas?" *The Hindu,* September 14, 2017. www.thehindu.com/news/national/who-are-chakmas/article61473775.ece

Wilmer, S. E. *Performing Statelessness in Europe.* Cham: Springer, 2018.

Xiang, Biao, and Johan Lindquist. "Migration Infrastructure." *International Migration Review* 48, no. 1, suppl (2014): 122–48.

Yao, Xine, *Disaffected: The Cultural Politics of Unfeeling in Nineteenth-Century America.* Durham, NC: Duke University Press, 2021.

Yea, Sallie. "Human Trafficking and Jurisdictional Exceptionalism in the Global Fishing Industry: A Case Study of Singapore." *Geopolitics* 27, no. 1 (2022): 238–59.

Yeo, Colin. "The Rise of Modern Banishment: Deprivation and Nullification of British Citizenship," in *Citizenship in Times of Turmoil? Theory, Practice and Policy,* edited by Devyani Prabhat. Cheltenham:: Edward Elgar, 2019, 134–50.

Zachariah, Benjamin. "Internationalisms in the Interwar Years: The Traveling of Ideas," in *The Internationalist Moment: South Asia, Worlds, and World Views, 1917–39.* New Delhi: Sage, 2015, 1–21.

Zhe, Bao Dao. "Part I. Falsification, Exploitation, Blood-Tear Fishery: Far Sea Fishing Trans-National Investigative Report." *The Reporter* (2017).

# List of Contributors

**Michel Agier** is an anthropologist, Professor at Ecole des Hautes Etudes en Sciences Sociales (EHESS, Paris), and Emeritus Senior Researcher at Institut de Recherches pour le Développement (IRD). His main interests are human globalization, exile, and urban marginalities. He is the director of the Department *Policy* at the Institut Convergence Migrations http://icmigrations.fr/ (2018–2022). Recent publications in English include *The Stranger as My Guest. A Critical Anthropology of Hospitality* (Polity Press, 2020) and *The Jungle: Calais's Camps and Migrants*, with Y. Bouagga, M. Galisson, C. Hanappe, M. Pette, and P. Wannesson (Polity Press, 2018).

**Paula Banerjee** is the IDRC Chair and the founding Director of the Centre of Gender and Forced Displacement (CGFD) at the Asian Institute of Technology, Bangkok. Earlier she was the Dean of Arts at the University of Calcutta and Vice Chancellor of The Sanskrit College and University, where she supervised thirty-two departments and ten research centers. She has served as president of the International Association for the Study of Forced Migration (IASFM) and as honorary director of the Calcutta Research Group, where she remains currently associated as a member of its governing body. She is a world-class leader who has a long research and publication record on gender and displacement in both South and Southeast Asia.

**Samata Biswas** is a teacher, writer, and media practitioner. She teaches English at The Sanskrit College and University in Kolkata, India. As part of the West Bengal Education Service, she worked at Haldia Government College (2009–2015) in the port City of Haldia, West Bengal, and then at Asia's first women's college, Bethune College (2016–2018), in Kolkata. At the 198-year old Sanskrit College and University (erstwhile Sanskrit

College), she teaches courses on gender, popular culture, cinema, partition, and literary representations of migration, slavery, and colonialism. She was educated at Presidency College and the English and Foreign Languages University, Hyderabad. In 2020, her co-edited volume *Situating Social Media: Gender, Caste, Solidarity, Protest* was published by Women Unlimited. In 2019, she developed the concept for a film titled *Calcutta A Migrant City* (https://youtu.be/fpREEq7Ar-Y), and in 2020 she worked on research, production, and subtitling of the film *Tale of a Migrant City*, with Debalina Majumder (https://youtu.be/w5CnRwKd3p8). Both films were produced by Mahanirban Calcutta Research Group (CRG), of which she is a member. In July–August 2021, she coordinated reading *Refugees, Reading Migration: An (Online) Orientation Course for College and University Teachers*. She runs the Forced Migration blog *Refugee Watch Online* (www.refugeewatchonline.wordpress.com) and is the book review editor of the international journal *Refugee Watch*.

**Ayşe Çağlar** is a professor in the Department of Social and Cultural Anthropology at the University of Vienna and a permanent fellow at the Institute for Human Sciences (IWM), Vienna. Çağlar has published widely on the processes and interfaces of migration, urban restructuring, dispossession, displacement, confined labor, and extractive and cultural industries, as well as on the entanglements between states and transnationalization processes, with a special focus on cities. In addition to her co-edited *Locating Migration: Rescaling Cities and Migrants* (Cornell University Press, 2010) and co-authored *Migrants and City-Making: Dispossession, Displacement, and Urban Regeneration* (Duke University Press, 2018) volumes, she is editor and co-editor, respectively, of *Urbaner Protest: Revolte in der neoliberalen Stadt* (Passagen Verlag, 2019) and the special issue "Displacements and Dispossessions," *Refugee Watch* 58 (2022).

**Nergis Canefe** (PhD & SJD) is a Turkish-Canadian scholar of public international law, comparative politics, forced migration studies, and critical human rights. She has held posts in several European and Turkish Universities and is a faculty member at York University, Canada, since 2003. She serves regularly on the executive board of several international organizations, including the International Association of Forced Migration Studies, and is the co-editor of *Journal of Conflict Transformation and Security*. She is a frequent public speaker on issues related to human rights, minority rights, and historical injustices. She has penned nearly one hundred scholarly articles and several books, including *Transitional Justice and Forced Migration* (edited volume, 2019, Cambridge University Press), *The Syrian Exodus* (monograph, 2018, Bilgi University), *The Jewish Diaspora as a Paradigm: Politics, Religion and Belonging* (edited volume, 2014, Libra Press, Jewish Studies Series), *Milliyetcilik, Kimlik ve Aidiyet* (monograph, 2006, Nationalism, Identity and Belonging. Istanbul: Bilgi University Publishing House), and *Turkey and European Integration: Accession Prospects and Issues* (2004, edited volume in collaboration with Mehmet Ugur, Routledge). Her most recent book is *Limits of Universal Jurisdiction: A Critical Debate on Crimes against Humanity* (University of Wales International Law Series, in press), to be followed by a volume on *Unorthodox Minorities in the Middle East* (Lexington Press) and *Comparative Politics of Administrative Law in the Middle East* (MacMillan Publishers). Her scholarly work has appeared in *Nations and Nationalism*, *Citizenship Studies*, *New Perspectives*, *Refugee Watch*, *Refuge*, *South East European Studies*, *Globalizations*, *Peace Review*, *Middle Eastern Law and Governance*, *Journal of International Human Rights*, and *Narrative Politics*. Professor Canefe is a trained artist, and her designs and murals have been showcased since 2008.

**Subhas Ranjan Chakraborty** retired from Presidency College, Kolkata, in 2005, but continued to teach as a guest teacher until 2013. He taught as guest faculty in the Department of History, Calcutta University, until 2018. He has written on the history and politics of Darjeeling, on aspects of forced migration during the colonial period, and on the French Revolution and the Balkans. He is currently a Vice-President of the Asiatic Society, Kolkata, and a member of the Calcutta Research Group.

**Sabyasachi Basu Ray Chaudhury** is a professor in the Department of Political Science, Rabindra Bharati University, Kolkata, and president of the Calcutta Research Group (CRG), India. He is also president at the Institute for Development Studies, Kolkata (IDSK). His areas of research interest include global politics, South Asian politics, migration and refugee studies, human rights, and sociology of labor. His recent publications include *Rohingya in South Asia: The People without a State* (co-editor, Routledge, 2018), *Rights after Globalisation* (co-editor, Sage, 2011), and *Internal Displacement in South Asia: The Relevance of the UN Guiding Principles* (co-editor, with Paula Banerjee and Samir Kumar Das, Sage, 2005). He was also Vice Chancellor of Rabindra Bharati University, Kolkata, from July 2012 to March 2023.

**Yu-Fan Chiu** is an associate professor at the School of Law, National Yang Ming Chiao Tung University. She studied in Taiwan and Germany and held doctoral scholarships from the German Hans-Böckler-Foundation and Ministry of Education (MOE), Taiwan. She has also worked in Chunghwa Telecom Workers' Union and the Industrial Union of Metal workers (IG Metall). After completing her doctorate at the University of Gottingen in Germany, she has researched and taught Labor and Employment Law since 2016. Her research focuses on the law issues about collective labor rights, migrant workers, and gender equality. Her current project examines the Legality of the Employers' Industrial Actions and its Scope of Constituting Unfair Labor Practices and Gender Pay Gap in the Platform Economy.

**Nasreen Chowdhory** is an associate professor in the Department of Political Science, University of Delhi. She obtained her PhD in political science from McGill University, Canada, taught at Concordia University, and later joined the University of Delhi. Some of her significant publications include "Displacement: A 'State of Exception' " in the *International Journal of Migration and Border Studies*, 2016; *Refugees, Citizenship and Belonging: A Contested Terrains* (Springer 2018); the edited volume *Deterritorialised Identities and Transborder Movement in South Asia* with Nasir Uddin (Springer 2019); *Citizenship, Nationalism and Refugeehood of Rohingyas in Southern* Asia, co-edited with Biswajit Mohanty (Springer 2020), and *Gender, Identity and Migration in India*, with Paula Banerjee (Palgrave 2021). She is Vice President of Mahanirban Calcutta Research Group, Kolkata, India.

**Elspeth Guild** is a Jean Monnet Professor ad personam in law at Queen Mary University of London and Emeritus Professor at Radboud University, Nijmegen, Netherlands. She is also a visiting professor at the College of Europe, Bruges, and teaches at Sciences-Po Paris. She regularly advises EU institutions on migration and asylum-related matters and has written studies for the European Parliament on the European dimension of the refugee crisis 2016, Euro-Mediterranean cooperation on migration. She advises the Council of Europe and has written two Issue Papers for the Commissioner for Human Rights, one on the right to leave a country, and the other on criminalization of migration. In 2017, she co-edited with Stefanie Grant and Kees Groenendijk *The Human Rights of Migrants in the 21st Century* (Focus Series, Routledge) and directed at the UN Global Compact for Safe, Orderly and Regular Migration.

**Efadul Huq** is an assistant professor of environmental science and policy at Smith College. Huq's research analyzes relationships between social-ecological change and regional development that shape livelihoods and ecosystems across urban and rural regions in the context of global displacements and climate change. His research and teaching span areas of environmental justice, international community development, urban sustainability, and political ecology, with a geographic focus on South Asia and the United States.

**Sibel Karadağ** is an assistant professor at Kadir Has University in the Department of Political Science and Public Administration. She is also 2021–2022 Mercator-IPC Fellow. Karadağ received her PhD in political science and international relations from Koç University in 2020, with the dissertation titled "Monitoring Migration, Governing Borders in the Aegean Sea: An Ethnographic Study of Practices, Subjectivities and Narratives." After completing her doctoral research, she worked as a postdoctoral researcher at Koç University Migration Research Center (MiReKoc) within ADMIGOV project. During the 2018–2019 academic year, she was a Fulbright Fellow at Yale University. Her research interests lie mainly in critical security and border studies, migration and mobility, politics of humanitarianism, sovereignty and citizenship, and social and political theory. In addition to numerous project reports, her research has been published in academic journals such as *Geopolitics, Turkish Studies, and Comparative Migration Studies*. Karadağ received her BA in social and political Science (2010) and her MA in European studies (2012) from Sabancı University. She received an MSc in social policy (2012) from LSE, with the Jean Monnet Scholarship.

**Sangbida Lahiri** is an assistant professor at the Centre for Communication and Critical Thinking, JKLU. She specializes in history and international relations in South and Southeast Asia. The title of her PhD thesis is "Emergence of the Student: History of a Political Concept in Colonial Calcutta (1905–1935)." Her thesis studies the evolution of modern political concepts in twentieth-century colonial Calcutta among students' groups. Sangbida has over twelve years of teaching and research experience. Before joining JKLU, she worked with a government survey project at Sonagachi Red Light district in Kolkata in 2022–2023. She was also associated with the National Human Rights Commission and the University of Glasgow as a researcher. Dr. Sangbida worked with the Calcutta Research Group and Jadavpur University on various research projects on women and labor migration. Formerly, she was a full-time journalist in Kolkata and worked with Ananda Bazar Patrika and Ei Samay, Bennet and Coleman Ltd. Co. where she was reporting on education, administration, politics, crime, women, and various other topics.

**Joyce C. H. Liu** is Chair Professor of the Institute of Social Research and Cultural Studies and director of the International Center for Cultural Studies and the International Program of Inter-Asia Cultural Studies at National Yang Ming Chiao Tung University. Her research focuses on geopolitics, biopolitics, border politics, internal coloniality, unequal citizens, epistemic decolonization, and artistic interventions. She is the author of six books and nine co-edited volumes. Currently, she is leading two ongoing joint research projects: "Conflict, Justice, Decolonization: Critical Inter-Asia Cultural Studies" (awarded by the Ministry of Education, Taiwan, 2018–2022), and "Migration, Logistics, and Unequal Citizens in the Global Context" (awarded by CHCI-Mellon Foundation, 2019–2021).

**Faranak Miraftab** is a professor of urban and regional planning at the University of Illinois, Urbana-Champaign. Her work, empirically based in Latin America, Southern Africa, and the United States, draws on feminist, transnational, and urban scholarship. Her research and teaching concerns the global and local development processes involved in the formation of cities and citizens' struggles to access dignified urban livelihood. Her most recent book, *Global Heartland: Displaced Labor, Transnational Lives and Local Placemaking*, received the ACSP's 2017 Davidoff book award and the ASA's Global & Transnational Sociology section book award.

**Jonathan S. Parhusip** is a PhD Student at the Institute of Social Research and Cultural Studies, National Yang Ming Chiao Tung University, Taiwan. His research interests include the politics of migration, the logistical chain of Indonesia–Taiwan migration industry, and Southeast Asian studies. His PhD research explores the employment practices of SEA migrant fishers onboard Taiwanese fishing vessels, migrant solidarity, and labor rights activism in Taiwan. His most recent article is titled "The Making of Freedom and Common Forms of Struggle of Runaway in Taiwan" (SAQ, 2021).

**Ranabir Samaddar** is currently the Distinguished Chair in Migration and Forced Migration Studies, Calcutta Research Group. He belongs to the critical school of thinking and is considered among the foremost theorists in migration and forced migration studies. He has worked extensively on issues of forced migration, the theory and practices of dialogue, identity politics, nationalism governance, postcolonial statehood in South Asia, neoliberalism, and new regimes of technological restructuring and labor control. The much-acclaimed *The Marginal Nation* (1999) and *The Politics of Dialogue* (2004) culminate his long work on historical and social affinities, geographical purviews, the concept of nation-state and borders, human rights, justice, and peace. His most recent works include *A Pandemic and the Politics of Life* with Women Unlimited in 2021 and *The Postcolonial Age of Migration* with Routledge published in 2020. Among his other works are *Migrants and the Neoliberal City* (Orient BlackSwan, 2018), *Karl Marx and the Postcolonial Age* (Palgrave McMillan, 2017), *Ideas and Frameworks of Governing India* (London & New York: Routledge, 2016), Passive Revolution in West Bengal—1977–2011 (Sage, 2013).

**Sucharita Sengupta** obtained her PhD from the Department of Anthropology and Sociology in the Graduate Institute of International and Development Studies, Geneva. Before joining the PhD program, she worked on issues and fields related to migration and forced migration studies as part of her work as a researcher at the Calcutta Research Group. She is interested in studying belonging, refugee agency, and resilience through the context of the Rohingyas living in the world's largest refugee camp, in Bangladesh.

**Shamna Thacham Poyil** is a PhD candidate in the Department of Political Science at the University of Delhi. Her research focuses on the narrative of statelessness of the Rohingyas and the politics of exclusion, where denial of citizenship is used as a strategy for ethno-political nation building in post-colonial Burma, rendering minorities like Rohingyas Stateless. Her recent publications include "Speaking the Language of the 'Other': Negotiating Cultural Boundaries through Language in Chitmahals in Indo-Bangladesh Borders," *Journal of Citizenship Studies* (2021); "National Identity and Conceptualization of Nationalism among Rohingya" in *Citizenship, Nationalism and Refugeehood of Rohingyas in Southern Asia* (2020), ed. Nasreen Chowdhory and Biswajit Mohanty; "The Global Compact of Refugees: A Viewpoint of Global South," *Refugee Watch* (2020); "The Idea of Protection: Norms and Practice of Refugee Management in India," *Refugee Watch* (2019) "Transitional Justice, Reconciliation and Reconstruction Process: The Case of the Former LTTE Female Combatants in Post-War Sri Lanka" with Dr. Nasreen Chowdhory in *Transitional Justice and Forced Migration* (2019), ed. Nergis Canefe (Cambridge University Press).

# Index